The Conversion of Scandinavia

ANDERS WINROTH

The Conversion of Scandinavia

VIKINGS, MERCHANTS, AND
MISSIONARIES IN THE REMAKING
OF NORTHERN EUROPE

Yale UNIVERSITY PRESS
New Haven &
London

Published with assistance from the Kingsley Trust Association Publication Fund established by the Scroll and Key Society of Yale College.

Yale University Press books may be purchased in quantity for educational, business, or promotional use. For information, please e-mail sales.press@yale.edu (U.S. office) or sales@yaleup.co.uk (U.K. office).

Set in Sabon type by IDS Infotech Ltd., Chandigarh, India.
Printed in the United States of America.

Library of Congress Cataloging-in-Publication Data

Winroth, Anders.
  The conversion of Scandinavia : Vikings, merchants, and missionaries in the remaking of Northern Europe / Anders Winroth.
    p. cm.
  Includes bibliographical references and index.
  ISBN 978-0-300-17026-9 (hardback) 1. Scandinavia—Commerce—History. 2. Vikings—Commerce—History. 3. Scandinavia—Economic conditions. 4. Economics—Religious aspects—Christianity—History. 5. Scandinavia—Religion—History. 6. Vikings—Religion. 7. Conversion—Christianity.   I. Title.
  HF3640.W56 2011
  948'.022—dc23
                                                            2011019106
A catalogue record for this book is available from the British Library.

This paper meets the requirements of ANSI/NISO Z39.48-1992 (Permanence of Paper).

10 9 8 7 6 5 4 3 2 1

Till Hjalmar och Elsa

Contents

Acknowledgments

During the more than ten years that work on this book has been in progress, I have incurred many debts of gratitude, which I am happy to acknowledge.

I wish especially to thank Roberta Frank warmly for more help than I could ever hope to list here. She has been a constant inspiration and great support, not least when we have taught Viking culture together. Several other colleagues have been kind enough to discuss the early middle ages with me, answering questions about specific problems, and some have read and critiqued excerpts from the book at various stages of completion: Jessica Eriksson, Paul Freedman, Walter Goffart, Eric C. Knibbs, Fred C. Robinson, and Nancy Wicker. I am most grateful to them all for sharing their ideas, insights, and expertise. My thanks also go to the anonymous colleagues who reviewed the manuscript for the Press, making many very valuable suggestions. It goes without saying that I remain responsible for the errors and omissions in the book.

My agent, Lisa Adams of The Garamond Agency, helped me hone the structure of the book and some of the prose, and she guided me through the mysterious process of finding a publisher. My editor at Yale University Press, Jennifer Banks, believed in the project from early on, edited the manuscript admirably, and brought the book into print efficiently. Her assistants, Christina Tucker and Piyali Bhattacharya, were of great help, patiently answering many detailed questions and moving things along very professionally. Ann-Marie Imbornoni did splendid work copyediting the manuscript with great care and sympathy. I am most grateful to all of them for all their valuable help and encouragement, which has made this a better book.

Marita von Weissenberg accomplished miracles as my assistant when I finished the manuscript, notably in acquiring the illustrations and the maps, using her own expertise in the field, her organizational genius, and her customary good spirits.

My students have been the first to hear about each piece of research and analysis that has gone into this book. They have been the best critics of my ideas at the same time that their ideas have inspired me. I am grateful for their patience and cheerfulness.

A book like this, which attempts to synthesize research done in many fields and published sometimes in obscure places, could not have been written without access to a world-class research library with breadth and depth in its collections of books, journals, and electronic resources. Yale University Library is an ideal environment for serious humanistic research, and I am grateful to the institution and its librarians, in particular Susanne Roberts and Emily Horning, who always cheerfully helped me find what I needed. I am also grateful to Kungliga Biblioteket, Stockholm, for making available to me a work space for research as well as its collections, which are particularly rich in materials about Scandinavia.

I thank the institutions and persons who kindly provided the illustrations, especially Nicolai Garhøj Larsson of Øhavsmuseet, Faaborg, and Annika Larsson of Museum Gustavianum, Uppsala, from whom I learned much.

I could not have written this book without being given time to do research, to think about the topic, and to draft and redraft the text. I am grateful to the John D. and Catherine T. MacArthur Foundation, Chicago, and to Yale University for financial support. I also wish to thank the Frederick W. Hilles Publication Fund at Yale University for a grant toward the costs of preparing the book for print.

Note on Names and Translations

In reproducing the names of persons and places, I have as a historian not tried to be philologically exact but rather striven for a readable text. Thus, I have in the text used relevant modern forms and as far as possible avoided diacritics and unusual letters. Thus, the Old Norse Austmaðr has become modern Swedish Östman, Æthelred has readily become Ethelred, and Hludowicus will simply be called Louis the Pious. I have not worried too much about being consistent, so I write Olav Tryggvason and Olav Haraldsson (for the Norwegian kings) and Olof Eriksson (for the Swedish king) rather than Óláfr, Olavus, Anlāf, Amlaíb, or some other philologically correct form. I have, of course, retained appropriate forms in the bibliographical references.

In the notes, I have referred to available English translations, when I have been aware of them, for the benefit of students and others who prefer to read the sources in translation. When I quote sources in translation, I usually reproduce the translation indicated but sometimes I have adapted it or even provided my own translation, without especially noting this.

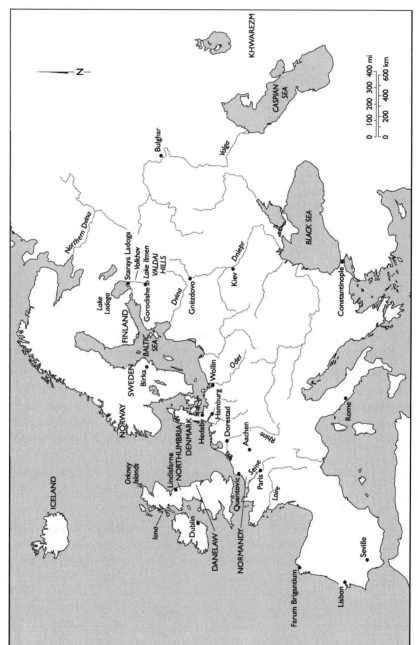

Map 1. Europe in the early Middle Ages. Cartography by Bill Nelson.

Map 2. Northern Europe in the early Middle Ages. Cartography by Bill Nelson.

Introduction:
Europe, Scandinavia, and Hallfred the Skald

In 988, a young Icelander, embarking on an ambitious journey, secured passage on a ship bound for Norway, where he was going to seek his fortune.[1] Unlike some other Scandinavians of the time, he was not a Viking sailing out to maraud along the coasts and rivers of Europe. This Icelander possessed an outstanding skill more valuable than martial prowess—the ability to write an extremely complex and demanding poetry called skaldic verse—and he was looking for an appreciative and generous patron. He particularly excelled at composing *dróttkvætt* stanzas, which praised and flattered princes through elaborate and complicated circumlocutions and an allusive style. There was only so much use for such poetry in princeless Iceland, where even the most powerful chieftains had paltry wealth and power in comparison to the great chieftains of mainland Scandinavia and the Norse principalities of the British Isles.

Our young poet, Hallfred Ottarson, had set his sights on the most powerful of chieftains in Norway, Earl Håkon Sigurdsson of Hlaðir (or Lade, as the place—now a suburb of Trondheim—is called in modern Norwegian). Håkon belonged to the famed family of the Lade earls, who since at least the ninth century had dominated the fertile region around the Trondheim fjord, Trøndelag. They also controlled the region to its north, Hålogaland, which was rich in reindeer, walruses, whales, and polar bears. Reindeer antlers, walrus ivory, whale hide twisted into strong ship ropes, and white bear skins were desired commodities that fetched high market prices in Europe. It was this access to arctic exotica and the surprising productivity (given its subarctic latitude) of Trøndelag agriculture that made Håkon rich and powerful. His family claimed divine descent through a son of the high god Odin, a claim that secured their power over other Norwegians. The Lade earls were kingmakers in Norway, and Håkon was in all but name king of Norway after he had freed himself in 986 from the more or less nominal overlordship of King Harald Bluetooth of Denmark. Only the most ambitious Icelandic poet would approach Håkon, and Hallfred was very ambitious.

Having indeed impressed Håkon with his ability to praise him with superbly composed dróttkvætt stanzas, Hallfred secured a position for himself as one of the earl's retainers. His gamble had paid off—he served a rich and generous patron, who rewarded him for his services. Earl Håkon gave him arm rings of gold and silver, provided him and his other retainers with weapons, perhaps decorated with the same precious metals, and kept him fed, clothed, and entertained. In return, Hallfred was expected to remain loyal to Håkon, praise him with poetry, and fight for him. He was not a mercenary fighting for money; his relationship with Håkon was more complicated than that. Håkon's gifts obliged Hallfred to give his poetry and his fighting prowess as countergifts.

Hallfred was Håkon's man. But had he chosen the right patron? After a few years, a new and dashing young prince made his way to Norway determined to contest Håkon's rule. Olav Tryggvason had raided as a Viking in both the Baltic and the North Seas for years. His greatest adventure was in 994, when together with the Danish king Svein Forkbeard, he led a host of Viking warriors on a great fleet of ninety-four ships, pillaging, plundering, and raiding all over England. They were successful everywhere. Only the burghers of London resisted them, much to the surprise of the Norse. As an Anglo-Saxon writer noted in his chronicle, "[The Scandinavians] suffered more harm and injury than they ever imagined that any town-dwellers would do to them." Thwarted, the Vikings attacked Essex, Kent, Sussex, and Hampshire, where they "wrought the greatest harm which any raiding-army could ever do, in burning and raiding and slaughter of men," until the English king Ethelred in desperation sent a messenger asking for peace. To make his suggestions more palatable, the king offered to pay them sixteen thousand pounds of pure silver to stop fighting.[2] Olav and Svein agreed, and when they got the money they handed out enough of it to their Viking followers to make them happy. This secured Olav's reputation as a very generous chieftain with luck in battle and great fund-raising abilities. He also had accumulated enough silver to continue to hand out valuable gifts to any warrior who wanted to join him. In 995 it was time to stop being a Viking, and to gain a more durable power base. And so he assembled an army and attacked the man with the most fame and wealth in Norway, Earl Håkon Sigurdsson of Lade.

The contest between Olav and Håkon took place on a playing field that was far from level. Håkon was rich, but he was no Viking. He had painstakingly built his fortune through Trøndelag's agriculture, his control of trade along the coast of Norway, the tribute that the Sami of Hålogaland paid him, and other such comparatively modest sources. Olav, in contrast, had as a Viking acquired great stores of silver in one fell swoop in England. Thanks to his greater fortune, Olav was able to assemble an army so large that he overshadowed Håkon, who did not stand a chance.

Håkon realized this and decided not to put up a fight. His followers had deserted him, flocking to the young and spirited Olav Tryggvason, the most generous chieftain. "The followers were sparse around the standard of the friendless prince who saved his gold," as the poet Sigvat Thordarson wrote a generation later about a similar situation. Sigvat used poetic hyperbole; the prince he wrote about had surely in desperation handed out all the gold he had. And so did Håkon Sigurdsson in 995 in a futile attempt to build up a band of warriors who would measure up to Olav's. He simply did not have enough wealth to be a credible competitor. Left behind by his warriors, he was reputedly killed by his own slave.[3]

Hallfred, our ambitious poet, was among those who abandoned Håkon to join the retinue of the victorious Olav Tryggvason. Olav, who soon was in a position to call himself king of Norway, rewarded him richly, with gold and a finely worked sword, as a proper prince should. But Olav's gifts came with an extra requirement, beyond Hallfred's duty to use his poetic skills in praise. The king had accepted Christian baptism as a part of his peace agreement with King Ethelred of England and he required his followers also to be Christian. Olav himself was Hallfred's sponsor and godfather in baptism, just as King Ethelred had been Olav's godfather.

Hallfred was not pleased about changing his religion, even though it meant that he now could count a new kind of kinship—the spiritual kinship that godfatherhood created—with the kings of both Norway and England. He was a poet, however, and as a poet, he needed the imagery of pagan mythology, which gave him fodder for the metaphorical circumlocutions, or kennings, employed in skaldic verse. Poets needed their mythology in order to communicate. They needed their audience to understand that an expression like "Endill's eel-land" simply meant "the sea," since Endill was a mythological sea king and eel live in the water. Or that "Hlokk's blizzard-skis" meant "arrows," since Hlokk was a valkyrie. Her blizzard was a battle, in which arrows glide through the air much as skis glide on snow. Skaldic poetry's attraction comes from the mystery of euphonious kennings, which demand both learning and intuition to understand.

Hallfred had made a very good living from his poetic talents and his knowledge of Norse mythology. He expressed his feelings about changing religion in a famous stanza:

> It's the creed of the sovereign
> of Sogn [Olav Tryggvason] to ban sacrifices.
> We must renounce many
> a long-held decree of norns.
> All mankind casts Odin's words
> to the winds; now I am forced
> to forsake Freya's kin
> and pray to Christ.[4]

Hallfred elsewhere claims to have been much pleased with the god of poetry, Odin, whose "grace wrought poems" and to whom he had "made fine sacrifices" (a phrase that we may take as a kenning for "produced fine poetry"). He must have felt that his entire livelihood was threatened if he no longer could allude to the old gods in his poetry. Yet he was otherwise appropriately proud to have a famous king as his godfather in Christian baptism, and mentioned that fact more than once in his stanzas.

Others in similar positions were less ambivalent about Christianity. A generation after Hallfred, the poet Sigvat Thordarson professed to have been very happy the morning when his king served as the godfather to his daughter Tofa. This ritual created a bond between king and poet as strong as any blood kinship. Henceforth, Tofa Sigvatsdottir had two fathers: Sigvat and her king. To serve as a godfather, to bring the new prestigious religion of Christianity to their followers, was another gift that kings like Olav Tryggvason could give their followers, a gift that made them happy to serve him.

Hallfred's story evokes a larger story about Scandinavia's joining Europe and at the same time changing it. Like Hallfred, but perhaps more willingly, Scandinavia embraced Christianity around the year 1000, at about the same time that northern kings introduced European-style government. Scandinavian traders had already for two centuries significantly boosted European commerce, for example by introducing liquid wealth, especially silver, from new sources. During the next few centuries, European civilization would experience unprecedented growth and development, an expansion that laid the foundation for European world domination in the modern era. Scandinavia had a role in this expansion.

The story of Hallfred helps us understand the mechanisms that brought Scandinavia into European civilization. It explains how early medieval Scandinavian political society worked. Chieftains like Håkon and Olav competed for warriors and poets (who were also warriors), and they did so by creating close personal relationships with their warriors that involved giving gifts, feasting together, and sharing rituals. The nature of these relationships explains a great deal about what happened in and around Scandinavia in the early Middle Ages, from the eighth through the twelfth century.

This was a dynamic period in Scandinavian history. It was at this time that the three Scandinavian kingdoms—Denmark, Norway, and Sweden—not only first took form as states but also converted to Christianity. The early Middle Ages in northern Europe saw long-distance trade grow to unprecedented proportions. It witnessed the rich development of ornamental art and high-quality workmanship in Scandinavia. It stands to reason that all these processes were somehow interrelated, that they represent different facets of one overarching story. Yet, historians usually treat them separately. By exploring the connections among the Christianization of the region, the flourishing of trade around the Baltic Sea, the creation of kingdoms, and the Viking raids originating there, a very different picture of early Scandinavian history emerges. But before discussing this, we need to broaden our horizons to all of Europe.

Scandinavia became a part of mainstream European civilization around the year 1000. When King Charlemagne of the Franks was crowned emperor in 800, he ruled over most of Christian western Europe: France, northern Italy, northeastern Spain, and western Germany. Southern Italy and much of the Iberian Peninsula were in the hands of the Byzantines and the Arabs. The British Isles were Christian, independent of the new emperor and divided into many kingdoms. The areas north and east of Charlemagne's empire, including most of Germany, eastern Europe, and Scandinavia, were not Christian and not organized into states. They were a poorly known and much feared backwater, considered an alien and barbaric wilderness.

During the centuries after 800, the area of western, Christian culture—of Latin Christendom—at least doubled, as it came to encompass much of eastern and northern Europe and, in due time, also the Iberian Peninsula. This was a momentous development; it caused the population of Europe to reach a critical mass, which made possible the great ascendancy of European civilization that continues to this day. That greater population laid the foundation for more intense land use, more commerce, the reorganization of government, the expansion of education, and military innovations, among the many developments of the high Middle Ages that make up the historical background of modern western society. Europe's expansion during the centuries around the year

1000 was, thus, not only a precedent for Europe's colonial expansion to other continents in the early modern period, but also a necessary precondition for it.

Scholars have devoted much attention to the *reconquista* from the Arabs of the Iberian Peninsula and to the expansion of the Frankish and German Empires toward the east, into the fertile plains of eastern Germany and Poland. These increases in European territory came about, in the main, through military conquest and agricultural colonization. Because scholars sometimes see the inclusion of Scandinavia into Europe in the context of the general expansion of European civilization, the patterns that held in continental Europe have often served as a template for understanding the further extension of European civilization into northern Europe. The "Europeanization" of this area is often portrayed in terms of conquest and colonization, if not by rulers through soldiers and settlers, then at least by the church through missionaries, who preached and persuaded. Scandinavians are, in either case, depicted as passive recipients.

This book presents a different interpretation of the Christianization and Europeanization of Scandinavia. Unlike many other European regions, Scandinavia *chose* to convert to Christianity and accept European culture. This conclusion invites historians of the European ascendancy to change slightly their accounts of the expansion of Europe, producing a richer history of what is usually, but not necessarily helpfully, called the Viking Age. Violent Vikings appropriating the riches of Europe make up only a single aspect of a greater and far more interesting story about Scandinavia's embrace of European religion, political culture, and economic systems. Thus, this book will go beyond the two stereotypical interpretations of early medieval Scandinavian history: the image of the Viking raids as great adventures and the depiction of Scandinavian Christianization and state formation as a kind of colonization. Instead, the book synthesizes Viking raids, northern European trade, Christianization, state formation, and other aspects of early medieval Scandinavian history. The result is an interpretative essay about, and a new model for, the integration of a region into European culture, which will enrich our understanding of medieval European history.

The error of perspective in traditional scholarship depends partially on the nature of the available sources. Most written sources from the period 750–1100 come from outside Scandinavia, from the parts of Europe that were already Christianized. Their perspective is that of Europeans as triumphant, if mostly figurative, conquerors of the barbarian north. Their story tells how Christian Europe brought Christianity and civilization to wild barbarians, who are portrayed as the beneficiaries of their civilizing influences. Just before the year 800, the Danish early-eighth-century king Ongendus was portrayed as "harder than a stone," so the missionary Willibrord failed to make an impression on him with his preaching.[5] In contrast, King Harald Bluetooth of Denmark was, according to the contemporary German historian Widukind of Corvey, "quick to hear" and he became "converted" in the 960s.[6] The use of the passive verb form (*conversus*) in describing his conversion is typical. It is the representatives of civilized Europe, the rulers and missionaries, who are the active players. The historian Adam of Bremen characteristically adhered to this perspective when he set out in the 1070s to write a book about "the deeds of the most holy fathers [the archbishops of Hamburg-Bremen] by whom the Church was exalted and the Christian religion spread among the pagans."[7]

In thus describing his enterprise, Adam expressed a commonplace. Christians spread the Word of God to the benighted pagans, in accordance with Christ's words to his apostles: "Go ye, therefore, and teach all nations, baptizing them" (Matthew 28:19). In fact, Adam's particular words were so much a commonplace that he had not formulated them himself; he copied them from a book by Pope Gregory I (died 604).[8]

The voices of the inhabitants of northern Europe were almost never heard in the contemporary source material. Written sources from inside northern Europe are few and far between and consist mostly of runic inscriptions and skaldic poetry, which tend to be terse, allusive, and enigmatic. Narrative texts, such as sagas and chronicles, were produced in northern Europe only from the twelfth century on and do not throw reliable light on events centuries before. Their authors were not necessarily as concerned with reporting historical fact as they were with using their creative imagination to shape attractive stories. The archeological material, on the other hand, is immense, and constantly growing. But it remains silent until put into an interpretative context. Unlike the sagas and chronicles, the spade does not lie, as the saying goes, but the spade does remain silent until modern interpreters make it talk.[9]

In this book, the voices of northern Europeans are heard again. We shall listen to what they have to say in their runic inscriptions and in their poetry. Taking our cues from such evidence, we will bring a better understanding to our reading of not only continental written sources but also the rich archeological material from northern Europe.

Early medieval Scandinavia is a lively research field in many different disciplines, such as archeology, history, numismatics, philology, and religious studies. A recent survey of research in the field contains contributions from some eighty experts, filling over seven hundred pages and weighing in at more than two kilograms.[10] My book could never have been written without so much existing splendid work by those scholars and countless others. The expert and not-so-expert reader will surely recognize most of the stories I tell and the specific details I examine, but I hope they will agree that the overall approach and interpretation are new. I have endeavored to synthesize existing work and fit it into a larger narrative and understanding of European history. I am grateful to be able to draw on the expertise of fellow researchers in this exciting field.

What the Scandinavian voices tell us is that European civilization extended into Scandinavia not because European powers wished it and worked for it through missionaries and armies, but because powerful people in the north thought this was in their best interests. They used Christianity to promote their own short-term political interests. The Christianization and Europeanization of the north is, thus, not a story of conquest and colonization, or of persuasion and preaching; it is the story of northerners willingly, indeed, eagerly, embracing European civilization. This willingness is how and why northern Europe became an integral part of Europe.

The story of the Saxons—a people living in what today is Germany—provides an instructive contrast. They were baptized en masse after Charlemagne, who "preached with an iron tongue," had defeated them. The emperor's iron-tongued preaching took the form of a thirty-year-long bloody war in which he once had several thousand prisoners of war summarily executed. Saxony (the regions just east of the Rhine River) then became integrated into the Frankish Empire, which meant that the inhabitants lived under the control of Frankish administrators, who outlawed paganism, threatening any recalcitrant pagans with death. Some Saxons were forcibly moved farther into the core Frankish lands to facilitate their integration. They did not have any other choice but to remain obedient and Christian, if they wanted to stay alive.

This template—conversion through military conquest followed by foreign occupation—does not apply to the Scandinavian countries or for that matter to Poland or to the Rus state centered at Kiev. Some Scandinavians, like the Danes, to be sure, lived under pressure from powerful Christian neighbors, who, it might have been feared, could take a page out of Charlemagne's playbook and invade, but this pressure is not a sufficient explanation for their acceptance of Christianity. For example, the Kievan Rus were more threatened by their immediate neighbors, the Muslim Bulghars and, particularly, the Jewish Khazars, than by the distant Christian empires of Byzantium and Germany. If neighborly pressure explains their conversion, they should have become Muslims or Jews. Instead the Rus opted to accept the Christianity of Byzantium, thus cementing a trading relationship with that empire. Neither Norway nor Sweden was threatened in any vital way by Christian outsiders when they adopted Christianity at the beginning of the eleventh century. Rather than being forced through conquest, the threat of conquest, or generalized political pressure from the outside, the pagans made a conscious choice to accept a new religion, because they were able to use that religion to their advantage.

But even when they do not buy into the "conquest and colonization" model, most modern scholars seem to take for granted that northern Europe was Christianized as a result of the persistent efforts of generations of missionaries. Their heroic work of preaching and baptizing eventually yielded fruit, despite temporary setbacks during "pagan reactions." The missionary preaches, and the pagan either is convinced to accept baptism or reacts negatively, often with violence. This is how things "should" be, in accordance with Christ's already quoted words and the gloss they received in early accounts of conversion. The responsibility for converting the heathens to Christianity fell on the shoulders of those who already were Christian. They sometimes felt this to be a heavy burden, as Pope Paschal I expressed in a letter from late 822 or early 823: "Since we are aware that some peoples who dwell in the North do not yet have knowledge of God, nor have they been reborn in the water of baptism, and they live in the shadow of death, and they idly serve creature rather than the Creator, therefore we have decided . . . to send this much revered brother, co-bishop, and friend Ebo, archbishop of the holy church in Rheims, to those regions to reveal the Truth."[11]

Ebo shared the pope's feelings in the matter, at least if we can believe Archbishop Rimbert of Hamburg, who was one of the most interesting medieval churchmen to write about the conversion of the north. In the 870s, he wrote that "Ebo himself was inspired by the Spirit of God and burned with eager desire to convert the heathen peoples and especially the Danes, whom he had often seen at the palace [of Charlemagne and his son Louis] and who, as he grieved to see, had been led astray by the wiles of the devil. In order to promote their salvation he longed to sacrifice himself and all that he possessed."[12]

These texts and others like them—there are plenty—are all about the desires and duties of the converter, known as "God's athlete" (*athleta Dei*).[13] The potential converts are portrayed as pitiful blank slates, the passive recipients of Christian benevolence, much as westerners in the eighteenth and nineteenth centuries liked to depict the original inhabitants of the regions that their governments and corporations were colonizing and their churches were missionizing. In fact, it is hard to escape the impression that nineteenth-century understandings of Christian mission still inspire modern understandings of the medieval conversion of Scandinavia.

An alternative way of telling the story of Scandinavian conversion is to begin not with the established narrative but with individual pieces of knowledge that we may extract from written and archeological sources. We may then construct our own story on the basis of that knowledge. A very different image of Scandinavian conversion emerges. Instead of the sudden and complete conversions achieved by missionaries and portrayed by medieval narrators, we see a slow and piecemeal assimilation of Christianity that extended over centuries. Thus, shifting the perspective from the missionary and his conquering sponsors to the recipients of Christianity, I will pose the question: what did Scandinavian leaders like Harald Bluetooth and Olav Tryggvason have to gain from converting to Christianity? The reasons for the success of Christianity must be sought among those who chose to become and remain Christians rather than among those who wanted to convert them.

The great driving force behind the conversion of Scandinavia was, I argue, the machinations of political leaders in northern Europe. Powerful chieftains lived there by the eighth century, as evidenced by their ostentatiously sumptuous graves as well as the archeological remnants of their residences, including their mead halls. But their power was essentially local. In addition, the power of such chieftains was not given once and for all: it was constantly contested. Competitors were always eager to take advantage of any weakness, and power could be as easily lost as it was gained. To gain, keep, and increase his power, a chieftain needed to be able to back up his claims with violence. Warriors were crucial; every chieftain needed warriors who were ready to kill at his command. Ambitious leaders built up loyal followings of warriors who made it possible to exert power over increasingly large groups of people. Chieftains worked hard to get and to keep their loyalty. This led to frequent, if not constant, warfare among them.[14]

In an era before they had access to the coercive powers of the state, chieftains needed to persuade, rather than to force, their warriors to follow them. A victorious warlord would always get followers because he was able to reward them with the spoils of victory. Victory equaled more booty, which equaled more gifts for more men, and more men equaled more victories. This basic equation governed how early medieval history played out in Scandinavia. Ambitious chieftains strove to strengthen the equation, especially by increasing the (perceived) value of the gifts they gave their warriors. This does not mean that the retinues of fighters surrounding Scandinavian leaders were made up of simple mercenaries, who fought for pay. By giving gifts, chieftains involved their warriors in a reciprocal relationship of gifts and countergifts. A warrior who had received a gift from his warlord was honor bound to reciprocate with his loyalty and fighting prowess. His manly worth depended on it, and chieftains strove to inspire this sense of honorable obligation in their followers.

Chieftains needed suitable gifts, and they used different strategies to give more of them. Some, like Olav Tryggvason, got more booty by sailing to Europe to plunder as Vikings. Others sought to refine the simple process of sharing booty, tribute, and plunder by using more-sophisticated means of persuasion. Many tried to make their booty last longer by employing artisans to work the spoils into beautiful artifacts. Centers for crafts and trade popped up all over Scandinavia during the Viking Age. This way, for the same "cost," chieftains had more gifts, and more attractive gifts, to distribute.

Others employed merchants who were able to acquire exotic objects, which were particularly valuable as gifts since they were rare and thus prestigious. Any minor chieftain could invite you to eat roast pork and drink mead out of cow horns, but only a select few could provide you with French wine in rare glass vessels and exotic walnuts for dessert. Local craftsmen made beautiful brooches and impressive clothes, but only truly well-connected and powerful chieftains wore or gave jewelry with carnelian beads from India, clothes with panels of luxurious Chinese silk, or peacock feathers. This is why Scandinavian chieftains participated in trade and organized artisans. They sold the products of the north, like polar bear and black fox fur, reindeer antlers, and walrus ivory, to the south, where they brought handsome prices, and they imported things that were rare and thus attractive in Scandinavia. Particularly ambitious chieftains would range farther afield, trading the even-richer furs of northern Russia and slaves captured during Viking raids and bringing home undreamed of riches in silver and gold from markets frequented by Arab and Byzantine merchants.

Chieftains further strengthened the ties with and among their followers, using religious and quasi-religious rituals to create social bonds as strong as family ties. The sacrificial meals of pre-Christian Scandinavia served this purpose, as did the customs of blood brotherhoods and the fellowships of warriors. Not content with homegrown traditions, ambitious chieftains imported Christianity, the most attractive foreign religion, just as they imported exotic trade goods. Christianity was a particularly desirable religion for a chieftain to share out among his followers for it was the prestigious religion of the most powerful people in Europe at the time: the English king and the Byzantine and Frankish emperors.

Some chieftains were more successful than others at playing the competitive gift-giving game. In the end, a few leaders stood out, having succeeded in creating for themselves stable kingdoms that they could pass on to their sons. This was the beginning of the history of the kingdoms of Denmark, Norway, and Sweden. This book ends with that beginning. It focuses on the preceding state of flux that existed during the Viking Age—a turmoil that produced some of the most fascinating episodes of European history.

I

The Dynamic Eighth Century:
Scandinavia Comes of Age

The pagan men from "the ends of the earth" in the north suddenly appeared on the European stage in around 780. Uncouth, unshaven, and—most importantly—unchristian, they were on the minds of rulers and intellectuals, a subject of wary conversation at the centers of power and culture in Europe, already before the beginning of the Viking raids. The Danes, in particular, were a political problem for the Frankish king Charlemagne, and all sorts of Scandinavians would soon become everyone's security problem, when the Viking Age began in earnest in 793.

The political and intellectual center of western Europe toward the end of the eighth century was Charlemagne's court, where the king "with a happy countenance" ruled his growing kingdom, and where the greatest minds of western Europe educated the king and the children of the Frankish elite. The court moved around with the hypermobile king. The court school, which eventually settled at the newly reconstructed palace in Aachen, was a serious intellectual powerhouse but also a playful and somewhat whimsical environment, where King Charles himself participated in intellectual games. Teachers and students wrote letters to each other, in which they showed off their rhetorical and poetical skills, and in which they competed sharply with each other. Two Italian intellectuals, who were among those Charlemagne had brought to his court, were particularly good at writing Latin verse in classical meters, and they entertained themselves, their king, the court, and the school with impish exchanges. Peter of Pisa was Charlemagne's own teacher of Latin, and he was also the king's ghostwriter of Latin poetry.[1]

"You never answered my question," wrote Charlemagne/Peter in a versified letter to Paul the Deacon, "whether you would prefer to be broken under heavy iron, lie in a wild prison dungeon when you are tired, or if you wish to consider carefully the face of pompous Sigifrit, who now holds his impious scepter over a pestiferous kingdom."[2] Sigifrit was king of the Danes, and he was a newly discovered enemy of Charlemagne when Peter wrote in the 780s.[3] Peter, speaking in the voice of Charlemagne, challenged Paul to go to Denmark and baptize Sigifrit, "who when he spots you will deprive you of life and art."

That an Italian schoolmaster, however distinguished an intellectual he was, would be able to convert and baptize the king of the Danes was so preposterous an idea that it was funny to Peter of Pisa. Paul was quick to pick up on the joke and heaped further abuse on Sigifrit in his very learned response, in which he several times quoted and alluded to Ovid, Virgil, Persius, and other classical Latin poets.

"If I were to be in such trouble as to behold Sigifrit's truculent countenance, I don't think that would be of much use," Paul responded, "for his uneducated heart lacks Latin speech, and his language is utterly unknown to me. I consider him an ape or a bristle-bearing brute. . . . Even though he is bearded and unshaven and very similar to a he-goat as he sets laws for the young bucks and rules over the goats," he will still be afraid of Charlemagne's weapons. Paul means that Charlemagne will put Sigifrit in his place with weapons, while his own Christian sermonizing would fail due to language problems. After military defeat, Sigifrit will become very gentle indeed and willing to be baptized. "Otherwise, he will come to us with his hands tied behind his back, and then Odin and Thor will be of no help to him."[4] Paul thought that Sigifrit, the archpagan, was so stubborn a pagan that only military conquest would suffice to convert him and, by extension, his people to Christianity. The method he recommended for Christianizing Sigifrit and his people was the same one Charlemagne was employing at the time against the Saxons.

Peter and Paul were not the only ones among Charlemagne's intellectuals to worry about the conversion of the Danes. In 789, their colleague Alcuin, who was also Charlemagne's teacher, asked a friend, an abbot in Saxony, whether there was any hope of converting the Danes.[5] The formulation of the question suggests that Alcuin did not expect an affirmative answer. No response from the abbot (whose identity we do not know) is preserved.

It is not surprising that Peter, Paul, and Alcuin worried and joked about the Danish king Sigifrit and his stubborn paganism in the 780s. The Danes had at the time become a political headache for leaders of the Frankish kingdom as Charlemagne was extending it eastwards across the Rhine. He had decided to conquer the Saxons in 773, and his first campaign there during that summer had been successful. The Saxons, however, unusually unwilling to be conquered, put up stubborn resistance, and it took thirty years and many very bloody summer campaigns to subdue them. Each summer they admitted defeat, were baptized, and gave hostages, promising to be faithful subjects of Charlemagne, only to take up their weapons again at the earliest opportunity.

To the north beyond the Saxons lived the Danes, who were a potential ally of the Franks, but they were in fact mostly hostile. When Charlemagne victoriously invaded Saxony for the third time in 776, the most important Saxon leader, Widukind, escaped the king's clutches by fleeing to Denmark, where the Frankish armies could not follow him. He came back in 778 and spurred on the Saxons to "revolt" once more against Charlemagne. The Franks suppressed the Saxons, again, and Widukind fled, again, but the sources do not tell us whereto. The Danes had at any rate become a player in the political game that Charlemagne was playing on his eastern border, and he was now forced to pay attention to them.

Indeed, Charlemagne soon took up diplomatic relations with King Sigifrit; a delegation led by a man with the Norse name Halvdan ("Halptani" in the Latin sources) showed up at a meeting of the important people in Charlemagne's kingdom in 782.[6] From that point on, the sources mention embassies in both directions now and then. It had become important for Frankish rulers to be in touch with the rulers of Denmark, and we may assume that it was important for the Danes to stay in contact with the most powerful ruler of Europe.

Soon enough, Scandinavians made their existence known in even more emphatic ways than by simply hiding a man whom Charlemagne considered a treacherous rebel. The "Viking Age" began in 793 with an armed attack on the defenseless monastery of Lindisfarne in northeastern England. Alcuin's reaction was twofold. First, he wrote a letter of consolation to the leader of the monastic community, Bishop Higbald.[7] He focused on the possible theological and eschatological implications of the attack (is it the "sign of some great guilt"?), and thus he talked of the attackers simply as "pagans," not "Danes" or "Northmen," although there is no reason to think that he did not know their origins. Indeed, in another letter where Alcuin refers to the unhappy fate of the "Church of St. Cuthbert" (Lindisfarne), he quotes the words of the prophet Jeremiah: "From the north an evil takes fire."[8]

Second, Alcuin wrote another consolatory text to the same addressee—a Latin poem consisting of 120 elegiac couplets—in which he attempted to put into context the "day when, alas, a pagan warband arrived from the ends of the earth, descended suddenly by ship and came to our land, despoiling our fathers' venerable tombs of their finery and befouling the temples dedicated to God." To soften the blow, Alcuin compared the sacking of Lindisfarne to the twofold destruction of the Temple of Jerusalem by the Babylonians and the Romans, the "barbarous ruins" remaining of "golden Rome," and the frailties of old age. Rather than blaming God and despairing, the monks of Lindisfarne ought to "appeal to His kindly mercy, so that He take tribulation away from us."[9]

After 793, as dangerous Scandinavians began to plunder and extort tribute all around northwestern Europe, they and their supposedly obstinate paganism captured the European imagination. It was in that context that Alcuin inserted an anecdote about Danish bullheadedness in the biography of St. Willibrord he wrote in 796 or soon thereafter. Alcuin claimed that Willibrord, whose main importance was as a missionary in Frisia before 714, had traveled the arduous way to Denmark, where he found King Ongendus "more savage than a wild beast and harder than any stone."[10] Needless to say, Willibrord did not accomplish anything with such unpromising material for conversion even though he was well received, or so Alcuin tells us. We recognize in Alcuin's story the same ideas as in the versified epistles of his colleagues and friends Peter and Paul: the Danes are obdurate in their paganism and there is no point in trying to preach to them or to convert them. When Alcuin wrote, the Frankish Empire was in the midst of conquering and converting Saxony. Peter, Paul, and Alcuin were trying to influence their king to go the same way with the Danes. There is, thus, no reason to suspect that Alcuin was reporting historical fact when he spoke of the encounter between Willibrord and Ongendus. He was simply commenting on the current political situation.

King Ongendus is mentioned in the Old English poems *Beowulf* and *Widsith* as King Ongentheow of the Swedes. We know from other sources that Alcuin knew "the songs of the heathen" (perhaps from his youth in England) and the names of persons who were mentioned in them. In a letter, he mentioned Ingeld, who also appears in *Beowulf*.[11] When Alcuin wished to include a story about Willibrord and a Danish king, he needed a name for that king. He found the name in the stuff of stories and poems that he knew, and he Latinized it as Ongendus. The fact that the king is mentioned in more than one source also does not mean that Alcuin was reporting the truth.

Peter, Paul, and Alcuin knew something about the threat of the Danes, but their writings do not exhibit any concrete geographical knowledge of the Scandinavian north. By the 820s, however, when another of Charlemagne's courtiers, Einhard, wrote a celebrated biography of his late master, he was able to describe the north of Europe better than anyone had before. He was the first writer to write of the Baltic Sea in a recognizable way: "A gulf of unknown length, but nowhere more than a hundred miles wide and in many parts narrower, stretches off towards the east from the western Ocean. Many tribes have settlements on its shores: the Danes and Swedes, whom we call Northmen, live along its northern shore and all the adjacent islands, while the southern shore is inhabited by the Slavs, Aisti, and various other tribes."[12]

Einhard was writing at a time when Carolingian intellectuals and kings no longer joked about the awful paganism of the Danes. They had become serious about finding allies and potential Christian converts in Denmark. They also knew more, since the Saxons had been pacified a generation earlier and many of them resettled all over the Frankish Empire. They must have brought geographical knowledge of their northern neighbors. A man who claimed to be a Danish king showed up in 826 at the court of Charlemagne's son and successor, Louis the Pious. Harald was baptized with his family and all his men amid pomp and circumstance at the Church of St. Albans outside Mainz and close to the imperial palace at Ingelheim.[13] This was a great triumph; the king of the Danes had submitted to Christ, and the emperor had been his godfather in baptism. Louis thought that the Danes would henceforth be allies. Unfortunately, Louis had misjudged the situation, and it turned out that Harald was not welcome back in Denmark, and he was unable to fight his way back, even with the reinforcements that his godfather provided. Harald became an imperial pensioner for the rest of his life. When the Carolingian Empire was split up among three brothers after the death of Louis the Pious, Harald even raided in the kingdom of one brother at the behest of another brother.[14]

Nevertheless, the 820s also saw the first organized religious missions to Scandinavia, first to Denmark, and then by the end of the decade also to Sweden. Archbishop Ebo of Rheims went to Denmark for the first time in 823, and his assistant Ansgar went to Sweden a few years later. The paganism of the north no longer seemed so impenetrable.[15]

The extension of Frankish interests toward the northeast and the incursion of Scandinavian pirates into western Europe had made Scandinavia a more distinct presence in the imagination of Europeans. Before 800, Charlemagne's courtiers had only hazy ideas of the geography of the north, while Einhard recognizably described the Baltic Sea. Scandinavia had, however, not been entirely unknown before Widukind fled to the Danes in 776. Learned geographers from the ancient Greeks on had included vague ideas of Scandinavia in their works, and they had supplemented their knowledge with what they could learn from merchants and soldiers. The historian Jordanes, writing in the 550s in Constantinople, knew for example that the Swedes "have splendid horses . . . [and] send through innumerable other peoples sappherine fur for trade." He was also able to report the names of several "peoples" living in

Scandinavia.[16] Still, Scandinavia definitively entered European history and the consciousness of Europeans only at the end of the eighth century. Why did it happen at that time specifically?

One answer is that the expansion of the Frankish kingdom toward the northeast put, especially, Denmark in closer touch with the "civilized" countries of Europe, but that is not the entire answer, nor even the most important one. The primary reasons for the appearance of Scandinavia on the European stage are to be sought inside Scandinavia, where things were rapidly changing in the eighth century. They would continue to change over the next centuries, leading in the end to the creation of Scandinavian kingdoms that adopted Christianity, notwithstanding the doubts of Paul the Deacon and Alcuin. As such, they took their place alongside other medieval European kingdoms, still perhaps to some degree exotic and strange, but no longer the utterly foreign and fearsome outsiders that Charlemagne's courtiers had imagined.

If the end of the eighth century marks a change in how seriously Europeans began to think about Scandinavia, that century also represents a watershed moment inside Scandinavia itself. It was during this period that the fundamental transformation of Scandinavian society that is the subject of this book began, as part of a long, drawn-out process. The remainder of this chapter will first sketch the power structure in eighth-century Scandinavia, as a kind of baseline for the transformation that will be described in the following chapters.[17] Then I shall highlight some of the changes that heralded the more fundamental transformation that Scandinavia experienced during the Viking Age.

Halls dominated the geography of power in Scandinavia during the eighth century.[18] They, or rather their archeological remains, are thus useful for providing an image of early medieval power. The tradition of building halls began around the fourth century, when they surely imitated, at least remotely, the audience halls, or *basilicae*, of Roman officials. Large buildings with a spacious interior, they had high ceilings and few inside posts supporting the roof (see figs. 1 and 2). Fireplaces at or close to their centers were not used for cooking or handicraft but provided light and heat. The real center of gravity in the hall was, however, the richly decorated high seat of the chieftain.[19] Here the chieftain sat, looking out over his guests and followers, whom he led in feasting, mead drinking, and sacrifices inside the hall, and in war outside it. It was here that the relationships that kept the group together were manifested and maintained.

In Scandinavian halls, archeologists have found evidence of the greatest luxuries of the time. Most spectacular are the sets of drinking vessels made out of glass, sufficient for at least half a dozen people, that have been found

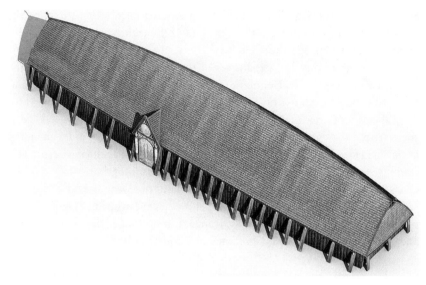

Fig. 1 The great hall in Lejre was the largest early-medieval building known from
the northern half of Europe. In its spacious interior, a chieftain maintained the
relationship with his warriors by feasting, drinking mead and wine, giving gifts,
and performing religious rituals. This careful computer reconstruction is based on
the archeology of the site, which provides good evidence for the architecture of the
hall, while the ornamental detail, although certainly contemporary, derives from
informed imagination. By courtesy of Nicolai Garhøj Larsen, EyeCadcher Media,
and Roskilde Museum.

in at least four different Scandinavian halls.[20] Single glass vessels have been
found in many other halls. Glass was not manufactured in early medieval
Scandinavia but had to be imported at great cost from the Frankish Empire
or even farther afield. Drinking was an important part of the ceremonies that
went on in the halls, as suggested in the early medieval poem *Beowulf*, which
describes what went on in King Hrothgar's hall, Heorot:

> [Hrothgar's queen, Wealhtheow] then went about
> to young and old, gave each his portion
> of the precious cup, until the moment came
> when the ring-adorned queen, of excellent heart,
> bore the mead-cup to Beowulf.[21]

The cup was precious, not so much because it was made from valuable
material or because of the liquid in it, but because of its associations with the
prestige and power of the chieftain. That prestige and power focused on the
hall and, specifically, on the high seat. No wonder that the loss of hall and

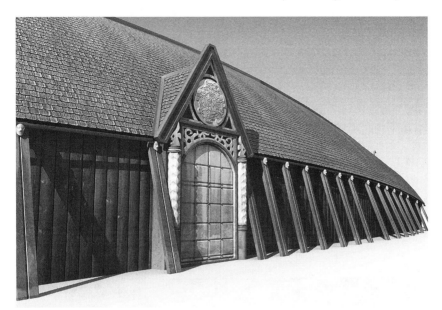

Fig. 2 The raking timbers supporting the roof made possible an open and roomy interior with few supporting pillars inside the Lejre hall. By courtesy of Nicolai Garhøj Larsen, EyeCadcher Media, and Roskilde Museum.

high seat, rather than the loss of human life, most grieved Beowulf when a fire-spewing monster harrowed his kingdom, "leav[ing] nothing alive":

> To Beowulf the news was quickly brought
> of that horror—that his own home,
> best of buildings, had burned in waves of fire,
> the gift-throne [high seat] of the Geats. To the good man that was
> painful in spirit, greatest of sorrows.[22]

Every chieftain had a hall and every hall discovered by archeologists is evidence of a chieftain's power. Because archeologists have discovered many halls in use in the eighth century, many chieftains must have held power at the time.[23]

An example of an eighth-century hall is Slöinge, situated on a ridge close to the Suseån River, in the Halland region in the southwestern part of the Scandinavian peninsula, today in Sweden.[24] Around 710, a chieftain constructed a new hall, measuring almost 30 meters in length and 8.5 meters in width at its broadest place. The hall succeeded other large buildings at the same site. Judging from the remnants that archeologists have found, Slöinge had been the home of resourceful chieftains already in the fifth and sixth centuries.

The chieftains residing in Slöinge had access to great wealth and resources, as is clear from the many glass shards found where the hall stood. Archeologists have uncovered shards from at least twenty-four different glass vessels, a very large number of vessels, especially considering that the settlement has been only partially excavated. Archeologists have also found fifty-seven *guldgub-bar*, thin golden foils with human images on them (see fig. 3). Some of these figures appear to embrace each other, even kiss. Most of them were found next to a roof-carrying post—a common place to find such figures. Similar gold-foil figures have emerged at some forty other Scandinavian archeological sites, usually in connection with halls or other places of high status. Their exact function is much debated, but most scholars think that they were used in a religious context. The finds at Slöinge suggest strongly that a powerful man resided in the hall there.

Fig. 3   A *guldgubbe* (thin golden foil with a human figure) from the hall at Slöinge. It is
uncertain which persons appear on *guldgubbar* and exactly what function these foils
had, but most agree that they had some kind of religious significance. Photo: Gunnel
Jansson, by courtesy of Statens Historiska Museum, Stockholm.

Slöinge was only one among many similar eighth-century halls spread over most of Scandinavia, from Borg on Lofoten, in northern Norway, to Gamla Uppsala, in eastern Sweden, to Dankirke, in southern Jutland, each a center of power, each the focus for a powerful man and his followers. Some thirty to forty Scandinavian halls from the first millennium have been excavated.[25] The extent of each chieftain's power would be clear when he invited his followers for mead drinking and feasting. Those who were loyal to him would come when he called, and their loyalty would be reinforced in the din of the mead hall. We may imagine that the power of all but the very greatest chieftains would be essentially local, but we must remember that his was a power not over territory but over people. The chieftain's power extended exactly as far as where the people were who answered his call. Some may have come from relatively far away, while others living quite close might have chosen not to come and drink mead with him, for whatever reason.

It is not hard to imagine how different chieftains with halls may have regarded each other with cautious suspicion, sometimes allying, sometimes falling out and waging war against each other, sometimes making peace or at least concluding an awkward truce. To burn down the hall of the chieftain you did not like was a strong strike against him, as we saw from Beowulf's reaction when his hall burned. Archeologists have indeed discovered that many halls burned down, sometimes but not always to be reconstructed again on the same spot. In Uppåkra, Scania, several of a sequence of halls situated on the same spot were burned. Three adults were burned with one of the halls around 400. To be sure, halls may burn for many reasons, not all of which have to do with war and defeat, but the ritualistic ways in which the glass vessels of some halls seem to have been destroyed suggest hostile acts.[26] *Beowulf* celebrates the deeds of the Danes' and King Hrothgar's mythical ancestors, who conquered many halls (here poetically represented by one of their most notable interior features, the "mead-benches" on which the followers of the chieftain sat):

> Often Scyld Scefing seized the mead-benches
> from many tribes, troops of enemies,
> struck fear into earls.[27]

Halls had been widespread before the eighth century. It is possible that the construction of halls, and thus competition over power, became more intense in the eighth century, but such a thesis would at the current state of research be based more on impressions than on hard data. The main point I wish to make by discussing the halls is that there were many people with power, if only a little power compared to later kings, in eighth-century Scandinavia.

On general grounds, we may expect those powerful persons to have competed with each other over what power there was, and this expectation is carried out by the evidence, as we will see in the following chapters.

When later medieval writers imagined the history of Scandinavia, they generally projected backwards their contemporary political situation, with a single king in each of the three Scandinavian kingdoms. They imagined, thus, "national" kings in the early middle ages, but we must be careful not to accept their ideas. Early medieval power in Scandinavia was fragmented, and its consolidation into the familiar three medieval kingdoms is part of the story that this book wishes to tell.

The dynamic eighth century is a suitable point to begin. The earlier form of the language, Proto-Norse, changed into Old Norse around the eighth century, and it was also at that time that the original Norse runic alphabet (*futhark*) of twenty-four characters was replaced with a set of sixteen runes.[28] These radical linguistic changes imply fundamental changes in society. Such changes are also visible in the archeological record.

Powerful persons carried out great building projects in the eighth century, demonstrating not only that they were able to command the work of many persons but also that they used the power they already had to increase their power. The largest early medieval construction in Scandinavia is the Dane-virke. This great earthen wall, reinforced with timber and accompanied by a ditch, stood two meters high and stretched seven kilometers across the base of the Jutland peninsula. It could not easily be flanked on its western side, where a marshy river presented obstacles. Its eastern end was at, or close to, the head of the Schlei, a long inlet of the Baltic Sea. The timber used for at least parts of it comes from trees felled in 737. The person who had the wall built may have wanted to improve defenses against attacking forces from the south, although constructions of this kind are actually not very useful militarily, except to demonstrate the power of the builder. He may also have used the wall as an early medieval counterpart to a toll barrier. Collecting tolls on overland trade would have made the powerful chieftain who controlled the Danevirke even more powerful.[29]

Not much earlier, in 726, a canal was built across the small island of Samsø, east of Jutland. Every ship approaching the two best routes to the Baltic Sea (through the Great and Little Belts, two of the Danish sounds) could be seen from the island. The canal made it possible to intercept quickly any ship that sailed into or out of the Baltic Sea by way of either channel. Thus, anyone who controlled the canal on Samsø could have charged a fee for any ship that sailed by, or simply have prevented it from passing at all. The Danevirke and the canal on Samsø would have taken many days for many men to build.

Their builders were powerful indeed to command so many man-hours, and both constructions would have made them even more powerful. It is possible that the building works were ordered by the same man, whose power would then have extended from the south of Jutland to the sea routes north of the Danish islands, but it is equally possible that the Danevirke was the response of one chieftain to another's construction of the Samsø canal.

The same may be said about another Danish construction of the early eighth century, the town of Ribe, on the southwestern coast of Jutland. It was originally founded around 704 to 710. The town bustled with artisans, such as shoemakers, potters, and jewelers, who produced goods that might have been useful for chieftains. Before Ribe was founded, artisans had for centuries worked at the hall of Dankirke, immediately south of Ribe. Dankirke is similar to the hall complex on the island of Helgö, in eastern Sweden, where artisans similarly produced artifacts useful for chieftains and had done so for centuries by 700. The chieftains at Helgö and Dankirke had artisans who worked close by, while the foundation of Ribe (established by the Dankirke chieftain, or by one of his competitors?) marks a new beginning. Ribe was a specialized site, no longer a hall with attached artisans, but a town built specifically and only for artisans (as well as perhaps traders). This was a harbinger of things to come. Within a hundred years, artisans would no longer work at Helgö, but there would be plenty of them at the town of Birka, on another island close by. Like Ribe, Birka was not organized around a hall. Other settlements for artisans and traders would sprout up around the Baltic and North Seas and at other convenient locations. While such towns multiplied, the halls met the opposite fate: more of them burned down and they became fewer and fewer. The hall at Helgö was destroyed around 800,[30] and the one at Slöinge disappeared at some point in the ninth or tenth century. In a few centuries, the plethora of chieftains in their halls would be replaced in Scandinavia by a few truly powerful men, who called themselves kings.

That change came out of the dynamism of the Scandinavian eighth century. So did the Viking raids, famously beginning around 790, and the wary attention that the Franks paid Denmark at about the same time. But the eighth century was only the beginning of all of these developments, which would truly take off in the following centuries.

2

The Raids of the Vikings

"Liberate us, Lord, from the wild Northmen who lay waste our country. They strangle the crowd of old men and of youth and of virgin boys. Repel from us all evil."[1] So prayed the inhabitants of the Frankish Empire in the ninth century, helping to give early medieval Scandinavians a reputation for being bloodthirsty and brutal pirates. The word "Viking" has in popular culture become associated with mindless violence. The Vikings were, however, not interested in violence and destruction for their own sake; their goal was to acquire wealth, which might gain their leaders the reputation of being generous chieftains, to whose standards warriors would flock. They went looking for wealth, destined for political use, wherever they were able, using whatever methods they had available.

The first Viking raid that made a lasting impression on the minds of Europeans took place in 793. Terrifying portents had, suitably, preceded it, as the *Anglo-Saxon Chronicle* reports:

> 793. Here terrible portents came about over the land of Northumbria, and miserably frightened the people: these were immense flashes of lightning, and fiery dragons were seen flying in the air. A great famine immediately followed these signs; and a little after that in the same year on 8 January [mistake for June] the raiding of heathen men miserably devastated God's church in Lindisfarne island by looting and slaughter.[2]

Lindisfarne was one of the classic Irish-inspired monasteries of northern England, original home of the Lindisfarne Gospels, the beautifully illuminated luxury copy of the Gospels that is today one of the greatest treasures of the British Library. The monastery occupied a striking spot on a tidal island off the coast of Northumberland. The famous scholar Alcuin, a native son of Northumberland living in voluntary exile at the court of Charlemagne, heard about this catastrophe and wrote a letter of consolation to the leader of the community at Lindisfarne, Bishop Higbald:

> Your tragic sufferings daily bring me sorrow, since the pagans have desecrated God's sanctuary, shed the blood of saints [monks] around the altar, laid waste the house of our hope and trampled the bodies of the saints "like dung in the street." I can only cry from my heart before Christ's altar: "O Lord, spare thy people and do not give the Gentiles thine inheritance, lest the heathen say, 'Where is the God of the Christians?'" What assurance can the churches of Britain have, if Saint Cuthbert and so great a company of saints do not defend their own? Is this the beginning of the great suffering, or the outcome of the sins of those who live there? It has not happened by chance, but is the sign of some great guilt.[3]

Alcuin's text demonstrates some of the sensibilities of an early medieval churchman. His language is elaborately rhetorical, suffused with scriptural quotations and allusions, and he sees the Scandinavian incursion in apocalyptic terms, understanding the Vikings as God's punishment for human sin. When he wonders whether the raid on Lindisfarne is "the beginning of the great suffering," this is not a premonition of the Viking Age; Alcuin wonders if the disaster in Northumberland might not herald the suffering that, according to the prophets, would pave the way for the end of the world. Like most medieval Christians, Alcuin was convinced that Christ's Second Coming could not be far off.

The world did not come to an end after the Lindisfarne raid, but many more raids, some even more disastrous, followed over the next centuries, both in the British Isles and on the European continent. The raids were, however, slow to get off the ground. The decades following the sack of Lindisfarne, in 793, saw mostly small and isolated raids in the north of the British Isles. The Vikings focused on raiding monasteries, which in general were undefended and easy targets. They looted the famous theologian Bede's old monastery at Jarrow (on the Tyne River, some distance south of Lindisfarne) in 796,[4] while the famous and rich monastery of Iona, off the west coast of Scotland, was repeatedly attacked, in 795, 802, and 806.[5] On the last occasion, sixty-eight members of the community were killed "by heathens," that is, by Vikings. Enough is enough, the abbot and the remaining monks thought, and they moved their monastery and the sacred relics of St. Columba from Iona to Kells, Ireland, in 807.[6] The Vikings continued their small hit-and-run raids, committing atrocities such as taking a large number of women captive (probably to be sold as slaves) from Howth, Ireland, in 821 and "shaking" the relics of St. Comgall from their shrine at Bangor, also in Ireland, in 824.[7] The reliquary was obviously worth a great deal more to the raiders than the bones of the saint, although the chronicler is more upset about the disrespect shown toward the sacred relics. Sometimes, however, defenders defeated them, as in 812 when two bands of "heathens" were "slaughtered" in Ireland.[8] During the first three decades of the ninth century, very few Viking raids on the European continent were recorded. The Frankish emperors and their annalists worried more about diplomatic relations with the kings of the Danes. Scandinavians carried out a major raid on Frisia in the Low Countries in 810: they ravaged the Frisian Islands and imposed a tribute of one hundred pounds of silver on the vanquished, but this was the only major raid on continental Europe recorded before 830.[9]

Things changed most definitely from the 830s, when Scandinavians began to appear more regularly, in larger and larger bands, raiding more widely along the coasts of Europe and venturing ever farther inland. They attacked, for example, the trade town of Dorestad in Frisia (in Carolingian territory) every year from 834 to 837, and only a storm prevented yet another attack in 838.[10] In 837, the cleric Prudentius resignedly noted from the viewpoint of the imperial palace at Aachen that "the Northmen at this time fell on Frisia with their usual surprise attack."[11] From a medieval observer's perspective, a Scandinavian attack was no longer completely unexpected. By the 840s, they had sailed as far as the Iberian Peninsula to plunder, and twenty years later the Mediterranean coasts of Spain, Italy, and Africa had been visited by the Northmen. From the 840s, they began to spend the winter in fortified encampments in Europe, rather than return home to Scandinavia with their loot. This made continued raiding the following year easier, and it was a harbinger of things to come. Eventually Scandinavians settled permanently farther south in Europe, never to return to their northern homelands (see chapter 4).

It is possible to chronicle the comings and goings of the Vikings in considerable detail throughout the Viking Age on the basis of the year-by-year summaries of contemporary history ("annals") taken down by churchmen everywhere in Europe; such an account would be a relentless and ultimately quite uninteresting succession of dates, more or less obscure place names, and sources. Instead, we may take a couple of years from the mid-840s as an example, affording a stark view of the havoc the Vikings were wreaking in Europe. By the middle of the decade, the three sons of Louis the Pious had achieved an awkward peace in their fratricidal struggles, and each of them was firmly ensconced in his separate kingdom. Arabs ruled much of the Iberian Peninsula, except for the north, where Christian kings prevailed. The British Isles were divided into many petty kingdoms, as was the usual state of affairs there in the early Middle Ages. Against this backdrop, different bands of Vikings show up just about everywhere in western Europe during the years 844–845.

To begin from the northwest, the Vikings were certainly in 845 a noticeable presence in Ireland. They took Abbot Forannán, of the great monastery of Armagh, as prisoner together with "his halidoms and following." The abbot returned safely the next year, with the relics of St. Patrick, surely in return for a great ransom, although the laconic sources tell us nothing about why he was returned. Probably a different band plundered Dunamase and killed Abbot Aed of Terryglass and Prior Ceiternach of Kildare "and many others." The *Annals of Ulster* also registers two Viking encampments in Ireland in 845, one on Lough Ree on the Shannon River (from where Connaught and Meath were plundered and several monasteries burned) and one at Cluain Andobuir. The Irish fought back and had some success. High King Niall mac Áeda "inflicted a battle-rout on the heathens in Mag Ítha," and Maelsechnaill took a further step toward his high kingship by capturing the Viking leader Tuirgéis, whose name in Norse must have been Thorgils. The Viking chieftain was ignominiously sewn into a sack and drowned in Lough Owel.[12]

We know nothing of what the Vikings might have accomplished in Scotland in the 840s, for there simply are no preserved sources to inform us.[13] The English sources are also silent regarding the mid-840s, for the events that the *Anglo-Saxon Chronicle* notes under 845 actually took place in 848: the Vikings were soundly defeated then. A party of men from Somerset and Dorset, under the leadership of two ealdormen and the bishop of Sherborne, "fought against a Danish raiding-army at the mouth of the Parret, and made great slaughter there and took the victory."[14] The *Annals of Saint Bertin* notes, under 844, that the Vikings launched a major attack on the island of Britain. "After a battle lasting three days, the Northmen emerged the winners: plundering, looting, slaughtering everywhere. They wielded power over the land at will."[15] The Viking victory described must be the one that the *Anglo-Saxon Chronicle* puts under the year 840, but which in reality happened in 843.[16]

If we do not know very much about England and Scotland in 844 or 845, we know more about the Continent. "In the same year [845] unbelievers [Vikings] invaded Christian lands at many points," wrote the annalist Gerward, who once had been the librarian of Emperor Louis the Pious at Aachen.[17] A large fleet attacked and laid waste the fortress "which is called Hamburg," including the future saint Ansgar's fledgling church. The pirates "seized the town and plundered it. . . . They came in the evening and they remained that night and the next day and night; and when everything had been burnt and destroyed they took their departure. The church there . . . and the monastery . . . were reduced to ashes. . . . Everything that was used in the services of the church and all [Ansgar's] treasures and possessions were lost by pillage and by fire during the enemy attack." Ansgar himself escaped with his life and his most prized possessions—the relics of the church—but without his cloak.[18]

The Vikings also attacked farther west. Gerward claims that the Frisians killed more than twelve thousand attacking Vikings, while six hundred were killed in Gaul.[19] The numbers are surely exaggerated and symbolic, as is the claim that 120 ships sailed up the Seine to Paris in March under the leadership of Ragnar. When the West Frankish ruler sent an army to stop them, they approached on both sides of the river. Ragnar simply attacked the weaker side, defeated it, and captured 111 prisoners (another no doubt symbolic figure). He had the prisoners hanged on an island in the Seine, in full view of the still-undefeated army contingent on the other side of the Seine. With this deliberate act of psychological warfare, Ragnar broke the remaining resistance of the Frankish army. Ragnar's men went on to plunder the rich monastery of St. Germain just outside Paris. King Charles the Bald negotiated for terms and agreed to pay Ragnar seven thousand pounds of silver, thereby persuading him to go away with his band of Vikings.[20]

The Vikings did relinquish Paris and the Seine valley, but they "devastated all the coastal regions, plundering and burning" farther south. Two annalists tell us, however, that God revenged his faithful by striking the Vikings "either with blindness or insanity, so severely that only a very few escaped to tell the rest about the might of God."[21] There is probably an element of pious wishful thinking in these accounts, which most likely are not independent of each other.

Farther south, in Aquitaine, another Viking force sailed in 844 unopposed up the Garonne, wreaking havoc on their way to Toulouse. Some of them appear not to have thought the plunder was sufficiently rewarding, so they turned back and instead sailed on to the Iberian Peninsula.[22] There they won a reputation of being "a pagan and overly cruel people." King Ramiro I of Asturias defeated them close to the still-standing second-century lighthouse then known as "Farum Brigantium" and now as the Tower of Hercules. "He killed many of their bands and he put fire to their ships," allegedly sixty vessels. Those who remained sailed on west and south, where they attacked Lisbon on 20 August 844, and then Seville on 11 November. There "they took booty and killed many Chaldeans [Muslims] with the sword and fire." Arab sources specify that Seville was taken by storm but also claim that the Vikings were defeated later in the year and that many of them were hanged.[23]

As we have seen, several different bands of Scandinavian raiders were active in 844–845 on the coasts and along the rivers of western Europe from Hamburg to Seville. Some of them, such as those attacking Hamburg, Paris, and Seville, must have been quite large. Later generations of Vikings would continue to raid in similar patterns, extending their raids even farther south, into the Mediterranean, as their bands grew even larger.

Scandinavians also raided north and east of Hamburg, even inside Scandinavia itself. This is easily forgotten, since their victims there have left few written testimonies, unlike those in western Europe. Soon after the missionary Ansgar visited the town of Birka, in eastern Sweden, around 850, the Swedes sacked the town "Apulia" on the other side of the Baltic Sea. The inhabitants of that town had recently defeated a band of Danes.[24]

A runestone from Västra Strö, in what is now the southernmost part of Sweden, was raised in memory of Ozzur, "who died in the north *i vikingu.*"[25] The word "viking" is here used as a verbal noun that means "raiding, harrying," so Ozzur had participated in a Viking raid to the north, one may guess somewhere else in Sweden or in Norway.

The Great Invasions of England

The raids in 844–845 were perpetrated by several largish but independently operating bands of Vikings. Within a couple of decades, however, huge contingents would occasionally gather for coordinated attacks, which could make kingdoms teeter and fall.

In 865, we hear for the first time about what the *Anglo-Saxon Chronicle* calls the "Great Army" (*micil here*) or even the "Great Heathen Army" (*mycel hæðen here*). This force of what must have been hundreds of ships and thousands of warriors would stay together for the next thirty years, waging war in both England and Francia, until it broke up in 896.[26] It would dramatically change the political and demographic makeup of England, which in 865 was partitioned among four kingdoms. The Great Army destroyed three of these kingdoms: Northumbria fell in 867, East Anglia in 869, and Mercia collapsed in 874. Only Wessex under Alfred the Great held out, and even that was close. The Vikings at first installed puppet kings in the conquered kingdoms, but soon Norse kings ruled them directly.

A Viking chieftain who became king was Guthrum. From his power base in East Anglia, he fought the last remaining Anglo-Saxon kingdom, Wessex, under King Alfred. In 878, the two kings agreed to make peace, and as part of the agreement Guthrum accepted baptism, with Alfred as his godfather.[27] In baptism he received the new name Athelstan, a good old Anglo-Saxon royal name. A preserved peace treaty, which may come from this occasion or, more likely, from somewhat later, lays down the boundary between Alfred's and Guthrum's realms.[28] This boundary more or less coincides with the borders of the Danelaw, the region in eastern England where many Norse settled, where Norse kings ruled, and where many place names as well as the genetic makeup of the population still testify to the influx of Norse-speaking Scandinavians.[29]

The Great Army stayed together, raiding and toppling kingdoms, for some thirty years. It is hard to imagine that many persons would have stayed in the army for its entire duration: the life expectancy of an early-medieval warrior cannot have been that long, and surely many returned home or settled in new homes when they were satisfied with the booty they had gathered. The army must have constantly resupplied its ranks with young Scandinavians, and perhaps also with non-Scandinavian would-be Vikings.[30]

After the breakup of the Great Army the raids continued. At that point, in 896, groups of warriors went off, "some to East Anglia, some to Northumbria, and those who were without money or property got themselves ships there, and went south across the sea to the Seine."[31] One imagines that the Vikings going to East Anglia and Northumbria settled there, while we know that those crossing over to the Continent under the leadership of Hundeus (or Huncdeus) raided in the Seine valley, continuing into the valley of the Oise. There the Carolingian king, Charles the Simple, who was working on taking back his father's and his brothers' French kingdom from the non-Carolingian usurper Odo, allied with Hundeus, against the strong advice of Archbishop Fulco of Rheims. Probably as a part of the agreement between Charles and the Viking leader, Hundeus accepted baptism, with the king as his godfather.[32] The sources have nothing more to say about Hundeus, but Charles got his kingdom when Odo died in 898.

Judging from the sources, raiding seems to have focused on the British Isles and the Continent at different periods. According to the *Anglo-Saxon Chronicle*, England was relatively at peace during much of the tenth century, until the raids resumed there about 980.[33] At first, they were small, but the raiding parties grew into formidable hosts of warriors. England suffered several great invasions during the period 991–1016.

Initially, the invading armies were content to ask for an appropriately great tribute, known in England as the danegeld. The army that invaded in 991, under the leadership of King Svein Forkbeard of Denmark and Olav Tryggvason, a future king of Norway, defeated the English forces at the Battle of Maldon, on 10 or 11 August 991, and collected a tribute of 10,000 pounds of silver. After assembling new armies (probably containing some of the same people) the Vikings returned to collect more danegeld: 16,000 pounds in

994, 24,000 pounds in 1002, 36,000 pounds in 1007, and 48,000 pounds in 1012. These raids culminated in Svein Forkbeard's invasion in 1013, which forced King Ethelred to escape to his wife's family in Normandy, and Svein became recognized as king of England. He soon died, in 1014, but his son Cnut organized a new invasion. He became king of England in 1017 and the next year imposed the last and the greatest of the danegelds, totaling 82,500 pounds of silver, to pay off his army.[34] He also became king of Denmark in 1018, when his brother Harald died, and expanded his power into both Norway and Sweden before his death in 1035.[35]

Cnut's success invited imitation. In 1066, the Norwegian king Harald Hardrada set out to invade England, but he was defeated and killed at the Battle of Stamford Bridge on 25 September. The Anglo-Saxon army, in turn, was defeated at the Battle of Hastings less than a month later, by a Norman army under Duke William, later known as "the Conqueror."

Harald's defeat at Stamford Bridge is a convenient and conventional end point for the Viking Age. Scandinavians continued to raid and plunder, to be sure, but less and less so in western Europe, where the various kingdoms became too well organized and too vigorously defended to provide the easy booty that they previously had. King Cnut's great-nephews, King Svein Estridssen's sons, tried to invade England in 1069 in collaboration with the Anglo-Saxon pretender Edgar Ætheling. They took York and plundered its castle before they were forced to retreat.[36] But Scandinavian raiders generally directed their energies elsewhere, for example to the east of Denmark, to the shores of the Baltic Sea. There is little difference between the goals and methods of the Viking raids of the tenth century and those of the Swedish raids in Finland in the twelfth, or for that matter those of the "pagan" raid in Sweden in 1188.[37] Only convention makes us label the tenth-century fighting "Viking raids," while the twelfth-century raids, depending on the perspective, are known as "crusades" (Swedes in Finland) or "pirate attacks" (pagans in Sweden).[38]

The Success of the Vikings

We may think of the Vikings as undefeatable, but their forces were not always successful. Sometimes, nature proved overwhelming, as when in 838 "Danish pirates sailed out from their homeland but a sudden severe storm arose at sea and they were drowned with scarcely any survivors."[39] At other times, the intended victims defended themselves. The warriors who came on 350 ships and attacked Canterbury and London in 851 were successful, putting to flight Beorhtwulf, the king of Mercia, and his army. They then went south, over the Thames and into Surrey, and were less successful: "King Aethelwulf and his son Aethelbald, with the army of Wessex, fought against them at Oak Field, and there made the greatest slaughter of a heathen raiding-army that we have ever heard tell of, and there took the victory."[40]

The sources, however, tell much more often of Viking successes, either in raiding and plundering or in trading threats for tribute, large amounts of valuables that European leaders used to pay off the would-be raiders. The exploits of the Norwegian Viking leader Olav Tryggvason in southern England in the early 990s represent a characteristic chain of events: "Here in this year [991] Olav came with ninety-three ships to Folkestone, and raided round about it, and then went from there to Sandwich, and so from there to Ipswich, and overran all that, and so to Maldon. And Ealdorman Byrhtnoth came against them there with his army and fought with them; and they killed the ealdorman there and had possession of the place of slaughter. And [994] afterwards they made peace with them."[41]

As part of the peace settlement, Olav would receive ten thousand pounds of silver. The English had put up resistance, but the Vikings defeated their army under ealdorman Byrhtnoth at Maldon, which became the subject of a rightly famous Anglo-Saxon poem extolling the tragic heroism of the ealdorman and his followers in the face of defeat.

Why were the Vikings so successful, not only in the 990s but much of the time?[42]

The explanation is not obvious from their numbers. The Great Army numbered in the thousands, but most raids were carried out by smaller groups numbering at most in the hundreds. European emperors and kings could field armies of superior numbers. A conservative estimate of the size of Charlemagne's army puts it at about five thousand warriors.

Furthermore, Viking weaponry was not in any obvious way superior to that of their victims.[43] Scandinavian battle axes, spears, and arrows were efficient, but Vikings nevertheless coveted Frankish battle swords, which were famous for their craftsmanship all over Europe and even in Baghdad. Scandinavian warriors often acquired Frankish swords; many were buried with them. The Franks were aware of the superiority of their weapons; Emperor Charles the Bald in 864 prohibited the sale of weapons to Northmen, on pain of death.[44]

The most important reason for Viking success was that the raiding bands were fast, adaptable, and cleverly opportunistic. They were able to attack where they knew the rewards were great and the defenses weak. They knew when to fight and when to escape, when to approach by ship and when to ride overland, when to accept tribute and when to plunder. Several groups of Vikings could band together quickly when needed and go their separate ways when this served them better. Indeed, a warrior band could even take employment with a European ruler to stave off another Viking band or to fight his other enemies, even his own family members: "To Sigfrid and Gorm and their accomplices he [Charles the Fat in 882] gave several thousand pounds of silver and gold which he had seized from the treasury of St-Stephen at Metz and from the resting-places of other saints, and he gave them permission to stay so that they could go on ravaging a part of his cousin's kingdom as they had before."[45]

Vikings are often in modern popular culture portrayed as warriors who were violent for the sake of violence itself, but for the Vikings, violence was the calculated means toward desirable ends. In this, they are not different from most political actors in world history. The early Middle Ages were as violent a period as any other. Any medieval or contemporary history of Emperor Charlemagne, for example, describes his frequent wars against one after another of his neighbors: the Lombards in Italy, the Basques, the Bretons, the Saxons, the Avars, and others.

Yet, Charlemagne's exploits are generally presented in a positive, almost triumphal light in medieval sources, as well as in modern accounts. Charlemagne was the victorious, strong emperor, who has now even become the symbol of the European Union, which has borrowed his name for a huge office building in Brussels. Almost all the medieval sources for his exploits, however, were produced by his subjects, some of the same writers who were greatly dismayed by the violence of the Vikings. The difference is one of perspective. As long as the violence was directed outwards, Frankish writers did not mind it, but when the Franks themselves became the victims of violence, they protested loudly. The same may be said about others who suffered Viking aggression. Since Scandinavians did not have much of a written culture in the Viking Age, the perspective of their victims on the Continent has dominated the modern view of the period, inspiring an understanding of Viking violence as unique and extraordinary.[46]

The Greed of the Vikings

The goals and methods of Scandinavian raiders were, in fact, very similar to those of Christian European rulers. In their raids they were primarily seeking portable wealth, which they could bring home, rather than opportunities for violence. The sources occasionally spell this out explicitly.[47] When, for example, the German king Louis III died in 882, the Vikings "exulted with exaggerated joy and no longer thought of fighting but instead of booty." Louis died without a son, so his brother Charles the Fat succeeded him, but Charles was far away in Italy at the time. The Vikings used the resulting power vacuum to plunder the great cities of Trier and Metz.[48]

Many examples show how the "minds of that greedy people caught fire at the prospect of getting money."[49] In 865, for example, "Northmen had got into the monastery of St. Denis, where they stayed for about twenty days, carrying off booty from the monastery to their ships each day."[50] St. Denis was the most important monastery of France, where kings from the Merovingians to the Bourbons were buried, and it had accumulated enormous wealth over the years. The Vikings must have been able to take home enormous riches from this raid, unless the annalist Hincmar of Rheims is correct in stating that they all died of disease in divine retribution: "The Northmen who had sacked St. Denis became ill with various ailments. Some went mad, some were covered in sores, some discharged their guts with a watery flow through their arses: and so they died."[51]

Other examples of the "greed of the Vikings" may easily be found in European chronicles. In 1048, for example, the Scandinavian chieftains Lothen and Yrling arrived at Sandwich in southern England with twenty-five ships. They "took untold war booty in men, in gold and in silver, such that no-one knew what it all was." After this success, they turned around to attack the island of Thanet, "wanting to do the same there." However, the local people withstood their attacks successfully and put the Vikings to flight. Instead, they raided in Essex, taking "men and whatever they could find." After these successful forays, they sailed off "to Baldwin's land" (Flanders) on the other side of the English Channel, where they sold their booty. The captured men would have been sold as slaves. Lothen, Yrling, and their Vikings thus exchanged their loot for precious metals that they could more easily bring home and feed into the gift economy. The *Anglo-Saxon Chronicle* tells us that afterwards they "travelled east from where they came earlier," supposedly back to Scandinavia.[52]

The "minds that caught fire at the prospect of getting money" are visible also in Scandinavian sources from the Viking Age. Early medieval Scandinavian literature often extols plunder and war booty and celebrates the heroes who were able to take it. This is true for some of the oldest remnants of that literature, like the ninth-century runic inscription on the great stone at the church in Rök in eastern Sweden that contains what may be brief allusions to a handful of then-famous stories. Readers are meant to fill in the context for themselves, which we moderns often are unable to do. One of the allusions hints at a story about war booty: "I say the folktale, which the two war booties were, which twelve times were taken as war booty, both at once from different men."[53] We no longer know what the story was about these war booties, although it is tempting to imagine a story with heroism, treachery, tragedy, and astounding riches. The important point is that there was a story, and that the sponsor of the Rök stone thought it worthwhile to include it in his inscription, suggesting that the idea of war booty loomed large in the imagination of ninth-century Scandinavians.[54]

Skaldic poetry provides further evidence. An example is a stanza composed by Kormak Ögmundarson in the middle of the tenth century. Kormak was an Icelandic warrior in the retinue of the Norwegian earl Sigurd, who resided in Lade, close to what is now the city of Trondheim. In one of his poems, Kormak boasts about his prowess by describing how he "one morning on Ireland" was coloring his sword red with blood "in order to conquer gold."[55] He had fought the Irish to conquer wealth. He is not likely to have gone there alone, but as a member of Sigurd's (or another chieftain's) band of warriors. We have seen earlier in this chapter that Vikings were able to win much wealth in Ireland.

Some Viking bands indeed accumulated great riches, as Europeans discovered when they occasionally defeated Vikings who had already been raiding for some time. When a group of Frisians, for example, in 885 defeated a Viking band, they found "such a mass of treasure in gold and silver and other movables that all from the greatest to the least [of the Frisians] were made wealthy."[56] Other Europeans who managed to overcome Vikings and take their encampments had similar experiences. Locally organized troops managed to conquer a Viking fortress in 923, only to find "an enormous amount of booty" and "a thousand captives." The captives also represented wealth, since they could be sold as slaves.[57]

It is tempting to think that many of the valuable objects and metals that archeologists have found in Scandinavia were booty from raids in Europe,[58] but it is difficult to distinguish stolen objects from what reached the north through trade or as gifts. The silver of a neck ring found on the island of Senja in the far north of Norway (above the Arctic Circle) was most likely taken as booty in Frisia. Or at least that is the interpretation suggested by a runic inscription on the ring: "We traveled to meet the valiant men of Frisia, we divided the spoils of the fight."[59]

What treasures the Vikings desired most becomes clear when one sees what they demanded when negotiating peace. In the poem about the Battle of Maldon, a messenger from the camp of the Scandinavians comes to Ealdorman Byrhtnoth with the following message:

> The brave seafarers have sent me to say to you
> That they will be so good as to let you give gold rings
> In return for peace. It is better for you
> To buy off our raid with gold
> Than that we, renowned for cruelty, should cut you down in battle.[60]

The Vikings wanted gold. Byrhtnoth refused the offer and was defeated and killed. Other leaders, in contrast, were happy to pay off invading Scandinavians: "King Charles . . . ordered a tax to be levied on the treasures of the churches and on all *mansi* [*mansus* = a tax unit for agricultural land] and on traders—even very small-scale ones: even their houses and all their equipment were assessed so that the tribute could be levied on them. For the Danes had promised that if 3,000 pounds of silver, weighed out under careful inspection, were handed over to them, they would turn and attack those Danes who were busy on the Seine and would either drive them away or kill them."[61]

In one exceptional case, an object that is known to have been looted and later exchanged for gold survives. This is a beautifully decorated Latin Gospel book, which was stolen from a church in England and then redeemed at some point between the 850s and the 880s, according to an Old English inscription on its first page: "I, Earl Alfred, and my wife Werburg procured this book from the heathen invading army with our own money; the purchase was made with pure gold."[62] Earl Alfred and Werburg explain that they did not want "these holy works to remain any longer in heathen hands." They presented the book to Christ Church in Canterbury with the stipulation that it should be read aloud every month for their souls and that of their daughter Alhthryth.[63] Ironically, the manuscript is now one of the treasures of the Royal Library in Stockholm, where it was acquired through perfectly lawful ways after the dissolution of the English monasteries in the sixteenth century. Whichever Vikings had gotten their hands on the book were able to return home to Scandinavia with pure gold in its stead.

Scandinavian raiders not only traded in looted artifacts for precious metals but also captured people for enslaving or for ransoming. Occasionally, Vikings were able to capture some person of great value, as in 858: "Another group of those pirates captured Abbot Louis of St. Denis along with his brother Gauzlin, and demanded a very heavy fine for their ransom. In order to pay this, many church treasuries in Charles [the Bald]'s realm were drained dry, at the king's command. But even all this was far from being enough: to bring it up to the required amount, large sums were eagerly contributed also by the king, and by all the bishops, abbots, counts and other powerful men."[64] Louis was a grandson of Emperor Charlemagne and served as the chancellor of his cousin King Charles the Bald.[65] Gauzlin was his half-brother and would later become both abbot of St. Denis and bishop of Paris. The "very heavy" ransom amounted to 686 pounds of gold and 3,250 pounds of silver.

Capturing these two ecclesiastical dignitaries was only the most spectacular Viking kidnapping; they constantly captured lesser persons. A band of Vikings who arrived in western Britain in 917, for example, raided "where it suited them" and took captive Bishop Cyfeiliog of Llandaff. King Edward the Elder of Wessex paid his ransom of forty pounds of silver.[66]

Raiding with weapons in hand was risky business. "He met death in viking on the western route," a Swedish runestone from around 1000 comments laconically.[67] Determined resistance could appear where it was least expected. Such risks explain why the Vikings often preferred to negotiate for a tribute. It seems that sometimes it was enough for them to show up in numbers and have some initial military success to be offered a payment in exchange for going away. Northmen were, for example, about to attack Frisia in 852, but when they received a "payment as large as they asked for, they headed off elsewhere."[68] When a group of Vikings sailed up the Loire River in 868, reaching Orléans unopposed, they were offered a ransom to save the city.[69]

The strategy of the Vikings was similar to that employed by many nomadic peoples of the Eurasian steppes: ensure that you are swift in appearing and disappearing, acquire a reputation for being dangerous and cruel, and people will be willing to pay you when you suddenly appear at their gates.[70]

Warriors who extracted tribute once from a population were likely to come back for more. In some places, Scandinavians succeeded in making a population pay tribute regularly. The *Annals of St. Bertin* notes that this happened in Ireland in 847: "The Irish, who had been attacked by the Northmen for a number of years, were made into regular tribute-payers."[71] The *Russian Primary Chronicle* reports, similarly, that Scandinavians ("Varangians") were able to collect regular tribute among the tribes of Russia from 859: "The Varangians from beyond the sea imposed tribute upon the Chuds, the Slavs, the Merians, the Ves', and the Krivichians."[72]

In the late tenth century, Vikings began to take tribute, as we have seen, from the weak English kingdom at intervals of several years. This danegeld increased in size with every collection and explains why more Anglo-Saxon coins (about forty thousand) have been found in Scandinavia than in England itself.[73] The reasoning behind the payment of such tributes is spelled out in the *Anglo-Saxon Chronicle* under the year 1006:

> Then there arose so great a terror of the [Viking] raiding-army that no-one could think or plan how they should be got out of the country, or this country guarded against them, because they had severely marked every shire in Wessex with burning and with raiding. The king began to plan earnestly with his councillors as to what they all thought most advisable as to how this country might be protected before it was entirely done for. Then the king and his councillors decided that, though it were hateful to them all, tax [tribute] must needs be paid to the raiding-army for the good of the entire nation. Then the king sent to the raiding-army and ordered it to be made known to them that

he wished there to be a truce between them, and that they should be granted tax and provisions; and they all accepted that, and they were provisioned throughout the English race.⁷⁴

Scandinavians who returned home with their share of the money evidently thought this was boast worthy. One of them was a Swede named Ulf. He had a runestone raised in Orkesta in the province of Uppland in eastern Sweden (see fig. 4): "And Ulf has taken three payments [*giald*; cf. "danegeld"] in England. That was the first that Tosti paid. Then Thorketill paid. Then Cnut paid."⁷⁵ The three other names mentioned are those of the Viking leaders who collected danegeld in 1006, 1012, and 1018 (the last is King Cnut). They had distributed the silver among their followers, among whom Ulf was one. Another participant in Cnut's conquest of England, a Norwegian named Bjor, was not as lucky as Ulf. He never got any share in the loot, and he never returned home. He "died in the retinue when Cnut attacked England," according to the runestone his father, Arnsteinn, had made in his memory.⁷⁶

Vikings who returned home to Scandinavia brought the booty they had won from raiding and tribute taking. The Viking chieftains Sigfrid and Gorm "sent ships loaded with treasure and captives back to their country" in 882.⁷⁷ Ulf paid for a boastful runestone, but others used their gains in other ways.

In exacting booty and tribute during expeditions to the south, Scandinavian leaders operated in the same way as rulers in Christian Europe.⁷⁸ Charlemagne fought wars against his neighbors almost every year, so much so that the writers of the *Royal Frankish Annals* felt obliged to point out the exceptional years when there was no war. Each war produced booty, as for example when the Frankish army in 796 entered the central fortification of the Avars and found enormous riches.⁷⁹ The Carolingians also received annual tribute from some other neighbors: 350 pounds of silver from the Beneventans and 50 pounds from the Bretons. It is no wonder that the Greeks, according to Einhard, had a proverb "If you have a Frank as your friend, he is not your neighbor."⁸⁰ Taking tribute from lesser rulers was such an ingrained part of Frankish politics that the cleric who penned the *Annals of Fulda* did not hesitate to upbraid Charles the Fat when he in 882 paid tribute to the Viking chieftain Sigfrid: "What was still more of a crime, he did not blush to pay tribute, against the custom of his ancestors, the kings of the Franks, and following the advice of evil men, to a man from whom he ought to have exacted tribute and hostages."⁸¹

The tribute and booty that Frankish rulers acquired was then distributed to the most prominent among the king's followers in return for their loyalty. After Charlemagne had received the treasure of the Avars and sent some of

Fig. 4 Ulf sponsored this runestone, now at the church of Orkesta north of Stockholm, to commemorate that he received from his chieftains a share in tribute payments extorted from England in 1006, 1012, and 1018. Photo: Bengt A. Lundberg, by courtesy of Riksantikvarieämbetet, Stockholm.

it to the pope, "he distributed the rest among his magnates, ecclesiastical as well as lay, and his other vassals."[82] Distribution of tribute and booty was the engine that drove the political economy of the Carolingians.

Scandinavian society functioned similarly. Tribute and booty taken by Vikings were distributed among the warriors of the Viking bands: the Swede Ulf, for example, received his share from three of the chieftains that he had followed during the first two decades of the eleventh century. Scandinavians sought riches by plundering and exacting tribute not only in Christian Europe but also closer to home. The sources tell us about only a few such raids and tributes, but this is to be expected outside the literate area of Europe, where there was no one to write down reports of such events.

An exception concerns a Norwegian chieftain named Ottar, who "lived the farthest north of all Norwegians." In the ninth century, he told King Alfred of England how he regularly collected tribute from the Sami population of northern Scandinavia: "That tribute consists of the skins of beasts, the feathers of birds, whale-bone, and ship-ropes made from walrus-hide and seal-skin. Each pays according to his rank. The highest in rank has to pay fifteen marten skins, five reindeer skins, one bear skin and ten measures of feathers, and a jacket of bearskin or otterskin and two ship-ropes. Each of these must be sixty ells long, one made from walrus-hide the other from seal."[83] This tribute made Ottar a "very rich man." As we shall see in later chapters, the items that the Finnas paid Ottar in tribute were very valuable, if they could be brought to the marketplaces of Europe. Ottar's tactic was essentially the same as Charlemagne's exacting tribute from his militarily weaker neighbors.

Ottar regularly collected tribute from the neighboring Sami, and, as we saw earlier, the Swedes exacted tribute from the inhabitants of "Apulia" by showing up with a great band of menacing warriors. We have every reason to believe that this kind of thing went on in Scandinavia long before we have sources that tell us about them. Indeed, the Danes had already in the sixth century attempted to raid in Gaul, according to the testimony of Gregory of Tours.[84] What happened in 793 and in later Viking raids was simply that Scandinavians became willing to travel farther to collect tribute and booty.

3

The Power of Gifts

On Palm Sunday, 25 March 1016, a great sea battle raged at Nesjar in southern Norway. Olav Haraldsson had returned to Norway with a band of warriors after many years as a Viking raider and mercenary soldier in Europe, and he planned to conquer the country. A critical moment came when Olav's fleet engaged the ships of Norway's current ruler, Earl Svein Håkonsson, the son of Håkon Sigurdsson, Hallfred Ottarson's first patron. The clash of weapons was loud, and many corpses floated on the water, which was colored red with blood, drink for the raven, claimed the eyewitness Sigvat Thordarson, who added that "never was [Olav's] fleet at a worse place." The outcome of the battle appeared to lie in the balance, but people kept showing up to join Olav: "The king's forces grow, for people from Opplandene want to support this man." Olav defeated Svein, opening the way for him to conquer Norway. Sigvat explains why people kept showing up to join the ranks of Olav's forces: "The generous obtained a much larger following for the battle than the stingy . . . but the ranks were thin around the standard of the friendless leader, who saved his wealth." Olav, having plenty of wealth after years of fund-raising in foreign lands, was known as a generous leader, and he easily recruited warriors to conquer Norway.[1]

The story demonstrates the dynamics of political power in early medieval Scandinavia. Such power was based on violence, and chieftains and kings surrounded themselves with armed retinues in order to be able to inflict violence on each other. They assured the loyalty of those retainers by giving them gifts of valuables and desirable objects, thereby creating an ongoing relationship between themselves and their warriors, a relationship in which the chieftains owed valuable and prestigious gifts and their followers owed support and loyalty. In creating such bonds between themselves and their warriors, Scandinavian chieftains were not doing anything that had not been done before. Since the beginning of history, people have linked themselves to others through exchange of gifts.[2]

Scandinavian Warriors

Dozens of magnificently furnished graves from several grave fields in the region around Uppsala in eastern Sweden vividly evoke the early medieval Scandinavian aristocratic warrior setting out for battle. Having disembarked from his boat, he is mounted on his horse, wielding sword, axe, shield, and spear. A leashed dog and a couple of extra horses carrying tools, food, and cooking utensils accompany him. He is prepared for a long campaign. He will cook for himself, roasting pork or beef on a spit or boiling vegetables or fish in a pot on a fire that he has started with flint and steel. After battle, he will sharpen his weapons with a whetstone and repair his equipment with knife, awl, and scissors.[3]

These graves are particularly rich in grave goods. The men buried in them were clearly important men, possibly chieftains. Graves with similarly militaristic grave goods dot the countryside of Scandinavia, even though most are not as richly equipped. Many typically contain battle axes, swords, arrows, knives, or spears. The man buried in Mammen, in Jutland, in the tenth century, for example, had two axes with him in the grave.[4] Such grave goods represent a warrior ideology, in which it was important to be seen, even in death, as an able and courageous fighter.

Examples of the same ideology are also apparent on the early medieval picture stones that are found on Gotland, the largest island in the Baltic Sea. These stones often depict warriors swinging axes, throwing spears, or standing with their swords raised or hanging in their sheaths. The warriors appear in boats, on foot, or on horseback.[5] Some picture stones depict fights, like the one that the antiquarian Per Arvid Säve found in 1850 inside the church of Alskog, Gotland. In the upper left-hand corner, the stone depicts two men fighting hand to hand. Each of them holds a shield in front of him and has a sword at his side. They seem to hold spears in their hands, and four spears (or arrows) are stuck in the shield of the man to the right. Spears or arrows in mid-air are approaching him, and at least one appears to be stuck in his chest. Another man seems to be hastening to the scene from the right with an axe, perhaps to help the man who is losing the battle.[6] This picture stone, like many others, extols the glories of war.

The martial ideology pervading early medieval Scandinavia also found expression in literature, with many Icelandic sagas celebrating the fierce manhood of its warrior heroes. While the sagas were composed in the thirteenth century or later, centuries after the Viking Age, their manuscripts often preserve poetry that had been composed in the early Middle Ages. This is the so-called skaldic poetry, written (mostly) as praise poems by poetically inclined retainers ("skalds") of kings and chieftains. The genre follows complex rules that make its interpretation difficult. Its statements are in any case often vague and elusive. Nevertheless, skaldic poetry provides an authentic window into how the aristocracy of the Scandinavian Viking Age thought. Much of skaldic verse is strikingly martial in tone.[7]

One example is the only skaldic stanza that has been preserved in contemporary writing by being inscribed on a ninth-century runestone. It honors a warrior with militaristic imagery. The retinue of Sibbe, the son of Foldar, raised the runestone in Karlevi on the Swedish island of Öland in memory of their leader. They summarized Sibbe's character using the circumlocutions (kennings) that are typical of skaldic stanzas: "In this mound lies he hidden who was followed by the greatest deeds (most know that), Þrúðr's performer of battle. Never again shall such a flawless battle-strong wagon-Viðurr of Endill's expanses rule land in Denmark."[8] By resolving the circumlocutions, the meaning of the poem becomes easier to grasp: "In this mound lies buried he who was followed by the greatest deeds (most know that), a warlike chieftain. Never again shall such a flawless battle-strong warrior chieftain of the sea rule land in Denmark." The circumlocutions are in themselves made up of warlike allusions. Þrúðr, whose name means "strength," was the daughter of the martial god Thor. Viðurr was another name for the god Odin, the warrior-god par excellence. The Karlevi runestone idealizes the image of the warrior chieftain; it is the same image that emerges from the warrior graves and picture stones throughout Scandinavia.

Competition among Chieftains

Olav Haraldsson and Svein Håkonsson fighting each other at Nesjar in 1016 were only two Scandinavian chieftains who tried to kill each other when competing for power and resources. Deadly competition was the normal state of affairs among chieftains.

A Norwegian chieftain who met a violent end was buried in a great burial mound in Gokstad, Norway, at some point soon after the middle of the ninth century. He was interred in his ship (more than twenty-three meters in length), which contained rich grave goods and at least twelve horses and six dogs. To get such a great burial, he must have been a powerful and wealthy person. Nevertheless, a recent examination of his skeleton has revealed that he was violently killed. He had been struck hard by a sword on the inside of his left knee, which must have made him fall. Another blow hit his right lower leg from the outside, and it was so powerful that it cut right through his ankle. The Gokstad man was also vigorously stabbed with a knife on the inside of his right thigh; this blow probably cut the great femoral artery and might have finished him off. The scars never healed, so they definitely come from his final, fatal battle.[9]

The *Royal Frankish Annals* tell us about another occasion when chieftains were killed through violence. They recount, briefly, what happened in Denmark after the "king of the Danes," Godfrid, was killed in 810 by one of his retainers: "[In 814,] Harald and Reginfrid, kings of the Danes, had been defeated and expelled from their kingdom the year before by the sons of Godfrid, against whom they regrouped their forces and again made war. In this conflict, Reginfrid and the oldest son of Godfrid were killed."[10] In other words, at least four chieftains, whom the Franks thought of as "kings" of the Danes, fought each other after the death of Godfrid. Two of them were killed. Modern historians tend to think of these kinds of events as bloody disputes about the succession to a kingdom, but that is applying the anachronistic standards of later history. There were no "kingdoms" with well-defined and stable assets or boundaries to fight over in Scandinavia at this point.[11] Godfrid had been a particularly powerful ruler, but his inheritance was up for grabs after his death. It was not self-evident that his sons, much less his oldest son, should inherit the power that their father had possessed. In fact, an examination of genetic material from bodies buried in prestigious graves in central Sweden shows that there is no absolute connection between social status and genetics in the early Middle Ages.[12] Each ruler had to assert power for himself, in competition with other chieftains.

The power of chieftains was often contested. Individual chieftains attempted to subjugate other chieftains, as did Harald, Reginfrid, and the sons of Godfrid, and some were successful. Toward the end of the tenth century, the skald Einar, for example, praised the Norwegian earl Håkon Sigurdsson for having subjugated sixteen earls.[13] Another skald, Sigvat Thordarson, praised King Olav Haraldsson in similar terms when he said that the king had subjugated the Norwegian region Opplandene, where earlier eleven men had ruled.[14]

Einar and Sigvat might have allowed themselves some poetic license when giving the numbers of competing chieftains that their heroes had defeated, but the basic point is clear: chieftains fought with each other for power. Those who were successful defeated other chieftains, expanding the extent of their power.

Giving Gifts

In order to fight each other, chieftains needed to surround themselves with an armed retinue that would fight alongside them when required. The Karlevi runestone was raised by the retinue (*lið*) of the dead Sibbe, and Sigvat Thordarson praised in the 1020s the retinue of Norwegian king Olav Haraldsson. His retainers, "who feed the raven" (a skaldic kenning for killing enemies in battle), hang up their helmets and byrnies on the walls of the king's hall. "No young king may boast of more splendid furnishings."[15]

Every ambitious chieftain faced the same problem: how was he to recruit and keep warriors in his retinue? His retainers, not simple mercenaries that fought for wages, were free men whose sense of honor would not have tolerated that kind of venal relationship. Instead, the chieftain needed to engage his warriors in close personal relationships. If they were not biological kin, they might create kinship through, for example, rituals of brotherhood, marriage alliances, and friendship formalized by drinking together in the chieftain's hall. Whatever their relationship, it was constantly reasserted through the exchange of gifts. It was their relationship with their chieftain that made warriors willing and eager to fight for him. How chieftains persuaded their warriors to fight for them would have important consequences for the history of early medieval Scandinavia. Had they simply needed to pay a soldier's wages, they could have focused on raising as much liquid wealth as possible. Appropriate gifts in a gift-giving relationship needed to be prestigious, which caused many chieftains to focus some of their energies on acquiring prestigious goods specifically rather than wealth in general.

When the warrior received a gift of something valuable and prestigious from his chieftain, he was required to give a countergift. His first countergift was his loyalty, unto death if necessary. This is how relationships of power were created in a society without states; rather than being obliged to perform military duty for his king (as in a full-fledged state), the warrior was persuaded by gifts to voluntarily perform that duty for his chieftain. The asymmetry of the interchange, with the chieftain giving more valuable gifts than the warrior, was an expression of the structure of political power: the more exclusive the gift, the higher the esteem of the giver, and the more power concentrated in him.[16]

Against this background, it is not surprising that early medieval literature and other sources often dwell on the giving of gifts. The court poetry of early medieval Scandinavia habitually praised kings and chieftains for being generous, as did Egil Skallagrimsson when talking around 962 about his friend Arinbjørn: "He is cruel to gold, who lives in the fjords; he is an enemy of rings and opponent of thieves."[17] In other words, Arinbjørn gives his gold away (to his warriors), making life difficult for thieves who may have planned to steal it from him.

The Viking Age skalds often mention their chieftains' largesse in giving out arm rings to their followers, as did Arnorr jarlaskald in a preserved fragment from the middle of the eleventh century:

> Fire of the stream [gold] was set
> between the wrist and shoulders of the Danes;
> I saw men of Skáney thank
> him for an arm-ring.[18]

Details of the northern European system of gift giving are sketched in the Old English poem *Beowulf*.[19] The young Beowulf was taken from his father when he was seven years old to be raised by King Hreðel and was clearly destined for Hreðel's retinue. The king gave him "treasure and feasting." After defeating Grendel, Beowulf and his followers received further gifts from King Hrothgar.[20] When Beowulf himself became a leader and a king, he also gave gifts to his retinue. When Beowulf fought his third, nameless dragon and his sword failed him, his follower Wiglaf "remembered the bountiful gifts bestowed on him":

> I remember the time that we took mead together
> when we made promises to our prince
> in the beer-hall—he gave us these rings—
> that we would pay him back for this battle-gear
> these helmets and hard swords, if such a need
> as this ever befell him.[21]

After this reflection, Wiglaf threw himself into the struggle to help his lord. Beowulf's gifts had their desired result in Wiglaf's case, but the other retainers did not dare to join the fight. At the same time Wiglaf (and the poet) sternly rebuked the cowards who did not defend their ring giver. They lost their honor by not giving their countergift. Similar criticism is implied on an eleventh-century runestone from the province of Södermanland in Sweden: "Olof[?] had the monument . . . made in memory of his son Björn, [who] was killed on Gotland. Because his followers fled, he lost his life; they . . . would not hold."[22]

The poet's description of Beowulf's gift giving is illuminating. The purpose of the gifts is clearly stated: the retinue gave their loyalty as countergift. Or as the tenth-century king Håkon the Good himself expressed it (if this stanza indeed is authentic): "My men repay well the gold and the [silver-]adorned spears. We engage in this battle. The contest of Hamðir's clothes [contest of the byrnie = battle] is at hand."[23]

Beowulf's gifts to Wiglaf had been, in the first place, the equipment of a warrior. Such gifts are also mentioned by the Norse skalds, for example, Thorbjorn hornklofi (c. 900), who described the lot of the warrior-retainers of King Harald Fairhair:

> Much are they given, the battle-famed, who throw dice at Harald's court.
> They are given goods and beautiful swords, Hunnish ore [gold or weapons?],
> and eastern slave girls.[24]

Another appropriate gift for warriors was rings, especially arm rings, and, accordingly, Beowulf is characterized as the "giver of rings" (*bēagas geaf* in Old English). Scandinavian rulers are also called "ring givers" in Norse poetry, and the skalds play with many different but synonymous expressions, for example, *bauga deilir*, *hringvörpuðr*, *hringstriðr*, and *hringbrjótr*. To be a "ring giver" is to be a good ruler.[25] Archeology confirms the importance in early medieval Scandinavia of rings (and other pieces) of precious metals (gold and silver), which are often found as grave goods (see fig. 5). In general, much silver survives from this period, not only in graves, but also in hoards that were deposited underground and never claimed. Treasures typically contain, often in large quantities, pieces of silver bars, silver rings, and coins. Two hoards found close to each other at Spillings, on the island of Gotland, in 1999 contain no less than 65 kilograms of silver, including some 520 arm rings.[26]

When studying archeological finds such as the Spillings hoard, we usually cannot know for certain whether any objects in the find were gifts or intended as gifts, although we may often suspect that particularly prestigious things would have been gifts. Occasionally, the circumstances are such that we may with some confidence posit that an object was a gift. During the winter of 970–971, a stoutly built man died and was buried in a mound in Mammen, in Jutland.[27] He rested on a down pillow and wore a splendid dress, which included gold sequins, marmot fur, and embroidered leopards and other animals. He was buried with two axes. The Mammen man was clearly an important warrior. One of his axes is famous for its rich decoration with silver-wire inlay depicting an animal and a plant (see fig. 6). Stylistically, it is very similar to the decoration on Harald Bluetooth's runestone in Jelling from about the same time. Scholars have for that reason concluded that it was

Fig. 5 In 1943 the farmer Göte Nilsson struck upon an invaluable treasure while digging
a ditch in Hägvalds, Gerum, on the Swedish island of Gotland. The ceramic jar
he unearthed contained a Viking Age silver treasure consisting of 1,912 coins, 4
silver spirals, and 31 other pieces of silver. The treasure testifies to early medieval
Scandinavians' desire for silver, and the variety of coins illustrates the reach of the
northern arc of commerce and exchange in the late tenth century: 1,298 Arabic
coins, 591 German coins, 11 from Bulghar, 6 English coins, 3 from Byzantium, and
2 from Bohemia. The youngest coin dates from 991, suggesting that the jar was
buried shortly thereafter. Photo: Raymond Hejdström, by courtesy of Gotlands
Museum, Visby.

created by artisans at Harald Bluetooth's court.[28] The most likely interpretation
is that Harald gave the axe as a gift to one of his followers, the man buried
at Mammen. Despite its obvious beauty, which still awes us today, the craftsmanship of the axe and its decoration is not great. Some of the silver inlay is
poorly attached to the iron axe, and it appears to have been done hastily.[29]
Were the workmen in a hurry because this was not the only similar axe they
were making? Were King Harald's most important followers coming to drink
and eat with him, and did the king want to give many of them beautiful axes
as party gifts? Did King Harald keep the Mammen man happy and loyal by

Fig. 6 A magnificent axe was buried during the winter of 970–971 in the richly
furnished grave of a warrior in a mound at Mammen, on Jutland, Denmark. The
ornamentation inlaid with silver wire is famous for its beauty and has given name to
the Mammen style of early medieval ornamental art. The axe may have been King
Harald Bluetooth's gift to one of his warriors. Photo: Lennart Larsen, by courtesy of
Nationalmuseet, Copenhagen.

giving him gifts like the famous axe? With its beautiful decoration, in a style
associated with Harald, and its hurried workmanship, the Mammen axe is a
token of friendship, not meant for use. As such it does indeed fit the bill for
a gift from king to follower.

The giving and receiving of gifts is intricately connected to early medieval
ideas of honor or personal worth. Gifts are identified with fame and honor, and
their value lies not so much in their economic importance or in their useful-
ness, but in their role in enhancing the esteem of givers and receivers. We can
observe this in *Beowulf*, where the poet dwells on the less utilitarian aspects
of gifts, their beauty and rareness. For example, Hrothgar's gifts to Beowulf
included, "a saddle, skillfully tooled, set with gemstones."[30]

Another aspect of the generosity of the early medieval leader was his hospitality. The feasts in chieftains' halls are a constantly returning topos in early medieval northern literature. In an eleventh-century praise poem, Arnorr jarlaskald extolled his patron, Earl Thorfinn of the Orkneys, for keeping his retainers in food and drink throughout the winter (and not only at Yule, as did other rulers):

> Through all the serpent's slayer [= winter] he,
> surpassing, drank the swamp of malt [= ale, beer],
> —the ruler practiced splendid hospitality then.[31]

As noted earlier, the *Beowulf* poet let Wiglaf remember his lord's hospitality in his hall, where "the mead was flowing." The tenth-century skald Kormak Ögmundarson praised his lord, Earl Sigurd, for his generosity with food, affirming that one should not bring food to the great man (as if he presided over a potluck).[32]

Early medieval halls, the sites of such hospitality, have been identified archeologically in many places in Scandinavia, for example, in Lejre on Seeland (Sjælland) and in Old Uppsala in Sweden.[33] The great hall in Lejre, built about 880, was 48.5 meters long by 11.5 meters wide—very great indeed. Succeeding two earlier halls on the same site, the hall in Lejre is the largest building known to have existed during the Viking Age in northern Europe. It was double the size of the largest early medieval English building that we know of, the Northumbrian palace in Yeavering. As we shall see below, the German chronicler Thietmar of Merseburg claimed that pagan sacrifices had taken place at Lejre, which was "the capital of this kingdom."[34] The halls were places where leaders were able to display their wealth and refinement. Sigvat praised, as we have seen, Olav Haraldsson's hall, with its sparkling war gear hanging on the walls. We hear of similarly ostentatious display in the Beowulf poet's description of Hrothgar's hall, Heorot, where his splendidly attired queen, Wealhtheow, served mead out of a decorated pitcher. Archeological finds of glass shards in halls confirm the image of luxury that the literature suggests. Glass was a luxury article useful for this kind of display. Leaders were able to reward their guests not solely by offering mead, beer, and wine in large quantities and of good quality, but by offering it in exotic vessels, for example, drinking glasses. Drinking vessels made of glass are often discovered in early medieval Scandinavian graves.

Interesting parallels to the feasts in Beowulf's and Thorfinn's halls are found in Scandinavian runic inscriptions. An eleventh-century runestone from the Swedish province of Småland eulogizes a dead man's generosity: "Vemund placed this stone [in memory of] his brother Svein, gentle with his followers and free with food, greatly praised."[35] Another relevant inscription was discovered in an archeological excavation in the Swedish town of Sigtuna in 1990: "The king is the most generous with food. He owns the most wealth. He is agreeable."[36] The text is inscribed on a cow's rib, which (it is tempting to assume) represents the physical remnants of a great feast in the eleventh or twelfth century. A literate guest may have expressed in this fashion his satisfaction with the food and his host.

The ability to give suitable gifts to his warriors was essential for any chieftain who strove to both maintain the status quo and expand his power. Without such gifts, the warriors were not honor-bound to offer up their loyalty to their chieftain. In fact, Sigvat Thordarson, himself a retainer, said as much in a poem entitled "Straight-speaking Song." When he felt that Olav Haraldsson's son Magnus was not as generous as his father had been, he threatened to transfer his allegiance to King Hardaknud of Denmark.[37] In other words, he threatened to abandon his king for another unless gifts were forthcoming more regularly. It is easy to imagine that chieftains could have been quickly abandoned by their retainers before a decisive battle if the opposing chieftain had the reputation of being the more generous leader. We know of at least one retainer who changed sides in connection with a battle, although we do not know if it happened before, during, or afterwards. Hallfred Ottarsson served the Norwegian earl Håkon Sigurdsson but transferred his allegiance to Olav Tryggvason when the latter arrived in Norway in 995.[38]

Various chieftains competed with each other for the loyalty of the same group of expert warriors, creating an inflationary spiral, with each giving ever-greater gifts. They thus needed increasing access to wealth. But greater wealth was not the only key to gaining and retaining a warrior following. Chieftains also sought out rare and exclusive gifts, which they brought to Scandinavia from far away. The value of such gifts resided partially in their being exotic, while other gifts gained value by being worked up by skillful artisans. Chieftains also made use of another kind of gift: by participating with their warriors in religious rituals, they created a bond of kinship with them that sometimes overlapped with the gift-exchange relationship. The practice led eventually to Scandinavia's acceptance of Christianity.

4

Carving Out Power

A decade and a half before the turn of the millennium, a young murderer named Erik was condemned to lesser outlawry by an Icelandic court. This meant that anyone could lawfully kill him at any point during the next three years if he remained in Iceland. He had to move away from the island, but this was not a terrible blow, for he did not have much of a position to uphold there anyway. He was a troublemaker and ne'er-do-well, who had already been forced to move twice after slaying several people. First he had moved with his father from Norway to Iceland, then from the main island to two smaller islands, Oxney and Brokey. When he had to move for the third time, he did not, like most people in a similar situation, choose to go east to mainland Scandinavia or south to the Norse-dominated areas of the British Isles. Instead, he daringly went west, to Greenland. Parts of the western coast of this otherwise glacier-covered island are rich grazing land, and the arctic waters around it teem with walruses, whales, and other valuable animals. Erik discovered that he could make a good living there, and he called the island "Greenland," for "he said it would encourage people to go there that the country had a good name." When the three years were ended, he went back to Iceland and began to recruit settlers who would come with him to live in Greenland. Many wanted to take this new opportunity, and they built dozens of farms in two settlement areas on the island. Greenland became a flourishing Norse settlement in the farthest northwest corner of the known world, and Erik became a great chieftain.[1]

This story relies on late sagas, which probably have exaggerated much, including the stark contrast between Erik the Red's sad life in Iceland and his subsequent success in Greenland. It stands beyond question, however, that he became a leading figure in Greenland, and the story captures something essential about the Viking Age emigration from Scandinavia. That emigration was in the first place an opportunity for leaders to carve out niches of power for themselves away from Scandinavia, where they might not have been powerful. They brought people with them, sometimes in large groups, but we should not think of this as a mass migration akin to the great migration of Scandinavians to the United States and Canada in the late nineteenth century. Some of the people who chose to follow successful Norse chieftains were not necessarily themselves Norse, as has been vividly proven through the genetic mapping of the modern population of Iceland. Despite what the medieval sagas say about Iceland's being populated through mass migration from Norway, Icelanders have Celtic genes as well as Norse genes.[2] Many Irish men and women came to Iceland, and not all of them would have come as slaves.

Erik the Red is an example of a Scandinavian man who took the opportunity to become a chieftain when it was given him. One of the earliest Scandinavian opportunists we hear of in the sources was a Danish man called Harald Klak. After the murder of the Danish king Godfrid in 810, Harald was one of the several would-be kings who fought for power in Denmark. He sought help from Emperor Louis the Pious, who was happy to oblige in order to gain influence in Denmark. Nevertheless, Harald's continued attempts to gain and hold onto power in Denmark were not very successful. In 826, he agreed to be baptized, with the emperor as his godfather, in a move perhaps calculated to inspire Louis to provide more help, which he did. It is hard to escape the impression, however, that Harald's real goal in accepting baptism was to be accepted into the Frankish Empire. In connection with the grand ceremonies marking the baptism of Harald, his family, and his followers, Louis gave him the Frisian county of Rüstringen as a base for Harald's operations against his competitors in Denmark. Harald never succeeded in gaining control of Denmark. Instead, he settled as a vassal of the emperor in the county given him. He had failed to gain a position of power at home in Denmark, but he succeeded in carving out a perhaps even better position in foreign lands (and actually not that far from Denmark).[3]

Erik the Red's and Harald's stories may be emblematic of Scandinavians' moves away from Scandinavia during the Viking Age. Individual leaders took every opportunity to carve out foreign lordships for themselves, and the annals of that period are full of men who succeeded: Ingolf in Iceland; Rurik in Russia and his namesake Rorik in the West Frankish Kingdom; Rollo in Normandy; Halfdan, Ivar Boneless, Guthrum, and Erik Bloodaxe in England; Olav (Amlaib in Gaelic) and Sihtric in Ireland; and so on in a long line, and there are still many more who must have existed but whose exploits have remained unsung in the preserved sources. They encountered very different situations where they settled. Some of them, like Erik the Red, came to largely uninhabited lands that were simply there for the taking. Others fought their way in (like many of the conquerors in the British Isles), while yet others, like Harald and Rurik, were happy to have their authority delegated to them by Frankish kings or Slavic tribes. Their main goal was power, and it did not matter much how they got it.

Scandinavian chieftains who chose not to build on their power base at home in Scandinavia moved in three directions to gain power elsewhere, bringing other Scandinavians with them. Some moved to the islands of the North Atlantic. Others moved to western Europe, and yet others to eastern Europe.

The Atlantic Islands

The first Norse inhabitant in Iceland was Ingolf Arnarsson, who moved there from Norway in the 870s. He settled in the south, at Reykjavik. Many others soon followed, so that the island was fully occupied by 930. Ingolf and his descendants were great chieftains residing in Reykjavik, which has maintained its predominance into modern times as the capital of Iceland.

Such is at least the story as told in the earliest written history of Iceland, the *Íslendingabók*, compiled in the early twelfth century by Ari Thorgilsson, and thus at a distance of centuries from the events Ari claims to retell. What he wrote may or may not have been what actually happened, but the exact names and personalities do not matter for our argument. What does matter here is that settlers like Ingolf moved to Iceland to become chieftains. That much is clear from the image of Icelandic society that is revealed by a reading of the *Íslendingabók* and other, later Icelandic sources.

The twelfth- and thirteenth-century Icelandic sources describe a society that was ruled by chieftains, or *goðar*. Each chieftain had his group of followers, or *goðord*. The chieftains and their followers often fought with each other, and the Icelanders worked out an elaborate system of managing the violence that stemmed from the competition between chieftains. Chieftains judged disputes among their own followers. Disputes between chieftains or between people who belonged to the goðord of different chieftains were settled at a regional meeting, or *thing*. If the disputing parties belonged to different regions, the matter was settled at the Althing, the annual meeting of the entire island.⁴

There must have been chieftains in Iceland from the beginning; how could this system otherwise have evolved? We must imagine, then, that Iceland was settled much like Greenland was under Erik the Red: would-be chieftains created chieftaincies for themselves by bringing settlers to the uninhabited island.

Iceland was, as we already have seen, a base for moving farther west, to Greenland. That island, in turn, served in the same way for an abortive move even farther west. Around the year 1000, a man was blown off course and discovered land southwest of Greenland. Leif, the son of Erik the Red, famously set out to explore this land, according to the much later sagas, which aimed at promoting Erik's family. They recount that Leif settled in "Vinland," as he called the new land, but that hostile contact with *skraelinger* (Native Americans) made him abandon his plans for a settlement, so he and his companions moved back home to Greenland. In fact, Scandinavians built a short-lived settlement on Newfoundland, which archeologists excavated in the 1960s. The presence there of a Native American arrowhead even gives some credence to the saga story about hostility between the Scandinavians and the skraelinger. The Greenlanders did not entirely abandon the lands to their west after the failed attempt at colonization. They went there to get timber and other commodities that they could not get on Greenland.⁵

Western Europe

We know the names of many Scandinavians who moved to different parts of western Europe to become leaders there, especially in the British Isles but also in France.

Scandinavian settlement of the British Isles proceeded from the north to the south. It began on the islands north of Britain: the Shetlands, the Orkneys, and the Hebrides. By the end of the Viking Age, the population of these islands was predominantly Scandinavian.⁶ Norse dialects survived there into modern times.

It is unclear exactly when Scandinavians began to live on these islands. Only in the late ninth century is there good evidence that they lived there.⁷ Historians have wanted to date the settlement to the eighth century because they imagine that the Vikings who raided in the British Isles from the 790s must have had a base closer to the places they targeted than Scandinavia itself.⁸ That is plausible enough, but the fact remains that there is neither textual nor archeological evidence that any Scandinavians settled there so early.

Around the middle of the ninth century, Viking raiders began to overwinter at several sites in Britain and Ireland. Early in 841, the Ulster annalist expressed, perhaps with some surprise, that "the pagans [are] still on Lough Neagh."[9] They began to build several fortresses—so-called *longphoirts*—that protected their boats, both on Lough Neagh and elsewhere around the island. They built one at Duiblinn (Dublin) in 841, and an annalist notes that they were still there in 842. In fact, they would stay in Dublin for the rest of the Viking Age, making it the center of a Norse kingdom.[10] No notable genetic traces of them have as yet been found in the modern Irish population, suggesting that the written sources recorded small groups of Scandinavians seeking power and lordships, not mass migration.[11]

In England, the Anglo-Saxon chronicler notes for the first time in 850 that "the heathen men stayed in Thanet over the winter."[12] That the Vikings wanted to stay over the winter suggests that they, leaders as well as followers, did not have much to go home to in Scandinavia. It is not surprising that they looked to settle permanently. In 874, a band of Vikings—part of the Great Army—led by Halfdan conquered land on the Tyne River in Northumbria. The Vikings became settled, and Halfdan created a kingdom for himself centered on York. Norse kings would rule York for most of the following hundred years.

Vikings similarly settled in other regions of England. Land in Mercia was shared out in 877, "a gang of Vikings [*hloð wicinga*] gathered and settled at Fulham on the Thames" in 878, and the raiding army settled and divided up land in East Anglia in 880.[13] The sources seem to describe a process whereby a chieftain settled and portioned out conquered lands to his warriors.[14] Such settlements obviously gave agricultural land to individual Vikings, but they also created lordships for their leaders. For a long period kings of Scandinavian ancestry ruled parts of eastern England, the Danelaw. Earlier in this chapter, I briefly mentioned Guthrum, who was king in East Anglia, and Halfdan had several Norse successors in York. Such leaders also ruled in Dublin and on the Isle of Man, the Hebrides, and the Shetlands.

The Scandinavians who settled in the British Isles assimilated relatively quickly with the Anglo-Saxons and Celts who were already there, although their genes are still discernible in at least some regional populations.[15] There is good evidence that the settlers married indigenous women. The resulting cultural mix may have been what made the *Beowulf* poem possible, although that is a highly controversial issue. The poem was written in Old English but treated matters that were entirely Scandinavian.[16] The cultural mix also created many hybrid place names in which a Norse personal name or word was combined with an English word, like Grimston (from the Norse male name Grimnir or Grim and the English *tun*, meaning "enclosure, dwelling, or town"). Other place names are entirely Norse, ending in *-by* (village), *-thorp* (hamlet), or *-eye* (island). The Scandinavian settlements also influenced the language of the British Isles, although Gaelic less so than English. Modern English is full of Norse loanwords, such as *they*, *seem*, and *wrong*. Some Norse words made it into both Gaelic and English, such as Old Norse *rannsaka* (search a house), which became *rannsughadh* (search, rummage) in Gaelic and *ransack* in English. By the end of the tenth century, Irish aristocrats had no qualms about borrowing Norse names such as Amlaíb (from Norse Óláfr), Ímar (from Ívarr), Ragnall (from Rognvaldr), and Sitri(u)c (from Sigtryggr), while the Scandinavians began to adopt Irish names even earlier.[17]

We should not imagine that the relationship between Scandinavians and the previous inhabitants of the British Isles necessarily was hostile. They often fought, but indigenous rulers also often allied themselves with Viking leaders. For example, when Ui Neill attempted to make themselves kings of Ireland, they used Vikings as allies or mercenaries.[18] Some Irish and English rulers successfully gained control of the Scandinavian colonies. The last remaining Anglo-Saxon kingdom in England, Wessex, conquered the Danelaw bit by bit. Athelstan (ruled 924–939) styled himself "king of the Anglo-Saxons and of the Danes" in an early charter, but later—after he succeeded in ousting the Norse king in York—he simply called himself "king of the English" or "king of the whole of Britain."[19] Later Anglo-Saxon kings would continue to rule over the Danelaw until the Danish king Svein Forkbeard conquered England in 1013.

Viking leaders seeking power on the European continent proceeded differently from their confreres in the British Isles. They did not so much conquer territory as move in with the approval of the local ruler, typically in return for some service. Thus we find a long sequence of Scandinavian men who served Frankish kings. Some simply served a Frankish emperor or king at his court, like the Dane Aslak, who, being "a companion of [King Charles the Bald's] palace," negotiated on the king's behalf with the Viking leader Weland. The result of the negotiations was that Weland and his Vikings would attack another group of Vikings, who were wreaking havoc in the Seine valley. Weland was paid in gold and silver.

Other Scandinavians followed in the footsteps of the Dane Harald Klak and served Frankish kings or emperors by agreeing to defend some part of the empire, thereby in effect becoming vassals. The most famous example is Rollo, to whom King Charles the Simple in 911 delegated a lordship at Rouen and thus also the defense of the mouth of the Seine River. Rollo's descendants would become dukes of Normandy. He had several less well known predecessors who gained lordships in the Frankish Empire. Members of Harald Klak's family obtained an area in Frisia, including the trading town Dorestad, to defend, and they seem to have done so very competently and in the main faithfully for long periods. Harald Klak's nephew Rorik controlled Dorestad and its surrounding region for twenty-three years in the middle of the ninth century, and during this period only two Viking raids are known to have affected the area. One of those happened in 857, when Rorik was in Denmark trying—unsuccessfully—to become king there. If Rorik was unable to gain power at home in Denmark, being in effect the Frankish subking in Frisia was not a bad fallback position. Two sources actually call Rorik "king" (*rex*), but he was a faithful vassal of four different Frankish kings. To defend Frisia, he obviously needed warriors, and one suspects that at least some of them were Scandinavian. Since there are no place names in Frisia that derive from Norse, scholars do not believe that any large contingents of Scandinavians settled there, as opposed to Normandy, where the traces of Norse are evident in the place names.[20]

Eastern Europe

Scandinavians found opportunities to exert power also in eastern Europe, but fewer details are known about that area because fewer written sources exist. They went to Russia to acquire trade goods, especially fur and slaves, but they soon discovered the rich markets that existed farther east and south. Scandinavians settled along the rivers, which functioned as the main arteries of communication in the vast eastern European plain.

The regions they moved into were sparsely populated. They had founded, for example, the town of Staraya Ladoga, close to Lake Ladoga near present-day St. Petersburg, already by the middle of the eighth century. The area around this town was inhospitable, filled with forests and bogs. Nevertheless, the site of Staraya Ladoga, on top of a ridge next to the Volkhov River, was attractive, for it provided access to the great fur-trapping areas to the east and north. The Scandinavians had clearly come to profit from the fur that they could get cheaply here and sell dearly elsewhere. Another attraction of the town was the river, which provided access to the interior of Russia, and ultimately to the rich Arab and Byzantine markets beyond it.

The oldest archeological layers in Staraya Ladoga, from the decades around 750, contain mostly artifacts of Scandinavian origin. There are, however, also some Finnish and Slavic objects, coming from the original inhabitants of the area. This suggests that Scandinavians, Finns, and Slavs were able to live alongside each other from the beginning of the town's existence. Just as the chieftains of Iceland did not rule over a population that was purely Norse—as modern genetics has shown—the chieftains of the Russian towns dealt with multiethnic populations.

In Russia, trade developed along the rivers, which were the main conduits of communication. Scandinavians followed the trade and settled in many of the towns that dot the banks of the rivers. The archeological remains of these towns suggest that they were melting pots in which the Scandinavians were only one of several ethnic elements. Scandinavian-type objects have been found in places like Riurikovo Gorodishe (the predecessor of Novgorod), Murom (east of Moscow, on the Oka River), and Timorëvo (northeast of Moscow). The presence of jewelry and other artifacts in Scandinavian styles does not necessarily prove the presence of Scandinavians, as styles easily spread among the different groups inhabiting the banks of the Russian rivers. There can be no mistake, however, that Scandinavians immigrated to these parts of eastern Europe.[21]

A Scandinavian by the name of Rurik was particularly successful in creating a lordship for himself and his descendants. The twelfth-century *Russian Primary Chronicle* tells the story of how Rurik gained power in the town of Novgorod.

> Discord thus ensued among [Slavic tribes], and they began to war one against another. They said to themselves, "Let us seek a prince who may rule over us and judge us according to the Law." They accordingly went overseas to the Varangian Russes: these particular Varangians were known as Russes, just as some are called Swedes, and others Normans, English, and Gotlanders, for they were thus named. The Chuds, the Slavs, the Krivichians, and the Ves' then said to the people of Rus', "Our land is great and rich, but there is no order in it. Come to rule and reign over us." They thus selected three brothers, with their kinsfolk, who took with them all the Russes and migrated. The oldest, Rurik, located himself in Novgorod; the second, Sineus, at Beloozero; and the third, Truvor, in Izborsk.[22]

The interpretation of this evidence as well as the archeological evidence has been fraught with controversy. The text is late, clearly has legendary elements, and cannot be literally true in all its details. It surely oversimplifies a chain of events that must have been considerably more complicated, and it appears confused, inviting differing interpretations. The *Chronicle* implies that Scandinavians rather than Slavs founded the Rus state (a predecessor of Russia), an idea that caused Russian nationalists to discredit this evidence in the eighteenth century. Given that several Scandinavians carved out principalities for themselves in western Europe, it is not surprising that some attempted to do the same in eastern Europe. The evidence from the west also teaches us, however, that the Scandinavians could assimilate relatively quickly with the other populations in these areas, so that it soon becomes meaningless to distinguish different ethnic groups. Rurik's descendants, according to the *Chronicle*, bear Slavic names after the first couple of generations. The archeological evidence from Russia points in the same direction.

The case of Russia shows, more importantly, how Scandinavians were taking opportunities when they were offered. Rurik and his two brothers moved in and became chieftains. The descendants of Rurik would rule Russia until the sixteenth century.

In this chapter, we have heard of two men who shared the Norse name Rørekr, which was transcribed as Roricus in Latin and Riurik in Old Slavonic. In addition to their name, they also shared an urge for power that they were unable to develop fully at home in Scandinavia, but both of them found and took opportunities to be rulers elsewhere in Europe, one in Frisia, the other in Novgorod. In this they were similar to many other Scandinavians who carved out power niches for themselves elsewhere when there was not enough maneuvering space at home. That is how Iceland and Greenland were populated, how great swaths of the British Isles came to be governed by Scandinavians, and how Carolingian kings acquired Norse vassals. The ways in which chieftains acquired power were different in different areas, which is why some of them seem to have brought large contingents of Scandinavians with them, while others brought few followers. The movement of people away from Scandinavia during the Viking Age is not primarily about migration, but about chieftains taking opportunities to gain power when those opportunities presented themselves.

5

Weland, Ulfberht, and Other Artisans

Chieftains used artisans to add value to their gifts. Instead of simply giving a bar of silver or a sword—valuable gifts in themselves—the chieftain might first have an artisan work on the gift, turning the precious metal into an exquisite piece of jewelry or embellishing the sword with gems. The same applies to other, less intrinsically valuable materials, such as bone, antlers, and wood, which expert artisans turned into objects of beauty that thrilled people across early medieval northern Europe and still excite and enchant museum visitors today.

The best artisans gained a legendary reputation. The Frankish sword maker Ulfberht became so famous that pirated swords signed "Ulfberht" circulated all over Europe and beyond. Well over a hundred of his swords, or pirated copies, have been found almost everywhere in northern Europe, from Iceland and Ireland in the west to Bulghar on the Volga River in the east (see fig. 7). There may well be many more, since thousands of rusty early medieval swords that lie in museums around Europe have never been X-rayed to see if the blades carry any signatures under the rust that envelopes them.[1]

Their art was so admired that such craftsmen were often thought of as having superhuman or magical powers. People liked to tell and hear stories about the archetypical but legendary smith Weland, who often turns up in early medieval art and literature.[2] Weland is depicted on the Gotland picture stone Ardre VIII, which was made in the eighth or ninth century (see fig. 8).

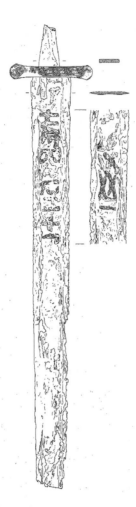

Fig. 7 A sword, almost half a meter long and with the Ulfberht "trademark," was found in the Elbe River at Hamburg. Such swords were very desirable during the Viking Age. Reproduced with permission from M. Müller-Wille, "Ein neues ULFBERHT-Schwert aus Hamburg: Verbreitung, Formenkunde und Herkunft," *Offa* 27 (1970), 66, fig. 1.

Fig. 8 Early medieval picture stones from the Swedish island of Gotland provide valuable
visual evidence for Scandinavian society and imagination at the time. This example
from Ardre shows several mythological scenes, including Odin's eight-legged horse
and the moment when the hamstrung Weland flies away from his prison with the
wings he has fashioned for himself. The image also shows the smithy with tongues
and the headless bodies of his victims as well as Bödvild walking away from the
scene of her violation. Photo: Bengt A. Lundberg, by courtesy of Statens Historiska
Museum, Stockholm.

Here, he has put on the eagle's wings that he has fabricated, and he is flying away from his smithy, tongs and hammers close by.[3] The Franks Casket in the British Museum is a box made out of whalebone in the early eighth century, probably in Northumbria (see fig. 9). It is carved with scenes drawn from different mythologies: Romulus and Remus, the Sack of Jerusalem, the Adoration of the Magi, and Weland the smith. Tongs, an anvil, and a hammer are clearly visible on the casket.[4] The casket and the picture stone are themselves the products of very skilled craftsmen.

Weland was no less famous in early medieval literature. The *Poetic Edda* devotes an entire poem to Weland—the *Völundarkviða*—which praises his skill as a jeweler:

> He beat red gold
> round the firm-set gem,
> he closed all
> rings well for the linden rope.

Fig. 9 An early-eighth-century casket made of whalebone, probably in Northumbria, England, contains scenes from Christian and pagan mythologies. Its front shows, to the right, the adoration of the magi and, to the left, Weland in his smithy. © The Trustees of the British Museum, London.

Stores of trinkets were there [in Weland's chest],
which, it seemed to the boys,
were red gold
and jewels.[5]

Weland was not only a goldsmith but a maker of warrior's gear. In *Völundarkviða* he sharpened the sword of King Niðuðr. Weland made byrnies, too, if we believe the *Beowulf* poet. When Beowulf implored King Hrothgar to allow him to fight Grendel, he stood up to speak, and the poet noted admiringly how his byrnie gleamed "with a smith's high art."[6] Beowulf was the greatest of heroes, so his gear also had to be the greatest. At the end of his speech, Beowulf reveals that his armor is even more exclusive than might have appeared at first. The legendary master smith himself had made it:

Send on to [Beowulf's uncle] Hygelac, if battle should take me,
the best battledress, which my breast wears,
finest of garments; it is Hrethel's heirloom,
the work of Weland.[7]

Weland comes across in art and literature as more than human. Indeed in the *Völundarkviða*, he knows how to fly like a superhero, or perhaps more like Daedalus, since according to the high medieval *Þiðreks saga af Bern* he fashioned his own wings.[8] Weland picked up many characteristics from the ancient mythological Greco-Roman figure of Daedalus, who among his many accomplishments invented the labyrinth. The medieval Latin expression for labyrinth is sometimes "house of Daedalus" (*domus Dedali*); in Old Norse, the corresponding term is "house of Weland" (*Völundarhús*). The way that the archetypical artisan Weland's stature was magnified in art and literature suggests how highly early medieval people thought of artisans and their skills.

The skills of early medieval craftsmen were considerable, and their output must have been enormous, for very much survives, at least of such artifacts that were made in durable materials. Those surviving products demonstrate real expertise in working with different materials as well as admirable artistry.[9] It is easy to understand that chieftains would use the skills of artisans in enhancing the value of their gifts. These skilled workers traveled around with their tools and raw materials in chests, just as Weland does in the *Völundarkviða*. Successful chieftains might have enough work for artisans to keep some always at their side, and those chieftains who were very successful created entire villages or towns for them.

Three aspects of the work of artisans are important here. Early medieval people experienced artisanal products as attractive and desirable, as we shall see in the first section, providing illustrations from literature. We will then examine the artistry of the craftsmen as demonstrated by surviving artifacts. Finally, a look at the archeological remains of towns and settlements that chieftains created for their artisans will help us understand the role of artisans in the gift economy of the early Middle Ages.

Artistry in Northern Literature

When northern literature of the Middle Ages mentions the gifts of kings and chieftains, it often dwells on the artistic merits of the gifts, showing that people at the time valued artistry. We see this in *Beowulf*, as we have already noted, when the poet dwells on the less utilitarian aspects of gifts, that is, their beauty and the refinement of their decoration. King Hrothgar's gifts to Beowulf included, for example, "a skillfully tooled saddle set with treasure"[10] and a sword "honored by treasure" (which means that it was decorated with something valuable, such as gemstones or gold).[11]

A ninth-century praise poem celebrating Norwegian king Harald Fairhair portrays the king as the stereotypical giver of valuables. But the poet also lets us know that the king's gifts have been worked by artisans. He points out that the king's poets are easily recognizable: "One sees on their armor and gold rings that they are friends of the king. They enjoy red and well striped cloaks, silver-woven swords, ring-woven byrnies, gilded straps, and graven helmets, arm-worn rings, which Harald gave them."[12] This is a king who not only can afford to give away good arm rings, cloaks, swords, byrnies, and helmets but also can afford to have artisans work on them, for example, twining the sword hilts with silver wire (which is what I take "silver-woven swords" to mean), and attaching golden or at least gilded buckles to the sword strap.

King Olav Haraldsson similarly gave his retainer Sigvat Thordarson a sword that was "wound with gold" and had a "pommel of silver." Sigvat was so pleased with the gift that he remembered it in the memorial poem that he wrote after the king's death. The poem, *Erfidrápa Óláfs helga*, follows the conventions of Norse court poetry with its kennings and allusive style. Sigvat also plays with the contrast between the sword and the pilgrim's staff: "War-weary, I left at home the gold-woven ringing wand [sword], which the king gave me, and I journeyed to Rome, when we put down the precious sword, a weapon with a hilt-knob of silver with which the hunger of the she-wolf's husband was stilled [with which the wolf was fed = the enemy was killed in battle], and followed the sacred staff [went on pilgrimage]."[13] Sigvat mentions that the sword, or rather the hilt of the sword, was decorated with gold and silver. In fact, many exquisitely decorated swords survive from early medieval Scandinavia.

Surviving Artistry

Swords, hilts, scabbards, and such give examples of the fine workman-ship that the *Beowulf* poet, Sigvat, and many others appreciated. Many early medieval swords survive to illustrate the poets' comments; from Norway alone, more than 2,500 swords from the second half of the first millennium have been found. Sword blades often carry decorative inlays of silver, brass, or iron. The cross-guard and the pommel were usually made of iron but may also have been made of silver or bronze with decorative inlays of silver or copper. The grip was usually made of some organic material (textile, leather, horn, or bone) but could be twined with silver or gold wire.[14]

One of the most famous early medieval swords, from Snartemo in Norway, was found by two farmer brothers in 1933 when they were breaking ground for new farmland. The sword had been placed in a grave in the early sixth century. Its hilt is superbly decorated with thin sheets of gilded silver with intricately designed animal patterns. The grave also contained other weapons, a gold ring, and a drinking glass with silver details. All of these things had been worked by skillful craftsmen, the sword almost certainly within Scandinavia. The man buried in the grave was clearly a warrior of some standing. We do not know, of course, whether he received the sword and the other things in his grave as gifts from his chieftain. Even if he had bought or stolen them himself, they would have raised his stature and helped him get followers.[15]

Another elaborate sword was found in Dybäck, in Scania, in southern Sweden. It was made in Denmark or England during the second half of the tenth century. Its grip is twined with gold wire, and the entire hilt (the pommel is now missing) is cast in silver and embellished with engraved and punchwork animals. On the upper guard, for example, are depicted in vigorous relief two symmetrical birds, and between them is a beast intertwined with a snake, which is biting one of the birds.[16]

Arm rings, the archetypical gift of early medieval kings and chieftains, are another Viking Age artifact that demonstrates exquisite workmanship.[17] Many arm rings are preserved from early medieval Scandinavia. Some of the rings are simple loops of metal of no particular artistic interest, although they are still of value because they are made of silver or gold. Others are the products of skilled artisanry. In 1999, archeologists found a hoard including 486 arm rings at Spillings, on Gotland.[18] (It also contained 14,295 coins, mostly from the Arab Caliphate, although one of them is a unique Khazar coin.) The Spillings arm rings are relatively simple with decoration in punchwork. Other preserved arm rings are more exquisitely worked out. Each of six golden arm rings found at Erikstorp, in Sweden, consists of two thin bars that have been twisted around each other, the ends narrowing into an elegant knot.[19] A gilded silver ring from Undrom, in northern Sweden, was cleverly shaped to look like a snake (see fig. 10). For such rings, the value of the goldsmith's work is added to that of the metal. The added value more than made up for the cost of the artisan's work.

Developing Styles of Artistry

The Viking Age relished "the effects of relief, of contrasting materials and colours, and of the interplay of light and shade on blank and decorated fields."[20] A single piece of jewelry might include many materials, such as gold,

Fig. 10 In early-medieval Northern literature, kings and chieftains are often called "ring-givers," for the typical gift that they gave to their warriors was an arm ring. This elegant example, made of gilded silver with niello, was found in Undrom, in the province of Ångermanland, northern Sweden. Photo: Sören Hallgren, by courtesy of Statens Historiska Museum, Stockholm.

silver, bronze, niello, glass, and paint, illustrating the multifaceted skills of the artisans who made it. The materials are usually worked to form elaborate patterns. They typically depict animal bodies in more or less simplified form. They include filigree and granulation in order to break up any flat surfaces that might appear. Such artifacts are the products of expert craftsmen.

While these aspects of Viking Age artistry remained the same or similar, style also developed throughout the period. Archeologists and art historians place artifacts into a sequence of different stylistic periods, some of which overlapped chronologically.[21]

At the beginning of the Viking Age, in the late eighth and early ninth centuries, the so-called style E dominated (it succeeded styles A–D in the pre-Viking period). The style is also known as the Oseberg style, since it is represented in the rich grave find in Oseberg from the 830s (see fig. 11). A pervasive motif, especially in the older varieties of the style, is elegantly formed animals with long, narrow, and curved bodies. Their limbs intertwine to form interlacing patterns, often in figure eights. The animals usually have small heads appearing in profile with large eyes. Their bodies are often filled in with purely geometrical shapes. The Oseberg ship, which was built between 815 and 820 and also buried in the mound, is ornamented in this style.

The Oseberg find also contains artifacts decorated in a more recent style, which features so-called gripping beasts, robust animals with their large heads seen full face, gripping everything they can with their hands and feet: themselves, their neighbors, or whatever other decorative detail is within reach.[22]

These styles were succeeded toward the end of the ninth century by the Borre style, so called from a ship burial in Borre, in Norway. A development of the Oseberg styles, the Borre style still has the gripping beast as a central motif. It is now, however, more boldly formed, longer, and more twisted. A new motif is the "ring braid" or "ring chain": two bands that are symmetrically braided, held together with circles or ovals, and surrounded by square figures.[23] From the Borre style on, Scandinavian artistic styles show increasing kinship with European art, especially British art. Scholars dispute in which direction the influence went.

The next style, the Jelling style, does not so much replace the Borre style as coexist with it during the tenth century. The object that gave the style its name is a small (only 4.3 centimeters tall) silver, gilt, and niello cup that was found in the early nineteenth century in the burial mound of King Gorm in Jelling, Denmark. The animals are now seen in profile, with open mouths, long pigtails in their necks, and a lip-lappet. Their bodies are even more elongated and ribbonlike, and they are often surrounded and intertwined with ribbons.

Fig. 11 The prow of the Oseberg ship (built at some point between 815 and 820) features exquisite carvings, which have given name to the Oseberg style. The ship was the last resting place of two women, who were accompanied in their mound-covered grave by many other objects, including furniture, wagons, sleds, textiles, and a walnut. Photo: Eirik Irgens Johnsen, © Kulturhistorisk Museum, Universitetet i Oslo.

On the Jelling cup, the animals face each other (fighting each other?) and are symmetrical and intertwined.[24]

Contemporary with the later phase of the Jelling style is the Mammen style, which developed from it around the middle of the tenth century. The animals are now more robust and their limbs end with plant tendrils. The style obtained its name from a magnificent iron axe buried with an important man in a mound in Mammen during the winter of 970–971. The blade of the axe shows, on one side, a bird with elongated, intertwined limbs and, on the other, an ornamental arrangement of tendrils, all executed in silver-wire inlay. Another famous example of the Mammen style is King Harald Bluetooth's great runestone in (confusingly) Jelling, where a great rampant animal (a lion?) is fighting a snake, giving the artist the opportunity to intertwine the elongated bodies of the two animals with each other.[25]

The plant and snake motifs are further elaborated in the Ringerike style, from the late tenth century until the middle of the eleventh. There are now masses of plant tendrils sprouting not only from the animals but also on their own. The composition is often symmetrical. The style "is full of speed and movement."[26] The Ringerike style was common also in the British Isles, where it may be found in the decorations of several manuscripts. It also appears on a famous runestone from St. Paul's churchyard in London.[27]

The final Viking Age style is the Urnes style, which flourished from just before the middle of the eleventh century into the high Middle Ages. It is exuberant and flamboyant, with large loops of narrow bands. The snakes and four-legged animals from previous styles are still there, and they still fight each other, but they are now depicted in a strongly schematic manner. They also typically bite each other. The style takes its name from the carvings of a portal in the stave church of Urnes, in Norway, made during the last phase of the Urnes style, when the animal-based ornamentation of the Viking Age had been drained of its vitality and become mannered and formulaic. Many examples of Urnes ornamentation survive also from Ireland, but few from England.[28]

Artisans, Chieftains, and Towns

Chieftains needed exquisite things to give to their followers. They could pillage beautifully worked artifacts in Europe, or buy them in the trade towns, but the chieftains might not have been immediately able to use such objects, since they had been made for purposes that were irrelevant in Scandinavia. So they used artisans to adapt them for their use. In fact, the Scandinavian ground has yielded many European objects that were retrofitted for new uses.[29] One example is a ninth-century silver fitting for a belt, which most likely comes from a cincture that girded a cleric's alb, since it is inscribed "I in the name of God, Ermadus made me." It was made into a brooch, probably in Denmark, where it was found. Many Carolingian metal fittings for belts and similar things were made into brooches in Scandinavia. A silver hoard buried during the second half of the tenth century on the Danish island of Lolland contains no less then 1,310 grams of silver, more than 90 percent of which was manufactured within the Carolingian Empire. Many of those pieces had been turned into brooches or pendants.[30]

Artisans traveled around Scandinavia offering their services to whomever could pay. A preserved artisan's chest from Mästermyr, on the Swedish island of Gotland, contains about 150 different tools, including two pairs of tongs, seven hammers, saws, two axes, two adzes, five small anvils, six bores, files, drills, knives, scissors, a gouge, a stamp punch, a chisel, and a whetstone. The versatile artisan who owned this chest was able to work in several different materials: iron, wood, bone, antlers, silver, and gold. Another artisan, whose chest was found in Tjele, in Jutland (Denmark), carried with him a few finished pieces of jewelry as well as raw materials in the form of chunks of bronze and lead. He also brought weights, probably so he could weigh and price the materials used.[31] A similar collection of tools, from the middle of the eighth century and belonging to a smith able to work with gold, silver, and iron, has been found in Staraya Ladoga.[32]

Traveling artisans like the owners of the Mästermyr and the Tjele chests were welcomed wherever they came, by lesser magnates or in peasant villages. Greater magnates wanted their own full-time artisans. They might not have needed to take as radical measures as King Niðuðr did, hamstringing Weland and imprisoning him on an island in order to keep him in his service. The greatest chieftains brought artisans together to live in towns, just as they often brought merchants to the same towns (see chapter 7). We shall examine two such sites, Helgö in Sweden and Ribe in Denmark, which archeologists have carefully excavated and examined. Both Helgö and Ribe at least started as artisans' centers rather than as trade towns. Artisans needed raw materials, some of which had to be imported, so these places naturally grew into trading centers.

HELGÖ

The island Helgö, in Lake Mälaren in central Sweden, was a major center for production and international trade from the third century.[33] It was most important in the period immediately preceding the Viking Age, yielding to Birka after 800 (or so it seems). Helgö is perhaps most famous for the spectacular, exotic objects that were found in the ground there: an Indian statuette of the Buddha (see fig. 12), an Irish bishop's crozier, an Egyptian

Fig. 12 The most striking artifact proving Scandinavian long-distance goods exchange is a
small bronze statuette of the Buddha, manufactured in India in the sixth century,
which was found on the island of Helgö, in central Sweden. Photo courtesy of
Statens Historiska Museum, Stockholm.

bronze ladle. The site is equally important, however, for the many artisans'
shops that once existed there. Archeologists have uncovered many buildings
where craftsmen of different kinds produced artifacts. Some worked with bog
iron from central Sweden, leaving behind a lot of iron slag.[34] Other artisans

made pottery or wove textiles. Perhaps most interesting in the context of my argument is the evidence for the many artisans who produced jewelry there.

Excavations have revealed about ten thousand fragments of molds and crucibles for casting precious metals, weighing some fifty kilograms all together. Some of the molds still contain remnants of the gold and bronze that were cast in them. With the help of these tools, goldsmiths produced ornaments of different kinds, including sword pommels, pins, belt buckles, and many different kinds of brooches, including some shaped like snakes and animal faces. Several brooches and other pieces of jewelry that at least approximately match the Helgö molds have been found from Högom, in northern Sweden, to Orsoy, in the Rhineland. The site also contains unworked materials, such as bronze bars, scrap metal, raw garnets, amber, and rock crystal.

Glass beads were produced at Helgö, probably from imported glass bars, but there is also evidence that glass might have been produced there. Much glass has been found on Helgö: some 1,600 pieces. This includes beautiful reticella glass, in which strings of colored glass were wound around thin transparent bars of glass and then partially melted. Polychrome beads made from this glass were used to make exquisite jewelry.

To make high-quality jewelry, glass beads, and such, artisans needed imported goods, so a site with many artisans, like Helgö, easily became a place for international exchange. Archeologists have uncovered plenty of evidence for this. Sixty-eight gold Roman solidi have been found on Helgö, which is about half of all the solidi found on the Swedish mainland. They have also discovered much Frankish, Finnish, Baltic, and Slavic pottery, further supporting the idea that Helgö became a trading place as well as a center for artisanal work.

RIBE

Ribe is another archeological site that bears witness to the need of chieftains to get suitable gifts for their followers.[35] Originally founded around 704–710, the town still exists on the western coast of Southern Jutland, in Denmark. At first, the buildings were laid out on irregular lots (as best as the archeologists can tell), but already in 721 or 722, they were arranged regularly along a street. The artisans worked on a series of parallel lots six to eight meters wide and twenty to thirty meters long. This means that some person had the power to impose this reorganization on the artisans who worked in Ribe. We suspect a powerful chieftain with an interest in having access to artisans, someone who controlled the site and needed to enhance the value of his gifts by having them crafted by experts.

The artisans in Ribe worked behind windscreens and in sunken huts (buildings partially dug into the ground), but they did not live in Ribe. At least, archeologists have not as yet found any settlements from the eighth century. The artisans were there for only part of the year. They were shoemakers, potters, comb makers, and jewelers working in bronze, lead, gold, glass beads, and amber. Since many of these crafts required raw materials that did not exist in the immediate surroundings of Ribe, the town early on became a trade town. Among the finished products that archeologists have uncovered are foreign pottery and glass vessels from Europe, whetstones and slate from elsewhere in Scandinavia, and glass beads from Europe and the Middle East.

The work that artisans did for their chieftains drove the rapid development of decorative styles during the Viking Age and created the first towns of Scandinavia. Chieftains organized Ribe and Helgö as centers for producing and refining the gifts they gave their warriors. This was a good investment, because the labor of artisans was comparatively cheap (some were surely slaves captured in Europe), and it made the gifts more attractive and thus more suitable for encouraging warriors to stay loyal. The artisans at these centers worked primarily for their chieftains, not for the market. During the Viking Age, however, trade towns developed in Scandinavia, as we shall see in chapter 7. It was only natural that places where artisans worked became trade towns as well. For starters, the work of expert artisans often required materials that had to be imported (gold, silver, amber, gemstones, glass, etc.). Also, people other than the chieftains were interested in acquiring their products, so trade tended to develop at artisans' workshops, whether they sold things on their own behalf or their master's.

6

The Lure of the Exotic

In the early ninth century, a slain Norwegian chieftain was buried in Gokstad with not only his ship, horses, dogs, and weapons but also a set of peacock feathers, still recognizable although badly decayed after a millennium underground. Peacocks may symbolically suggest Christian belief in resurrection or Roman belief in Juno, but on a more fundamental level the presence of exotic feathers, which must have been extremely rare in early medieval Norway, signals a wealthy and important man, whether he acquired them as a treasured gift, as booty, or as trade goods.[1] The Gokstad man's peacock feathers illustrate the value Scandinavian society put on exotic goods, things that had been transported from afar. Rare and unusual objects were used to extol the wealth and influence of the chieftains who carried them, and they were used in the gift exchange system to strengthen the ties between a chieftain and his warriors.

For Scandinavian chieftains, in general terms, to give an exotic object was better than to give something homespun, and thus they worked to acquire such objects, by plundering or by taking tribute (as described in chapter 2). We know that they did, since many Viking Age European objects have been found in Scandinavia.[2] The chieftains could also acquire them through trade, which will be the subject of chapter 7.

Some truly remarkable exotic objects have come to light in Scandinavia. The most spectacular is the small Buddha statuette in bronze from the sixth century that was excavated on the island of Helgö in Lake Mälaren in Sweden. Archeologists were called in when workers, who were digging a hole in order to raise a flagpole, found an early medieval baptismal ladle of bronze. The archeologists excavated several spots on Helgö from 1954 to 1978, uncovering an early medieval center where many artisans were active from the third century at least to around the year 1000. In addition to the Buddha, they also found part of an Irish bishop's staff. A few high-status objects like these are not evidence either for religious rituals on the site or for long-distance trade. Such things tended to be given as diplomatic gifts, be taken as war booty, or change hands in other noncommercial ways.[3] Other finds at Helgö, like the masses of foreign raw materials for use by goldsmiths, are, however, evidence for trade, demonstrating that Scandinavia participated in networks of long-distance exchange.

In both archeological finds and in literature the Scandinavian love for exotic objects is evident. The subject is enormous, and I will give only a few examples of the kinds of exotic goods that we know made it to Scandinavia and were likely used in the gift exchange system.

Walnuts

"The king does not forget his men," was Sigvat Thordarson's grateful comment when his lord, Norwegian king Olav, gave him and another retainer an exotic delicacy. The king had given them nuts: "The renowned king of the people sent nuts to me; this king does not forget his men; it will be a long time before I devote more art to praise-poetry. But the lord, bold towards men, often bade us divide them in two, Ottar, just as we would a father's legacy: my speeches are ended."[4]

It is hard to know what to do with this poem. Should it be taken at face value as praise in return for a desirable gift? Or might Sigvat's intent have been ironic? Is he poking fun at the king's less than royal gift of a few nuts, which to boot he was required to share with his nephew, the skald Ottar svarti? Sigvat was certainly capable of complaining about insufficient royal gifts. Later in life, in his "Plain-speaking Songs" (*Bersöglisvísur*), he would upbraid Olav's son King Magnus for being too parsimonious with gifts to his followers.[5]

If instead we take the poem at face value, then it would seem that Sigvat was sufficiently impressed by the gift to write a skaldic stanza about it. If so, one suspects that the nuts might not have been something as trivial as ordinary hazelnuts (indigenous to Scandinavia and a common component of the early medieval diet), but something more exotic. Walnuts were royal nuts, as modern systematizers recognized when they gave the species the Latin name *juglans regia* (royal acorn). The natural habitat of the walnut tree is Central Asia, and the Romans planted it in the Balkans and in southern Germany. Carolingian emperors and the monks at St. Gall planted much-desired walnut trees in their gardens so that they might have easy access to this delicacy.[6]

The example of Sigvat and the walnut demonstrates yet another way in which chieftains and kings competed with each other to give as valuable gifts as possible to their warriors. Only the truly well-connected and truly powerful could give rare and exotic gifts like walnuts. The bureaucracy of the caliph in Baghdad recognized the value of giving walnuts as gifts to foreign potentates. The embassy that traveled on his behalf in 921–922 to Bulghar brought walnuts to be used as gifts. Ibn Fadlan reports that they gave some to Oghuz notables on their way through the steppes east of the Caspian Sea.[7]

We know from archeological evidence that walnuts made it to Scandinavia during the early Middle Ages, and that Scandinavians appreciated them. At least one walnut was buried in 834 with the women who found their last rest in the gloriously furnished grave in Oseberg in Norway.[8] Their grave contained what is today the best preserved Viking Age ship and numerous exquisitely decorated artifacts. Very important persons were buried under such circumstances, and whoever arranged for the Oseberg burial thought that walnuts were appropriately prestigious delicacies for such persons. We know that walnuts came to Scandinavia through trade because archeologists have found remnants of them in Scandinavian trade towns. During excavations of a single modern building lot in Lund, they found almost a liter of hazelnut shells but only a single walnut shell from the eleventh century.[9] In Hedeby no less than six walnut shells have come to light, suggesting that walnuts were among the luxury goods that were traded at such places.[10]

Silk

Thousands of people were buried in a large grave field surrounding the Swedish town of Birka. The soil conditions are so favorable there that even some very fragile materials have survived, including textiles. One artifact from the graves, a small, conical, finely worked silver mount that was probably made in the Dnieper region, in what is today Ukraine, has remnants of silk inside it. It was, thus, once attached to the point of a cap that was at least partially made of silk, an exotic and expensive textile during the early Middle Ages. The Birka graves have also revealed hundreds of fragments of silk that served as collars, panels, or cuffs of dresses. More silk has been found in graves in Valsgärde, not far from Uppsala (see figs. 13 and 14). The techniques for weaving the silk were so different in China and the Middle

East (the two places where the Swedish silks might have originated) that it is possible to distinguish between Chinese silk and silk made in either Syria or Byzantium. At the very least a handful of the silks found at Valsgärde were in fact produced in China. They must have reached Sweden via caravans that traveled on the Silk Road and then through Bulghar or Kiev or some other trade town in eastern Europe. Most of the Birka silks, however, come from Syria or Byzantium.[11] Other prestigious burials in Scandinavia also contain silk, for example in Hedeby; in Mammen, in Jutland; in the Oseberg burial in Norway; and in Eura in western Finland.[12]

Literature often talks about silk as the prerogative of chieftains. Einar Helgason's poem *Vellekla*, for instance, says that Earl Håkon wore silk around his head. Perhaps he had the kind of silk cap that was buried in Birka.

> The guileless [chieftain] subjected seven counties—
> a silken band guards [his] brow—
> it was a lucky turn for the country.[13]

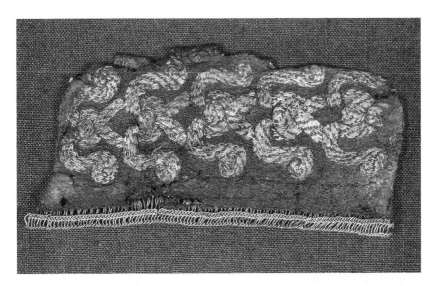

Fig. 13 A warrior was buried in the tenth century in Valsgärde, close to Uppsala, Sweden, in his boat and with many grave goods, including two pieces of silk, this one in the form of a cuff (although it might have made up some other detail of, for example, a bishop's liturgical clothes). The piece appears to have been worked on several times at different places. The silk was woven somewhere in the Middle East, and the embroidery in silver lamella is of a type associated with western European ecclesiastical milieus, while the border probably was added in Scandinavia or in a place influenced by Scandinavians, such as Russia. Photo: Teddy Törnlund, by courtesy of Museum Gustavianum, Uppsala.

Fig. 14 A silk collar(?) with embroidery in silver lamella, found in a boat grave in
Valsgärde, illustrates the love of exotic luxuries among Scandinavian warriors.
Photo: Teddy Törnlund, by courtesy of Museum Gustavianum, Uppsala.

The purpose of this stanza—as with most skaldic poetry—was to flatter
the chieftain. It succeeds in doing so in three ways. First, it boasts that Earl
Håkon was able to dominate seven counties (*fylki*), thus supposedly beating
his neighboring chieftains in battle or in recruiting warriors. Second, this was
a good thing for the people living in this area. Finally, he wore silk around his
head, which means that he was the real thing, a chieftain with the resources
to acquire such exotic luxuries.

Rock Crystal

A lot of jewelry has been discovered in the Birka graves and in other
Scandinavian graves from the early Middle Ages. Many pieces of jewelry were
manufactured in Scandinavia, as far as we may judge from their style and
execution, but many of the materials that went into making them were
imported.

Among those materials is rock crystal. In the early Middle Ages, rock
crystal was polished into many different shapes. In Scandinavia, surviving
early-medieval rock crystals appear in many different forms: flat, round,
octahedral, hexagonal, and elongated. Rock crystal beads from Hedeby are
of the simple, round variety. They are thought to have come from Harz in
Germany.[14] The many-faceted beads found in central Sweden, however, probably derive from the East, since they were manufactured with sophisticated
methods seemingly unknown in Europe. This is certainly true for a crystal bead
encased in blue glass, which was found in a tenth-century grave at Birka. The
technique was used only in Egypt at the time. Crystal beads mounted in silver
foil with characteristically Slavic decoration have been found on Gotland.[15] It
is also likely that the rock crystal in that jewelry came from the East.[16]

Wine

When the Norse god Rig came to a mansion, the third and most distinguished dwelling he visited in the poem *Rígsþula,* he was served a splendid and plentiful meal:

> Fresh game and pig's flesh
> and fowls roasted.
> There was wine in a flagon,
> ornamented goblets.[17]

The poet implies that wine was served at the rich man's table in Scandinavia. The grapes used for making wine do not grow in Scandinavia, so the wine that Rig was offered must have been imported. The closest wine-producing area was in the north of the Frankish Empire, where grapes had been grown, for example, in the Rhine and Moselle valleys since Roman times.

In fact, there are other good reasons to suspect that wine was imported to Scandinavia. When the Frankish missionary Ansgar arrived in Birka in the ninth century he met the Christian widow Frideborg, who had wine set aside for her last rites.[18] Imported ceramic bottles that are thought to have contained wine have been found in Helgö and in Birka in Sweden.[19] The walls of wells in Hedeby are often made out of reused wooden barrels. They were made from silver fir, which grew nowhere close to Hedeby. Such trees grew in the Upper Rhineland, close to wine-producing areas there, and the most obvious explanation for their presence in Hedeby is that the barrels came to the town filled with wine.[20] During the period of the late Roman Empire, sets of Roman-style drinking utensils were buried in Scandinavia together with their owners. In Öremölla in southern Sweden such a set has been found.[21] It includes two drinking vessels of glass, a large bronze bowl (for mixing the wine), a ladle, and a sieve (to remove sediments from the wine).

The Vikings liked wine. They often demanded and got wine as part of the tribute that European rulers paid them to be left in peace.[22] Godfrid was a Scandinavian in service to Emperor Charles the Fat. He was much favored by his emperor, having lands in Frisia and even being given as wife Gisela, the illegitimate daughter of King Lothar II. Godfrid, however, grasped for more, and in 884 he tried to blackmail the emperor into expanding his territory to include two wine-producing regions in the Rhine valley.[23]

The Vikings who obtained wine did not necessarily drink it themselves. Wine was a valuable trade commodity that they could sell for silver. Sometimes, however, the Vikings did enjoy the wine they got their hands on. In 1012, drunken Vikings martyred St. Alphege, also known as Archbishop Aelfheah of Canterbury, by pelting him to death with bones, horns, and finally the butt of an axe. They were "very drunk" on wine that had been brought from the south.[24]

Glass and Tatinger Pitchers

Any Scandinavian who could afford wine could also afford to serve it in appropriate vessels, just as those found in the grave from late antiquity in Öremölla, mentioned above. A tenth-century grave in Barkarby in central Sweden contains no less than six glass vessels, one of which was certainly made in Egypt, and the remaining five probably in the Middle East.[25]

Grave number 854 in Birka contains the remnants of a Viking Age man who was buried with a drinking vessel made of glass and a fancy pitcher of Tatinger ware (see fig. 15). The pitcher is of high quality and was shaped on a rapidly spinning potter's wheel, a technique not practiced in Scandinavia until later.[26] After firing, the potter decorated the pitcher by attaching thin, hammered tin foil in different patterns. The Birka man's pitcher is divided into several zones by horizontal lines. Each zone contains a row of small rhombs, and around the neck are long, vertical parallel lines.

This pitcher is one of several similar Tatinger pitchers that have been found in a broad swath of northern Europe from southeast England to Staraya Ladoga. A pitcher has even been found as far north as the Lofoten Islands of northern Norway, above the Arctic Circle. Tatinger pitchers are usually discovered in prestigious contexts such as rich graves, and they have been found in most of the trade towns of northern Europe: Hamwic, Dorestad, Ribe, Hedeby, Kaupang, and Helgö in addition to Birka and Staraya Ladoga. They were made somewhere in the northern Frankish Empire during the late eighth and early ninth centuries and were clearly high-status items not available to everyone.

This chapter has only touched on some of the masses of exotic goods that archeologists have discovered in Scandinavia. The point should be clear, however, that Viking Age Scandinavians who had the means to do so liked to surround themselves with exotic goods. They liked to wear silk and semiprecious stones when serving wine poured from Tatinger pitchers into glass vessels to accompany their dessert of walnuts. It is tempting to imagine that such was the scene that the poet wished to conjure up when he described the reception King Hrothgar gave Beowulf and his men in his great hall, Heorot:

> Wealtheow went forth
> Hrothgar's queen, mindful of customs;
> adorned with gold, she greeted the men in the hall,
> then that courteous wife offered the full cup . . .

Fig. 15 Tatinger pitchers were luxury artifacts manufactured on rapidly spinning potters' wheels somewhere in the Frankish Empire. The patterns on the pitcher were created by attaching hammered tin foil. Birka grave no. 854 also contained a glass drinking vessel. Photo: Sören Hallgren, by courtesy of Statens Historiska Museum, Stockholm.

[Much later, still in Heorot:]

> Glad sounds rose again,
> the bench-noise glittered, cupbearers gave
> wine from wondrous vessels. Wealtheow came forth
> in her golden crown . . .[27]

As the Beowulf excerpts illustrate, exotic and beautiful things were used not only as gifts but also as conspicuous luxuries, which chieftains used to decorate themselves, their wives, and their halls. What really mattered with such things was, at any rate, their symbolic value, enhancing the standing of the chieftain who owned them and gave them away. Chieftains went to great lengths to acquire rare objects, sending merchants to distant markets, cultivating friendships with even more-powerful rulers, and plundering wherever they could, in order to use exotica to tie their warriors ever closer to themselves.

7

Networks of Trade

The northern trading network was important not only because it supplied chieftains with exotic items but also because it created wealth, making it possible for those same chieftains to remain in the gift-giving business and thus to retain power. This trading network, the creation of chieftains and kings, also exported merchandise, particularly the furs and slaves to which northerners had easy access.

A surprising archeological find strikingly illustrates the reach of the northern trading network. People who had traveled far often visited Hedeby, at the southwestern corner of the Baltic Sea, so it was nothing out of the ordinary when a distant traveler arrived there at some point in the tenth century. This traveler, however, had the misfortune of dying during his visit, for reasons that we cannot even guess. He was buried in one of the many thousands of graves that surround the town, and his grave was excavated and examined in the 1960s. After a millennium his body had disappeared entirely, but some of his grave goods remained. Among these was a very unusual triangular bronze bowl of a type otherwise known only from Ireland. The bowl carries a runic inscription, which at first raised no eyebrows because Scandinavian utilitarian goods were often inscribed with runes. But this inscription surprised its discoverers, for it was not written in Old Norse but in a Turkic language. Its message is, however, universal: "Consider [this] advice: Drink! Love ardently! Obey!"

The language of the inscription places the origin of the bowl firmly in eastern Europe. It probably acquired its runes among the Volga Bulgarians, a Turkic-speaking people living in and around their trade town Bulghar, which was situated on the Volga River a little east of where Moscow now is situated. If the bowl is indeed Irish, its presence in Hedeby testifies that it moved back and forth across the entire width of northern Europe, from Ireland to Bulghar and then halfway back, ending up in southern Denmark.[1]

Was the bowl's owner Irish or Bulgarian? Had he also covered the same distances as the bowl? That is impossible to guess; for all we know, the owner might have been a Dane who acquired this exotic bowl in Hedeby, as the last in a long line of owners.

In the previous two chapters, we explored how trade served the gift exchange system. In chapter 5, we surveyed the achievements of artisans often working with imported raw materials. We examined evidence of Scandinavians' appreciation of imported and rare goods in chapter 6. This chapter looks at the efforts chieftains made to acquire such goods. I will argue that chieftains got involved in trade in several ways, by engaging in trade themselves, by having their agents engage in trade, or by establishing and controlling trade towns, creating networks of trade in the north.[2] Those networks in turn were connected to other networks in both western and eastern Europe, creating a great northern arc of trade, which linked western Asia with western Europe via the Baltic Sea, rather than—as previously—via the Mediterranean.[3] Flourishing from the early ninth century well into the tenth, this vast network was concentrated on a series of trading places spread out along the waterways of western, northern, and eastern Europe. Perhaps the most important consequence of this giant distribution system was to bring Arab silver on an unprecedented scale into silver-starved northern and western Europe.[4] Most of the dirhams that arrived there would have been melted down to produce western coinage or jewelry such as arm rings and brooches. Still, from Sweden alone more than eighty thousand dirhams survive from 587 hoards that were deposited in the ground at some point between the 790s and the 1090s. From the entire Baltic region, some two hundred thousand dirhams have been registered.[5]

Scandinavian Trade Towns

During the early Middle Ages, dozens of centers for goods exchange, or trade towns, were active in and around Scandinavia.[6] A few are known from literary evidence, but archeologists have found remnants of many more. Together they bear witness to what must have been substantial movement of goods in Scandinavia.

A Norwegian chieftain called Ottar (or Ohthere, in the Old English of the source) visited the court of the Anglo-Saxon king Alfred in the late ninth century. He told the king about how he earned a living. We have encountered him before, as an example of a tribute-taking chieftain. He collected from the Sami fur, feathers, whale bones (which may refer to walrus ivory as well, see figs. 16 and 17), and ropes made from walrus hide and sealskin. These goods were plentiful around his home in northern Norway and very attractive on the European market. Ottar told King Alfred how he would set sail southward to sell these goods. He sailed for a month along the coast of Norway to a trade town in southern Norway that he called Sciringes healh. (The second part of the compound means "hall," so the

Fig. 16 Walrus tusks could be carved into beautiful objects with a sheen similar to that of elephant ivory, and they were valuable products of the Arctic north, which made chieftains like Ottar in northern Norway and Erik the Red on Greenland into wealthy men. This early medieval tusk was found in Reykjavik, Iceland. Photo: Gudmundur Ingólfsson, by courtesy of Minjasafn Reykjavíkur, Reykjavik.

Fig. 17 Walrus ivory was used to make many kinds of luxury objects, including the hooked
        tops of pastoral staffs carried by high-ranking church officials, such as bishops
        and abbots. This twelfth-century crozier was discovered in 1993 in a grave in the
        Swedish city of Sigtuna. Photo: Jacques Vincent, by courtesy of Sigtuna Museum.

place name is prima facie evidence that the market there grew up around a
chieftain's hall.)⁷

Archeologists believe that they have found this town south of Larvik on
the western side of the broad mouth of the Oslo Fjord in southern Norway.⁸
Now called Kaupang, this is clearly a place where goods from far away
passed through. Excavations have revealed, for example, a few coins from the
Frankish and Anglo-Saxon kingdoms as well as twenty Arab dirhams. Most
of the pottery excavated there originated in Denmark or Frisia, but a third of
it comes from the Rhineland and a tenth is Slavonic. The pottery had traveled
across the sea to reach Norway. Kaupang flourished only briefly, in the eighth and
ninth centuries, and was never as important as Ottar's next destination: Hedeby.

Ottar recounted how it took him five days to sail from Sciringes healh
to Hedeby, which is situated on the eastern side of the base of the Jutland
peninsula. Hedeby is a classic archeological site, which has been extensively
excavated during most of the twentieth century. The site appears as a substantial trade town. It is situated at the end of a forty-kilometer-long and
narrow inlet (the Schlei) from the Baltic Sea, not far from the modern city of
Schleswig. At Hedeby, the Jutland peninsula is very narrow, only some seven
kilometers across, so it would not have been difficult to transport goods across
land from the North Sea or a river running into it.⁹

Hedeby was a large settlement. The archeological deposits extend over twenty-four hectares, and archeologists estimate that some twelve thousand graves are spread around the town. A settlement existed there already in the eighth century (and perhaps even earlier), but it appears as a trade town only from the early ninth century. The Arab diplomat Ibrahim ibn Yakub al-Turtushi visited Hedeby in its heyday in the tenth century and reported on the visit. There are freshwater wells inside it, and it is inhabited by both pagans and Christians, he said. The inhabitants mainly eat fish, and their singing is the most awful he has ever heard. "It is a groan that comes out of their throats, similar to the bark of the dogs but even more like a wild animal."[10] It is hard to know what to do with all the details of al-Turtushi's report, which survives only at second or third hand in medieval Arab encyclopedias, but it is very interesting that he claims both Christians and pagans lived in Hedeby. We know from other sources that a church had existed there since the first half of the ninth century.

Hedeby lost much of its importance and population after the year 1000, and disappeared entirely around the middle of the eleventh century.[11] As a trade town, Hedeby was replaced by Schleswig.

The evidence for goods exchange in Hedeby is plentiful. Archeologists have found many articles deriving from far away. Among the goods that Ottar claims he brought to Hedeby, the furs, feathers, and sealskins would not have left archeological traces. The ground has, however, yielded walrus bones, walrus ivory, and reindeer antlers. Ottar does not mention that he traded in antlers, but he says that he owned six hundred reindeer, so we may guess that he would have sold their antlers as well as their skins.

We saw in the last chapter that King Olav Haraldsson's retainer Sigvat Thordarson was happy to have received walnuts from the king. Archeologists have found remnants of more than six walnuts in Hedeby.[12] This suggests that Hedeby was one of the trade towns through which Scandinavian chieftains were able to acquire this delicacy, as well as many other exotic wares. The ground in Hedeby has, in fact, yielded many such trade articles, including foreign jewelry; Arab coins; amber; bars of iron, lead, silver, and brass; mercury; silk; glass; pottery; cornelian; and rock crystal. Many of these things originated further south in Europe, but some are of Asian origin, like some semiprecious stones, some of the silk, and the Arab coins. Hedeby was clearly a pivot in Scandinavian trade.[13]

A trade route went from Hedeby to the town of Birka, in Sweden, which was the only Scandinavian trade town to compete with Hedeby in size and importance.[14] The town was situated on the island of Björkö, west of Stockholm in Lake Mälaren, which at the time was a bay of the Baltic Sea.[15] The town extended over about thirteen hectares, and there are at least two thousand graves in the vicinity. Birka flourished at about the same time as Hedeby, from around 800 toward the end of the tenth century. When Archbishop Adalbert of Bremen visited the site in the 1060s looking for the grave of his predecessor, Unni (who had died there in 936), Birka was in ruins, and he could not find the grave.[16]

Just as in the case of Hedeby, there is plenty of evidence that goods from far away passed through Birka. Archeologists have found many exotic artifacts in the excavated graves: silk, cornelian beads, amber, foreign pottery, and jewelry. Outside of the graves, archeologists have also found evidence for Scandinavian goods that must have been meant for export. There survives a large number of claws from various animals with valuable furs, including foxes and marten, but few bones from the same animals. These finds suggest that the animals were roughly skinned when they were caught. The skins were then sent to Birka, where they were prepared for sale, the claws being removed and discarded in the process, so that the skins could be traded to the south and east of Europe and beyond.[17]

The literary and archeological evidence for Scandinavian trade towns demonstrates how those towns fit into the efforts of chieftains to attract and keep retinues of warriors. On the one hand, the towns and their merchants produced income for chieftains. Chieftains like Ottar could bring their goods to the towns to exchange them for other more or less exotic gifts for their followers. It is hard to imagine that Ottar could have done that without giving a valuable gift to the king who controlled Hedeby. Most trade in Viking Age Scandinavia was barter, as there were no strong states that were able to uphold the value of currency. Silver and gold coins were used in trade, but their value was determined by their weight and purity. This is the reason why people in Scandinavia needed the kinds of exact scales that have been found in graves in Birka, Hedeby, and elsewhere. Scandinavian rulers began to issue coins around the year 1000, indicating that the process of bringing the Scandinavian kingdoms into being had advanced so far that kings were able to impose a value on coins that was higher than their contents of precious metal.[18]

Scandinavian Trade in Western Europe

We know of Scandinavian trade in western Europe in two different contexts: the temporary markets set up by Vikings after raiding and taking tribute, and the network of trade towns around the North Sea. Merchants transported goods between the trade towns and other points in Scandinavia.[19]

In plundering western Europe, the Vikings must have picked up valuables that they had no wish to bring back home. Some of these, like slaves and cattle, might even have been too bulky or too difficult to transport long distances. It made sense to exchange such goods for silver or other easily transported valuables by setting up a market, as we know that some Vikings did. For example, during the peace negotiations after their defeat in 873 at Angers by the forces of King Charles the Bald, a band of Vikings "requested to be allowed to stay until February on an island in the Loire, and to hold a market there."[20] In this way, Vikings stimulated trade not only in their homelands but also in western Europe, where, for example, slaves were exported at an enormous profit across the Mediterranean.[21]

More important than such temporary markets were the trade towns on both sides of the North Sea, principally on the south coast of England and the north coast of the Frankish Empire. The most important English trade towns were Hamwih (at Southampton), Ipswich, Lundenwic (London), and Jorvik (York). Significant on the Continent were, particularly, Dorestad and Quentovic. Dorestad flourished between the early seventh century and the third quarter of the ninth century on the lower Rhine in what is today the Netherlands. Quentovic was situated some ten kilometers from the Frankish coast, close to the Canche River, and experienced its heyday in the eighth and ninth centuries. Both Quentovic and Dorestad were well situated for trade with the inland Frankish Empire (via the rivers) and England across the sea.[22]

No one doubts that there was ample contact between Scandinavia and these western trade towns. Excavations in western Europe have brought to light artifacts originating in Scandinavia and vice versa. For example, very many millstones have been found in Denmark that were made out of basalt from the quarries in Mayen, in the Eifel Mountains upstream from Dorestad, on the Rhine. They have also been found at almost every major excavation of Scandinavian rural sites, and a lot of them have been found in Hedeby and Ribe. Archeologists have found more than seven hundred fragments of mill-stones and four hundred fragments of unworked basalt in Dorestad, which was clearly a transit point for the trade in Eifel basalt.[23] Similarly, Norwegian whetstone and soapstone have been found in western Europe as well as in Hedeby. It is likely that Ottar's Sciringes healh was a transit station for the trade in these stones.[24]

There is also literary evidence for trade connecting Scandinavia with western trade towns. Rimbert's ninth-century *Life of Ansgar*, for example, vouches for contact between Birka and Dorestad. Rimbert mentions a Christian widow living among pagans in Birka, in Sweden. She stipulated that after her death her things should be sold and that her daughter should bring the money to

Dorestad to give away to the poor and to the church. We are also told that this was done when she passed away.[25]

There can be no doubt that much trade passed peacefully between Scandinavia and western Europe at the same time that Viking bands were acquiring goods in violent ways.

Trade in Eastern Europe

Important trade routes between Scandinavia and the Arab Caliphate passed through eastern Europe during the Viking Age. Medieval writers testify to separate pieces of this trading link, but the most impressive evidence for it are the tens of thousands of Arab coins that have been discovered in the soil around the Baltic Sea as well as along the banks of the rivers of eastern Europe.[26]

Several literary sources mention trade between Scandinavia and eastern Europe. Adam of Bremen, for example, tells us that one may sail from Birka to Russia in five days. He also mentions that Slavs and Samlandians[27] regularly come to Birka to trade. A traveler visiting King Alfred in the late ninth century, a man with the Anglo-Saxon name Wulfstan, told of sailing from Hedeby east along the southern shore of the Baltic Sea to a town called Truso. He sailed day and night for five days, probably using a sounding lead to stay at an appropriate distance from the shore on this shallow coast.[28] Archeologists believe that they have identified Truso, from excavations in the village of Janów Pomorski, on the delta of the Vistula River.[29]

The location of Truso near the mouth of the Vistula, one of many rivers in the region, is key for understanding the routes that Scandinavian trade followed in eastern Europe. Since most of Poland, Belarus, European Russia, Ukraine, and the three Baltic states extend over a flat plain with few mountains, their rivers flow calmly and are navigable almost to their sources (as long as the water supply is sufficient).[30] It is possible to travel from the Baltic Sea to either the Black Sea or the Caspian Sea by means of several routes without ever rising above two hundred meters in altitude. Waterways are available for most of the way.

Several Viking Age trading communities were strung along the banks of the rivers of eastern Europe. Scandinavians had penetrated these trade routes already in the ninth century. Towns close to the outlets of the rivers into the Baltic anchored the routes. Among them are, in addition to Truso on the Vistula, Wollin at the mouth of the Oder and Staraya Ladoga on the Volkhov, where it empties into Lake Ladoga, which drains into the Baltic via the short Neva River. Written sources mention trade routes extending from these towns, and other routes may be inferred on the basis of geography and archeological finds.

Most important among the written sources is the so-called *Russian Primary Chronicle*, written in Old Slavonic, which describes a trade route between the Baltic and the Black Seas: "A trade-route connected the Varangians with the Greeks. Starting from Greece [Byzantium], this route proceeds along the Dnieper, above which a portage leads to the Lovat'. By following the Lovat', the great lake Il'men' is reached. The river Volkhov flows out of this lake and enters the great lake Nevo [Lake Ladoga]. The mouth of this lake opens into the Varangian [Baltic] Sea."[31]

Archeological findings and other written sources fill in the picture of this route. We shall follow the route in the direction opposite to that of the chronicler, that is, from the north to the south. Beginning in the inner reaches of the Bay of Finland, which is the easternmost tip of the Baltic Sea, a ship would then sail up the marshy Neva River at the site of St. Petersburg. The river, today short and slow flowing, would have been even shorter and slower in the Viking Age, since the water level of the Baltic Sea was higher then than now.[32] Several rivers flow into the Ladoga, the most important of which for long-distance trade was the Volkhov. The town of Staraya Ladoga lies on a ridge alongside the river twelve kilometers upstream from Lake Ladoga, surrounded by impassable bogs and forests.[33] Founded in the middle of the eighth century at the site of a small Finno-Baltic settlement, the town had strong connections with Scandinavia from the start, as evidenced by Scandinavian-style artifacts in the oldest settlement layers. By the end of the tenth century, the town covered some ten hectares before it was sacked by the Norwegian earl Eirik Håkonsson of Lade.[34]

Continuing up the Volkhov, a traveler would arrive at Novgorod, the city built on the banks of the Volkhov just north of where it drains out of Lake Ilmen. The Viking Age town was built on a hill two kilometers south of the present city center. To distinguish it from Old Novgorod, which was settled in c. 930, scholars call it Riurikovo Gorodishe ("Rurik's fortress").[35] Gorodishe occupied at least ten hectares and was settled at the latest in the middle of the ninth century.

Several rivers empty into Lake Ilmen. The Old Slavonic chronicler recommends the Lovat, but several other routes are possible, including the Msta, leading in the direction of the Volga River system. Following any of the rivers upstream, a traveler would come to the Valdai Hills, the tallest spot on the Eastern European Plain, reaching 343 meters above sea level. As the Old Slavonic chronicler knew well, many important rivers originate in those hills, the hydrographic center of the plain; some examples include the Dnieper, which flows into the Black Sea; the Volga, which flows into the Caspian Sea; and several rivers whose waters flow into the Baltic Sea.[36] Among those is the Western Dvina, which empties into the Baltic Sea at Riga.

The Old Slavonic chronicler tells us that travelers on the route he describes portaged their boats between the Dnieper and the Lovat. Portaging a boat—dragging it overland between two bodies of water—is a laborious procedure. Before canals were built (often at the sites of old portages), this was how travelers moved between inland waterways. Modern reenactments have shown that the procedure is perfectly possible, even using the technology that was available in the Middle Ages.[37] River travelers are likely to have used much smaller boats than the oceangoing Viking ships that have been found, for example, in the Gokstad grave or at Roskilde.[38]

At commonly used portages, man-made changes in the terrain served to facilitate the passage. Each crew portaging their ship overland would as a matter of course remove some of the more obvious obstacles in their way, such as shrubbery, smaller rocks, and trees. After the passage of a few ships, a path began to form. This path would, simply by use, have become more and more hollowed out, forming a shallow trench. Such trenches are still visible at old portages, for example, near Briare, in north-central France, where (until a canal was built in 1642) ships were portaged between the Seine and the Loire, at the point where the two rivers are closest to each other.[39]

Local inhabitants and rulers could also assist portaging crews by maintaining and improving the portage path itself, for example, by smoothing the sides of the trench. The most enterprising portage managers lined their trenches with a revetment of timber, like the portage trench that has been identified at Draget, on the isthmus between two bays of Lake Mälaren, in Sweden.[40] To portage a ship through a smooth, timber-lined trench must have been considerably less time-consuming than to drag it over rough and trackless terrain. The person who had taken the trouble of lining the trench with timber or had otherwise facilitated portage could reasonably charge a fee or expect a gift from each passing ship.

To portage a ship is labor intensive, not only because it is hard work but also because the ship and its freight must be protected against attacks while it is being portaged. The Byzantine emperor Constantine VII Porphyrogennitos recounts how Rus travelers kept "vigilant watch for the Pechenegs" (a nomadic people with a reputation for ferocity) when they portaged their ships in order to avoid the Dnieper cataracts.[41] Ships' crews would welcome assistance, even when it came at a price. People living in the neighborhood would find it lucrative to assist in portaging ships, whether by providing protection, by making available additional manpower or the use of animal power, or by offering repair service to ships damaged in the process. In this way, a portage could feed the local economy and even stimulate the growth of a city. The city of Smolensk in Russia, for example, first grew up in the late ninth century at one of the most important portages connecting the Dnieper with rivers draining into the Baltic Sea.[42] Archeological investigations in Old Smolensk (Gnëzdovo), situated a few kilometers west of the modern city, have revealed numerous workshops, where ships could be repaired. This suggests that Gnëzdovo was a place where ships were repaired after being damaged during portage.[43]

The journey downstream on the Dnieper is described both by the Old Slavonic chronicler and Emperor Constantine VII. A traveler would reach Kiev (known as a great city by Adam of Bremen[44]) and its large trading suburb Podol. The continued journey toward the Black Sea would lead to the great Dnieper cataracts, which greatly interested Constantine. Over sixty-two kilometers, the river drops thirty-three meters, or so it did before the Dniepropetrovsk hydroelectric dam was built in the 1930s. Constantine gives the Rus and the Slavonic names of the seven rapids, and he tells us how the Rus maneuvered their boats through the smaller ones. But at the greatest of the rapids, which Constantine claims was called "Aifor" in the Rus language and "Neasit" in Slavonic, the Rus disembarked. Some men were deputized to watch against attacks, while the rest conducted the slaves and carried the other goods past the barrage by land, for six miles: "Then, partly dragging their boats, partly carrying them on their shoulders, they convey them to the far side of the barrage."[45] After loading the boats up again, the Rus continued to the next rapid.

Cossack river pilots took pride in being able to go by boat through all of the Dnieper rapids even after a canal bypassing them was built in the eighteenth century.[46] The Gotlander Ravn (or Hrafn) was not so fortunate, according to the testimony of a tenth-century runestone on Gotland, in Sweden: "Hegbjörn raised this brightly colored stone [and his] brothers Hrodvisl, Eysteinn, Emund [?], who have had stones raised in memory of Hrafn south of Rofstein. They came far in Eifor . . ."[47] The four brothers announce that they had previously raised stones in Ravn's memory, perhaps closer to the place where he died. They claim to have come far into "Eifor," which corresponds to Constantine's "Aifor." In other words, it seems that Ravn and his companions (including perhaps the four brothers sponsoring the runestone) tried to go by boat through the greatest of the Dnieper rapids, but that he died in the process.

A runestone on the island of Berezanyi, which is located at the mouth of the Dnieper, where it flows into the Black Sea, bears an inscription in Old Norse: "Grani made this mound in memory of his comrade Karl."[48] This demonstrates unambiguously that Scandinavians had traveled at least this far, and probably farther, during the Viking Age.

A Viking Age traveler also had the option of turning to the east at the portages of the Valdai Hills, to seek the Volga River. The Old Slavonic chronicler spells out this option: "The Volga rises in this same forest [at the Valdai Hills] but flows to the east, and discharges through seventy mouths into the Caspian Sea. It is possible by this route to the eastward to reach the Bulgars and the Caspians."[49]

The Bulgars, distant cousins of the Bulgarians of the Balkans, resided around the upper Volga, east of what is today Moscow. A little south of the confluence of the Kama River with the Volga, they had a trade town called Bulghar.[50] In 922, an Arab embassy from Baghdad visited Bulghar. One of its members, Ahmad ibn Fadlan, wrote a report about his experiences in the far north, so we can read a first-hand account of events in Bulghar.[51] He witnessed the cremation of a dead Rus chieftain in a great ship as well as Rus traders who arrived on ships on the Volga. Ibn Fadlan tells us that these merchants sold furs and slaves, and Arab geographers confirm that Bulghar was a center for the fur and slave trade. Its inhabitants traveled north to northern Russia, where some of the best fur in the world could be acquired.[52]

The identity of the Rus, whether they were Scandinavian settlers or Slavs or something else, is controversial. Scholars appear in recent years to have agreed that "Rus" is not an ethnic label but rather denotes a group of merchants active in eastern Europe. As we saw in chapter 4, archeological evidence suggests that Scandinavians were among the merchants of the towns in the region.[53]

From Bulghar, several routes led south. Travelers following the Volga downstream, either by boat or overland along the river, would come to the Khazar Empire and its towns in and around the Volga delta. They would pay a tenth of the value of their cargo to the Khazars. Another route would take travelers around the Khazars, going southeast to reach the Silk Road to China and to the cities of Khwarezm, a region of the Caliphate in Central Asia, around the Amu Darya River, southeast of the Aral Sea. This was the route that ibn Fadlan had taken from Baghdad to Bulghar.

When archeologists find artifacts, for instance, silk and Arab coins, in Scandinavia that came from far away, we should not automatically assume that Scandinavians brought them the entire distance. Trade normally happened through many intermediaries, although there were some Scandinavian travelers who in fact did go long distances, as is illustrated by runic inscriptions. Several Swedish runestones mention men who died in "Särkland" (land of the Saracens), in other words, in the Arab Caliphate.[54] A Swedish runestone from the early eleventh century is more exact about where in the Caliphate a certain young man traveled and, unfortunately, met his death: "Gudleif set this staff and these stones after his son Slagve. He met his end in the east in Khwarezm" (see fig. 18).[55]

We cannot know whether Slagve and the men who died in Särkland were traders or something else. In the eleventh century the Swedish chieftain Ingvar organized a raiding expedition to the Caspian Sea, which, however, encountered stiff resistance in the Arab Caliphate. Many of its participants died. The tragic fate of the expedition was so famous that a high-medieval Icelandic saga, *Yngvar's Saga*, treated it with great imagination but without providing much useful information. More than twenty preserved Swedish runestones were raised in memory of companions of Ingvar. His brother Harald came

Fig. 18 At some point in the early eleventh century, Gudleif raised a runestone, now at the ruined church of Stora Rytterne, Sweden, in memory of his son Slagve, who "met his end in the east in Khwarezm," providing a striking illustration of the long journeys that early medieval Scandinavians undertook. We do not know why Slagve traveled all the way to Central Asia, but he might have gone there as a merchant, a raider, a mercenary, or even as a slave. Photo: Jessica Eriksson. Reproduced with permission.

with him on the expedition but did not come back. Their mother raised a stone in Harald's memory:

Tola had this stone raised in memory of her son Harald, Ingvar's brother.

> They travelled valiantly
> far for gold
> and in the east
> gave [food] to the eagle.
> [They] died in the south,
> in Särkland.[56]

Part of the inscription is in the meter of *fornyrðislag*, an Old Norse verse form, and it includes a kenning that is well known from skaldic poetry: to give food to the eagle means to kill enemies. The verse thus tells us that Ingvar and his brother Harald went east to raid, and not to trade (or at least that is what their mother wanted readers to think). They used routes that traders had explored before them. Their expedition was not much different from those of Vikings sailing west on routes that traders had explored before them.

Chieftains and Trade

We have, thus far, surveyed a northern trading network following navigable water in a great arc from the North Sea via the Baltic Sea to the rivers of the eastern European plains. The network flourished in the ninth and tenth centuries and then withered. Its fortunes may be studied in some detail through the record of Arab silver coins (dirhams) reaching the Baltic Sea. Some 80,000 dirhams deposited in the ground between 670 and 1090 survive from Sweden. The corresponding figure for Poland is 37,000 and for Russia, Belarus, and the Ukraine together 207,000. This enormous influx of silver began as a slow trickle at the very end of the eighth century, became substantial by the middle of the ninth century, and declined noticeably in Scandinavia at the turn of the millennium. The stream continued a little longer in eastern Europe.[57] The most likely interpretation for this is that rulers in eastern Europe became strong enough to keep the profits from trade with the Arabs, and not let Scandinavian entrepreneurs take home the income from their sale of furs and slaves, which in any case they had acquired in eastern Europe. It is tempting and probably correct to see the slowing of dirham imports to Scandinavia as related to Vladimir the Great's creation, in the late tenth century, of a strong state centered on Kiev.[58]

The ninth- and tenth-century flowering of trade in northern Europe is a unique phenomenon; never before or since has trade traveled in quite the same ways. The influx of silver from the Caliphate fed the economy of Europe, which was beginning to take off. Much of the silver was surely made into western coins. But why did trade flourish here at exactly the time when it did? The preconditions were in place, certainly, with the silver mines of Afghanistan churning out silver, but the fact that the opportunity for trade existed is not sufficient explanation for why it actually happened.

Scandinavian chieftains did not know about the newly discovered silver mines at the extreme eastern end of the Caliphate, nor would they at first have known the entire potential of trade. They had their own particular reasons for getting involved in trade: they wished to increase their income and to acquire prestigious and exotic goods that they could use in competitive gift-giving. They could easily lay their hands on wares that could be bartered in the markets, either at home in Scandinavia (as Ottar did) or away from home. There was much that they could sell, such as whetstone and soapstone from Norway, iron from Sweden, and fur from all over northern Scandinavia. Particularly important were furs and slaves.

It was probably to get more and better-quality furs that Scandinavians first expanded their activities into northern Russia.[59] Staraya Ladoga was ideally situated to reach this natural resource via the waterways east of Lake Ladoga, and Scandinavians were among the first settlers there. Bulghar was similarly situated for the same purpose, and from the beginning its trade was oriented toward the lucrative Arab market. When Scandinavians discovered that it was possible to sell fur in Bulghar, they sought contact with the town, and through it with the Arab market, via the rivers of eastern Europe. The rich dirham finds of Scandinavia bear witness to their success.

A similar argument may be made about slaves, which was another important commodity traded by Scandinavians. The etymology of the word itself in most western European languages (as well as for the Arab word for "eunuch," *siqlabi*) suggests that most slaves were Slavs. Staraya Ladoga and other trade towns in eastern Europe served well as bases for slave raiding.[60]

Trade turned out to be a profitable pursuit for Scandinavians. Profit and the desire for exotic goods explain the flourishing trade of the Viking Age. It came about because of the political needs of Scandinavian chieftains. This idea is supported by the archeology of the Scandinavian sites where trade was carried out. Most Scandinavian trade towns were laid out in regular lots, with straight streets organized on a grid system. This suggests that they did not come about spontaneously or grow organically but rather were established and controlled by a governing authority. This pattern is very clear in Hedeby. The town is laid out over twenty-four hectares within a semicircular earthen rampart bordering on the harbor. Several parallel streets extend inland from the harbor, and wooden houses occupy regularly shaped lots along the streets.

Hedeby was founded by King Godfrid of the Danes. The *Royal Frankish Annals* recount how in 808 Godfrid launched Hedeby as a center for trade: "But Godfrid before his return [after fighting the Slavic Obodrites on the southern shores of the Baltic Sea] destroyed a trading place on the seashore, in Danish called Reric, which, because of the taxes it paid, was of great advantage to his kingdom. Transferring the merchants from Reric he weighed anchor and came with his whole army to the harbor of Sliesthorp."[61]

Sliesthorp is another name for Hedeby. A foundation date of 808 fits well with the dates archeologists are able to assign to the earliest datable houses in Hedeby. They are built with timber from wood felled as early as 811, but not earlier.[62] Since not all wood is suitable for exact dating (depending on how it was cut and on its state of preservation), this date is close enough to 808 to safely conclude that Hedeby was founded as a trade town in that year.

Godfrid's actions illustrate my argument. The Obodrites competed with the Danes for power around the southwestern corner of the Baltic Sea. One of the ways in which chieftains in the area competed was by having access to the goods provided by traders. By forcing the traders in the Obodritian trade town Reric to move to his own newly founded town in Hedeby, Godfrid not only deprived the Obodrites of this advantage but also acquired it for himself. In addition, and as the source points out, it was lucrative to control a successful trading center, since traders had to pay landing fees and other "taxes."

We are unusually well informed about the foundation of Hedeby, but everything we know about other trade towns in the north suggests that powerful chieftains were behind their establishment as well. Most of them were laid out on regular grids. This applies to Birka, in Sweden, where parallel streets led from jetties jutting out into the harbor. It also applies to Ribe, in Denmark, where an early-eighth-century settlement first established on irregular lots gave way within a few years to regularly shaped lots delimited by ditches along a street.[63] Wollin, at the mouth of the Oder, featured square blocks with four houses each, and its harbor was regularly laid out with quays and protruding jetties.[64] The literary sources support the conclusion that chieftains governed the trade towns. When Ansgar visited Hedeby and Birka in the first half of the ninth century, each was governed by a representative of the king.

Chieftains sponsored the trade towns. In competition with each other, they used trade to gain the advantage and for at least three ends. First, they were able to collect "taxes" (as the writer of the *Royal Frankish Annals* expresses it), probably in the form of landing fees and customs fees, from traders who visited their trade towns. Second, they earned riches by selling commodities like fur and slaves. Throughout the Viking Age, they brought home undreamed of quantities of Arab silver from the markets of eastern Europe. Tens of thousands of Arab dirhams have been found in the ground of northern Europe, and that does not account for all the coins that were melted down by smiths in the trade towns to make jewelry or simple silver bars. Third, chieftains also used trade to acquire exotic luxuries that were particularly effective in gift exchange, like the walnuts we know of from Norway or the semiprecious stones that have turned up all over Scandinavia.

8

The Story of Conversion

At the same time that the northern trading network was flourishing and the Vikings were acquiring wealth and an unflattering reputation in Europe, the Scandinavian homeland became Christian. The coincidence is striking and seems to require explanation.

The fundamental nature and sheer scope of this religious change are clearly apparent in a comparison between two European travelers in the north. They visited Scandinavia more than three centuries apart, and they had very different experiences. One visitor was a cardinal who would become pope and the other a monk who would become archbishop. Both owed their promotions to their travels in Scandinavia.

In 1152–1154, Cardinal Bishop Nicolaus Breakspear of Albano traveled around Scandinavia. He did not go there to convert the Scandinavians, like Ansgar or Poppa; that had already been done. Nicolaus was a bureaucrat, an administrator who had been sent to organize and regulate Christianity in Scandinavia, so that the region could be integrated into the universal church as a regular church province. He was welcomed everywhere, holding great church councils in both Nidaros, Norway, and Linköping, Sweden. Historians think the cardinal celebrated Christmas 1152 in Trondheim. No cardinal had ever been so far north, above sixty-three degrees latitude, and no one else would go again for a very long time. Nicolaus would have experienced days that lasted less than four and a half hours from sunrise to sunset. On his way back to Italy, he stayed with Archbishop Eskil of Lund. At the time, Scandinavia had some twenty bishops, most of whom were natives, and the cardinal must have met at least all of the Swedish and Norwegian bishops. Breakspear's trip to the north was so successful that he was elected pope (the only Englishman ever on the throne of St. Peter), taking the name Adrian IV, not many days after he returned to Rome. Norway, Sweden, and Denmark were clearly Christian kingdoms by the 1150s.[1]

His trip stands in stark contrast to that of the Frankish monk Ansgar, who in 829 with his companion Witmar obtained passage on a merchant ship going to Birka, in Sweden, where they hoped to convert the population to Christianity. Pirates attacked the ship, so the two monks had to swim to safety and then walk the rest of the way. In Birka they encountered a few Christians, some of whom were captives. Their success there was otherwise underwhelming; people liked to listen to their message, Ansgar's pious biographer Rimbert claims, but that is faint praise indeed in a hagiographical text meant to extol the sanctity of its hero. Rimbert makes much of the conversion and baptism of the town prefect Heriger. It is clear, however, that the Christian community Ansgar created in Sweden was small. It would continue to have a precarious existence as the northernmost outpost of the German bishopric that Ansgar managed to secure for himself through a combination of political maneuvering and outright forgery.[2]

The contrast between these two visits in the ninth and the twelfth centuries could hardly be greater. Cardinal Nicolaus visited lands that in the eyes of the church were already so Christianized that they could be given an ordinary ecclesiastical organization. Ansgar visited a predominantly pagan country, at some risk to his life. Other clerics whom Ansgar sent to Birka were killed, either there or on the way.[3] The religious landscape of Scandinavia had undergone a radical shift between the early ninth century and the mid-twelfth, becoming Christian in the interval. How that happened and why is less obvious. This will be the focus of this and the following chapters.[4]

Many circumstances have obscured the process of conversion in Scandinavia. One of the most important problems is the ambiguity of the word itself: "Conversion" can mean many different things, just as a "religion" is never monolithic but rather a system of beliefs and practices.[5] When studying the Scandinavian conversion to Christianity, we need to be careful to distinguish among different meanings of the word. On the one hand, conversion might refer to how Christian ideas and practices slowly infiltrated Scandinavia. Through archeology, we may study this slow seepage in the adoption of Christian burial practices and the embrace of Christian symbols. This process began as soon as the Roman Empire had become Christian and continued after the church had become firmly established in Scandinavia, when the church continued to work on implanting Christian ideas and practices into the population. We may talk about this kind of conversion as "Christianization."

On the other hand, there was the institutional conversion of the region. During this process Scandinavian kings destroyed pagan temples, built churches, established dioceses, and introduced Christian kingship. This process began later and played out faster. It began when Ansgar had the first churches in Birka and Hedeby built in the 830s. It continued with the conversion and baptism of rulers, and the process was for all practical purposes completed when Pope Alexander III created Scandinavia's third (and last medieval) archbishopric, Uppsala, in 1164.[6] Or perhaps a better end point would be when bishops first crowned Scandinavian kings, which happened in Norway in 1163 or 1164, in Denmark in 1170, and in Sweden in c. 1210.[7] The institutional conversion represented the alliance between the church and kings in Scandinavia. This kind of conversion was more a political event than a spiritual process.

Adding to the problems of understanding the Scandinavian conversion is that the different kinds of conversion are primarily illuminated by different kinds of sources. Generally, the archeological material tells us about the process of Christianization, while the written sources focus on institutional conversion, on the baptism of chieftains and kings, and on the building of churches and the installations of bishops. Each of the written sources, to boot, is driven by an agenda that must be deconstructed before one may start using it as a source. To combine the two kinds of source material successfully is, thus, difficult, unless one sets conversion against the broad background of early medieval Scandinavian society.

As seen in the written sources, the conversion of Scandinavia played out in three main phases. The missionary pioneers came first, among whom the most famous was the monk Ansgar of Corvey (died 865), who went on to become an archbishop with the special assignment to convert Scandinavia. Ansgar did not convert any kings or other really important persons. That would come later, in the second phase, playing out approximately between 960 and 1020, when a series of Scandinavian kings converted to Christianity, as celebrated by medieval Christian writers. The final phase of the conversion process was the establishment of a regular church infrastructure, especially the institution of bishoprics with fixed sees, a process for which Cardinal Nicolaus provided the capstone. This process of institutional conversion played out against the background of the much slower process of Christianization, which will be described and interpreted in chapters 9 and 10.

Missionaries

The first missionary known to have gone to Scandinavia was Archbishop Ebo of Rheims, who went to Denmark in 823.[8] The political situation was that Charlemagne had defeated, pacified, and forcibly baptized the Saxons living between the Rhine and the Elbe. Carolingian religious policy now took aim at the peoples that resided beyond them: the Scandinavians, primarily the Danes, to the north and the Slavs to the east. Emperor Louis the Pious assigned this important mission to his childhood playmate, Archbishop Ebo of Rheims, who obtained from Pope Paschal I a privilege appointing him papal legate to Scandinavia.[9] He was joined on his journey to Denmark by Bishop Willerich of Bremen. Ebo returned at least "several times," converting "many" to Christianity.[10] Indeed, after he had participated in the (eventually) failed coup against Emperor Louis the Pious, Ebo in 834 slipped away from Rheims at night, taking with him as much silver and gold as he was able to carry on his way to Scandinavia (*ad Normannos*), where he apparently expected to find a safe haven. Helping him to flee were "some Northmen, who were familiar with the routes and ports of the sea and the rivers running to the sea."[11]

We know very little about the details of Ebo's mission, for the sources do not tell us much. We are much better informed about the work of the monk Ansgar, who became one of Ebo's collaborators in the northern mission in 826 or 827.[12] Ansgar later became archbishop with residence in Bremen, and his successor in this job, Rimbert, had good reasons for promoting the cult of his predecessor as a saint. Rimbert also needed to provide a believable context for the documents that both he and Ansgar had forged in order to carve out an archbishopric for themselves. This explains why Rimbert's *Life of Ansgar* appears to be unexpectedly forthright (for a hagiographic text) about Ansgar's missionary work; Rimbert's main purpose was not to exaggerate Ansgar's success as a missionary.[13] Ebo, in contrast, had a checkered career; perhaps born a serf, he was deposed after rebelling against the emperor and imprisoned in Fulda monastery, and eventually he was made bishop of Hildesheim. No one was particularly interested in promoting him as a saint. Hence, there is no biography to tell us about his work. For this reason, modern accounts of the conversion of Scandinavia devote much space to Ansgar and barely any to Ebo. We should be aware, however, that this imbalance reflects the one-sidedness of the sources. Ebo's missions to Denmark might have been more successful and more significant than appears from the sources. The same may be said about many other missionaries, including Ebo's relative Gauzbert, who was active in Sweden in the 830s and early 840s.

Charlemagne and his son Louis strove to expand their empire, and they used Christianity to reach that goal. By having the Saxons baptized, the father brought them into the Christian commonwealth of his empire. In 826, the son had an opportunity to put the Danes in a similarly subservient position. He took it. The Danish king, Harald, who had lost a power struggle in Denmark, appeared in the empire and declared himself ready to be baptized if the Franks would help him win back his power in Denmark. Harald was one of several people who wished to be kings in Denmark after the death in 810 of King Godfrid, and the Franks had already in 819 helped Harald win back his kingdom.[14] At that time, he had recognized the overlordship of Emperor Louis the Pious. Seven years later, he was again driven into exile. The emperor became his godfather when Harald was baptized at Mainz with his family and four hundred followers. This made Harald into a son who should be obedient and respectful to his father Louis.[15] After these festivities, Harald sailed north on the Rhine, but he did not have much success in Denmark. Instead, he settled with his followers not far from Denmark, in the Frisian county of Rüstringen, given to him by Emperor Louis, as we have seen in chapter 4.

Ansgar preached and taught among Harald's followers for some time, but then he moved on to what he, or rather his superior, Ebo, hoped would be more-fertile fields in Sweden. Envoys from the king of the Swedes had arrived at Worms to ask Emperor Louis that preachers be sent to their homeland. Louis assigned this task to Ansgar and his companion, the monk Witmar. The two missionaries went to Birka, the trade town in Sweden, where they found some Christian slaves. Several others agreed to be baptized, including the prefect of the town, a man called Herigar, who "a little later" built a church on his property.[16] Ansgar and Witmar stayed in Birka a year and a half before returning to the Frankish Empire in 831.

The conversion of Scandinavia had until now been a high-profile Frankish project that was run by one of the greatest churchmen in the empire, Archbishop Ebo. Now politics came in the way. The relationship between Louis the Pious and his grown sons had never been happy, at least not since the birth of Charles (the Bald), from their father's second marriage. The sons, led by the oldest brother, Lothar, rebelled against their father in 833, and Ebo took the side of the sons, which was awkward when Louis was able to defeat the rebellion the following year. While the emperor treated his sons with the greatest leniency, he deposed Ebo from the archbishopric and sent him more or less as a prisoner to the monastery of Fulda in Saxony.

This left the northern mission without a leader. The solution was to have both Ansgar and Gauzbert (perhaps Ebo's nephew) consecrated bishops without sees, or missionary bishops, with responsibility for Denmark and Sweden, respectively.[17] Since only bishops are able to ordain priests, consecrate churches, and perform confirmations, bishops were needed in the missionary field. The emperor gave Ansgar and Gauzbert each a monastery, the income from which could be used to support their missions.

The 840s were not a happy time for Ansgar and Gauzbert. The latter was thrown out of Sweden and one of his priests was killed.[18] Ansgar's base was a church in the Frankish fortress of Hamburg. After the death of Louis the Pious in 840, the Frankish Empire was divided among his sons, and Hamburg and Ansgar wound up in the kingdom of Louis the German, while the monastery of Turholt that was supposed to support Ansgar's conversion work with its income ended up in the kingdom of Charles the Bald. The relationship between the royal half-brothers was not very harmonious, and Ansgar was consequently deprived of the income from the monastery that was his due. In addition, Vikings attacked and burned Hamburg to the ground in 845, as we saw in chapter 2. Ansgar escaped with his relics and his life but without his cloak.[19] Ansgar lost all he had, and whatever Gauzbert had accomplished in Sweden was destroyed.

Both Ansgar and Gauzbert eventually landed on their feet. Gauzbert became an ordinary bishop, with his see in Osnabrück, and appears to have had no particular wish to return to Sweden, which had to do without Christian clergy for almost seven years. Ansgar then sent the anchorite Ardgar to Birka, probably after reaching an agreement with Gauzbert, to whose mission field Sweden, strictly speaking, belonged.

Ansgar followed a different path. Having lost the financial support of the monastery that Louis the Pious had given him, he tried to create a bishopric for himself, centered on Hamburg, by annexing the territory of the bishoprics of Bremen and Verden that was north of the Elbe River. To that end, Ansgar created a false story that Louis the Pious in fact had given him an archdiocese in Hamburg. To support that story, he changed the text of the authentic privileges that Emperor Louis and Pope Gregory IV had given him when the mission to Scandinavia was reorganized. Ansgar had little success in this endeavor for the time being, but he was instead, in 848, made an ordinary bishop, like Gauzbert, in the diocese of Bremen. Having access to the resources of a bishopric meant that Ansgar was able to take up his conversion work again. Also, Ansgar got to keep Hamburg, which was in the diocese of Verden, though he had to compensate the bishop there for the lost territory by ceding some of Bremen's territory to Verden.

Within several years after 850, Ansgar gained the Danish king Horik's permission to enter the country. He constructed a church at Hedeby, where there were already many Christians that had been baptized elsewhere.[20] Ansgar had not forgotten about the Swedes, so he also went back to Birka at this time. Herigar had died since Ansgar last left Birka, but other Christians remained.

Ansgar managed to come to an agreement with the king, who permitted him to construct a church. Gauzbert's nephew Erimbert was left in Birka, so that "he there might celebrate the divine mysteries with his [the king's] help and protection."[21] Erimbert stayed in Birka for three years, until a replacement, Ansfrid, showed up. Ansfrid was a Dane who had been educated by Ebo and sent to Birka by Gauzbert, Ebo's relative and the bishop nominally in charge of Sweden. Ansfrid returned to Germany after 859, and Ansgar sent a new priest to Birka, Ragenbert. He did not get very far, however. Danish robbers attacked and killed him on his way to Hedeby, where a ship lay ready to transport him to Birka. Instead, Ansgar sent a man born in Denmark called Rimbert (probably a different Rimbert from Ansgar's successor and biographer).[22] He was the last priest in Birka about whom the sources tell us.

When Ansgar returned to his cathedral in Bremen from his second trip to Birka, he had to attend to the fate of the church in Denmark. King Horik had died and was succeeded by a relative of the same name, Horik II. The prefect of the town of Hedeby had taken the opportunity to close down the church there. Horik II, however, had the prefect deposed, and called for Ansgar to visit him, which Ansgar did, at some point in the late 850s. The king allowed the church in Hedeby to be reopened, and he also allowed the use of church bells, which "had earlier seemed horrid to the pagans." The king's decision is strikingly illustrated by a Viking Age church bell that archeologists have found in the harbor of Hedeby. It may have been dropped from a ship and have sunk to such depths that it could not be rescued in the Middle Ages (see fig. 19).[23] In addition, the king allowed another church to be built in Ribe, a trade town on the west coast of Jutland.[24] This was Ansgar's last Scandinavian trip, as far as Rimbert tells us.

Politics would again intervene in the 860s, but this time to Ansgar's advantage. Both Hamburg and Bremen were within the kingdom of Louis the German, who worked against his nephew, King Lothar II of Lotharingia. Lothar's marriage was without issue, but he strove to divorce his lawful wife and instead marry his mistress, with whom he already had several children, who would then have become his lawful heirs. Louis hoped to appropriate at least a part of Lothar's kingdom if the latter died without a legitimate successor, and thus he opposed the divorce. Louis also wanted to diminish the power of Gunthar, the archbishop of Cologne, who was one of Lothar's supporters. As bishop of Bremen, Ansgar was subject to the archbishop of Cologne, but at the request of King Louis, the pope made Ansgar a missionary archbishop of the Danes and the Swedes, retaining the bishopric of Bremen, which effectively removed that bishopric from the jurisdiction of Cologne. This happened in 864, the year before Ansgar's death. His death means that

Fig. 19 In the 850s, the missionary Ansgar persuaded King Horik of Denmark to give him permission to hang bells in the churches in Ribe and Hedeby, according to what his successor Archbishop Rimbert of Hamburg-Bremen stated in the *Life of Ansgar*. The story gained striking confirmation when archeologists found an early-medieval church bell in the harbor of Hedeby. The bell appears to have been dropped from a ship and sank to such depths that it could not be rescued. Photo courtesy of Wikinger Museum Haithabu, Schleswig.

the source, Rimbert's *Life of Ansgar*, which provides all these details about the mission in Scandinavia, ceases to be useful. The written sources contain very little information about missions over the next century.

It is therefore impossible to know much about how the churches that Ansgar had created in Scandinavia fared. The historian Adam of Bremen claims, in the 1070s, that the Swedes and the Danes soon relapsed into paganism,[25] and this is the story usually repeated in modern scholarship. I would like to focus instead on what Adam says elsewhere, when he tells us that the mission in Scandinavia grew continuously from Ansgar's days to his own.[26] The reason why we know almost nothing about Christianity in Scandinavia after 865 is simply that we lack sources, and that Adam likewise lacked sources.

The only two medieval sources that treat religion in Scandinavia during the century after Ansgar's death are Adam's history from the 1070s and the anonymous *Life of Rimbert*.[27] Rimbert may have been intended as Ansgar's successor both to the missionary archbishopric and to the bishopric at Bremen, but the political situation changed soon after the death of Ansgar. Lothar II capitulated, and King Louis the German no longer had any reason to infringe on the jurisdiction of the archbishop of Cologne, who would in any case become Louis's subject when Lothar died without a successor. However, Ansgar's fictions about an archbishopric at Hamburg now came into play, for Rimbert "succeeded" Ansgar as archbishop there. Rimbert also became bishop at Bremen, and he died in 888. The *Life* claims to have been written during the lifetime of his successor, Adalgar, who died in 909.[28] It does not matter much whether this is true, for the *Life* is devoid of concrete detail and therefore not much use as a historical source. The text talks about Rimbert "frequently" calming storms through prayer on his way to Scandinavia and providing priests for the congregations there.[29] These passages are so generalized that it is hard to avoid the impression that they simply are clichés. On other subjects, such as his consecration, the *Life of Rimbert* contains more specific information.[30]

Adam reproduces the *Life*'s statements about Rimbert's mission and adds similar general statements about Rimbert's successor, Adalgar, claiming that he appointed priests for the mission to the heathen.[31] About Bishop Unni, Adam knows that he went to Denmark and Sweden; he died at Birka on 17 September 936. Unni's followers buried his body in Birka but brought his head back to Bremen, a claim that was strikingly confirmed when archeological excavations in Bremen cathedral revealed a grave the size of a head, exactly where a twelfth-century source claims that Unni's grave should be.[32] Adam states that Unni was the only "teacher" who dared to go to

Scandinavia in the seventy years since Ansgar's death, but this simply means that Unni was the first cleric that Adam knew to have gone to Sweden after 865.[33]

Adam clearly had very few sources for the seventy-one years between the death of Ansgar (865) and that of Unni (936), but he skillfully used whatever sources he had to produce a coherent narrative. In addition to the *Life of Rimbert*, he used some annalistic works for information about general German history. He also seems to have had access to a brief list of the archbishops of Hamburg-Bremen, which provided him with their death dates and the length of their episcopates. The only concrete detail in Adam's account of Unni's trip to Sweden is the date and place of his death and the fact that his followers brought his head back to Bremen. It is likely that Adam found such details in that list of bishops. Adam appears to have taken this information and then added such detail as he thought ought to apply: Unni had a difficult crossing of the Baltic Sea, in the footsteps of St. Ansgar; the people of Birka were often assailed by pirates, so they blocked their harbor with cunning artifice; many kings had held bloody sway over them; Unni obtained permission to preach from those kings; he preached to and saved many lapsed Christians; and when he decided to return home, he fell sick and died. "This is enough to know; if we said more, we should be charged with a lying disposition."[34] Clearly, Adam did not know details about Unni's mission, only that he died in Sweden. We should not conclude from Adam's testimony that Unni was there to restart the mission; he might have gone to Sweden to visit an outlying parish, as a good bishop should. If any of Unni's predecessors had similarly gone to Sweden or Denmark and did not happen to die there, Adam would not have known about it, and thus we would not have heard about it.

We may conclude from this examination of Adam's work that when Adam said that Christianity in Scandinavia had lapsed after the death of Ansgar, he did not know this for a fact. He was extrapolating from the limited information that was available to him. We should thus discount his narrative and instead approach the evidence, archeological as well as literary, that we do have with an unbiased mind. That information suggests that Christian practices and beliefs continued in Scandinavia.[35]

There are, for starters, clues in Adam's own text that Christianity survived between Ansgar's death in 865 and Unni's visit in 936. Writing about Denmark's suffering under pagan tyrants during the episcopate of Hoger, from 909 to 915, Adam points out that "there was left in Denmark a little of the Christianity which Ansgar had planted and which did not entirely disappear."[36] It is hard to know if he had any good reasons for saying this, but since he otherwise liked to emphasize how the barbarity of the times destroyed everything Ansgar had planted, it is tempting to think that something other than Adam's speculation is behind this statement.

Unni's successor, Adaldag, created three regular bishoprics—Hedeby, Ribe, and Århus—in Denmark in 948.[37] It is hard to imagine that this would have been possible had not Christianity already been established in Denmark when Unni visited a dozen years earlier. There was still a church in Hedeby when Ibrahim ibn Yakub al-Turtushi visited the town in 965/966 in the service of the caliph of Cordoba (see chapter 7). Most of the inhabitants, however, "worshipped Sirius," that is, they were pagans. When the Saxon monk and historian Widukind of Corvey in the 960s wrote about the contemporary conversion of Danish king Harald Bluetooth, he said that the Danes were Christians of old.

In other words, there is some written evidence that Christianity continued in Scandinavia after Ansgar's death. Adam of Bremen in the 1070s had almost no information about Scandinavian Christianity in the century after Ansgar's death, but that does not mean that there was none. The sources do not tell us in exactly in what form and to what extent the religion survived, but judging from archeological sources the seepage of Christian ideas and practices into Scandinavia was going strong during the entire Viking Age (as we shall see in chapter 9). The Christianity that existed in Scandinavia was most likely not strictly organized in a way that pleased the clergy of Bremen, that is, in a hierarchically structured church under the supervision of the archbishop. That would also explain why the cathedral archives contained so little information about Christianity in Scandinavia in the century after Ansgar's death.

Kings

It was in the tenth century that Christianity really put roots down in Scandinavia, to such a degree that kings converted and called themselves Christians. This happened at a different pace in different parts of Scandinavia. Denmark was first—since it was closest to Christian Europe—Norway second, and Sweden last.

DENMARK

The first Christian king to rule Denmark, Harald Bluetooth, came to Christianity only as an adult.[38] When his father, Gorm, died in 958 or 959, Harald gave him a grandiose pagan burial at their residence in Jelling. He put his father's remains, with a horse and many grave goods, in a small Bronze Age burial mound and then added more earth to make the mound truly grand. Close by, he built a second mound of equal size, perhaps for himself, but it never contained anyone's body. Burials in such great, magnificently furnished mounds were long out of fashion in the tenth century, and Harald was gesturing back to the religion of former times. Gorm's was not just an ordinary pagan burial; it was a self-consciously and ostentatiously anti-Christian burial. It forcefully made the point that Harald and his father were pagans. The only reason to make this point so emphatically was to make it perfectly clear to everyone that Harald was *not* a Christian. In this way, Harald showed his independence of Christian rulers in Europe, perhaps especially the German king Otto who would soon, in 962, be crowned emperor.[39] Harald nonetheless converted to Christianity within a decade of his father's burial, in the mid-960s, although the narrative sources do not agree on the events that led up to his conversion.

Adam of Bremen claimed that the conversion was the result of Emperor Otto's invading Denmark and forcing the defeated Harald to be baptized. This is a story that Adam appears to have made up from whole cloth in order to make clear that the Danes received Christianity from the Germans and thus should remain under German ecclesiastical rule—a hot political issue during the 1070s, when Adam was writing. Otto's invasion is not mentioned in any source older than Adam, including, significantly, Widukind of Corvey's *Deeds of the Saxons* from the 960s, in which the author celebrates Otto's prowess as a political and military leader of Germany. It is hard to imagine that Widukind would not have mentioned Otto's triumph over the Danes had it actually happened. Adam was trying to counter the contemporary attempts of the king of Denmark to free his church from the supervision of the archbishop of Hamburg-Bremen. His *History* was meant to convey the impression that the Scandinavians still needed to remain under the tutelage of their German ecclesiastical superiors.[40]

The monk Widukind of Corvey wrote his *Deeds of the Saxons* within a few years of King Harald's conversion. He claims that it came about after Harald witnessed the cleric Poppa undergo the ordeal of fire by carrying a heated piece of iron. The story is likely Widukind's invention: the ordeal is a Christian practice and works only in a Christian context, so it is distinctly out of place in Harald's pagan surroundings.[41] Poppa's ordeal and other events in the story, including Harald's baptism (which Widukind did not mention), were in the twelfth century portrayed on a series of gilt copper plates (see fig. 20).

Interestingly, a third story survives, and it is Harald's own. At the exact midpoint between the two mounds in Jelling, he placed a large runestone in memory of his parents, which says, "King Harald had this monument made in memory of his father Gorm and in memory of his mother Thyre; that Harald who won for himself all Denmark and Norway, and made the Danes Christian."[42] The runestone includes a magnificent depiction of the crucified Christ. Again, Harald was emphatic and ostentatious; everyone should know that he and his parents were Christians. Unfortunately, his words are brief,

Fig. 20 About the twelfth century, the conversion of King Harald Bluetooth was portrayed
        in a series of gilt copper reliefs on the front of the altar in the church of Tamdrup,
        Jutland, Denmark. The artist imagined the king's baptism to have taken place in
        a barrel of water and to have been performed by Poppa as bishop. Other reliefs
        from the same series depict Poppa's miraculous ordeal by fire. By courtesy of
        Nationalmuseet, Copenhagen.

and he does not provide any context for his conversion, although the impression Harald wishes to convey is that his conversion, like that of the Danes, was to his own credit.

Harald also Christianized his father posthumously in another way. He moved Gorm's decomposed body from the mound to a grave inside the church that Harald had built next to the runestone.[43]

There can be no doubt that King Harald converted to Christianity in the 960s. We do not know why and in what circumstances. The narrative sources each push their own agenda. Adam wants the conversion to be a result of German intervention the better to defend the rights of his own (German) church in Bremen over Christianity in Scandinavia. It is harder to discern Widukind's purpose, except that he wants the conversion to be the result of the miracles worked by a Christian cleric. Harald must not have converted on his own initiative, although this is what Harald's own account implies. In chapter 10, I will suggest that it might be useful to take him at his word.

NORWAY

In the written sources, the conversion of Norway is tied to a sequence of kings who were baptized abroad and brought their faith home.[44] They also brought with them clerics and bishops, mostly from England. Their baptism happened either as a result of growing up in England or in connection with Viking raids around the North Sea. They all faced and were defeated by pagan opposition from the chieftains in Norway. This is at least how their stories are told in the great thirteenth-century compilation of kings' sagas in Old Norse, the *Heimskringla*.[45] Modern historians of Norway have not been able to break free from the influence of this text, which uses history to make several points about contemporary Icelandic society. The similarity of the stories of the several Christianizing Norwegian kings invites us to be suspicious. Did the authors of the *Heimskringla* and previous royal sagas adapt the story of those kings to a common model?

Håkon Adalsteinsfostre had been given as a foster son to King Ethelstan of England.[46] He became a Christian there and tried to propagate the religion when he in 934 became king of Norway. The resistance of the magnates was too great, so he apostatized.

Håkon's nephew and successor Harald gråfell likewise attempted to Christianize Norway, and likewise failed. He had grown up and been baptized in Northumberland, where his father, Erik Bloodaxe, was king of York after being forced out of Norway (yet another chieftain who was more successful at keeping power outside Scandinavia than within it).

The next Christian king of Norway was Olav Tryggvason. He raided as a Viking in both the Baltic and the North Seas. Together with the Danish king Svein Forkbeard, he attacked England and pressed the English to pay sixteen thousand pounds in tribute in 994. As part of the peace agreement, Olav was baptized with the English king Ethelred as his godfather. (Svein had been baptized already, since at least the conversion of his father, Harald Bluetooth.) Olav used the tribute to finance his takeover of Norway. As king there he had some success in converting the population, but again some magnates and especially

Earl Erik resisted the new religion, the earl allying himself with the Swedish king Olof Eriksson and Olav's former comrade in arms Svein. Together they defeated Olav in the great sea battle of Svöldr in 1000. The pagan earl Erik could now rule Norway under Svein's overlordship.

Another Olav, Olav Haraldsson, finished what Olav Tryggvason had begun. He was baptized in the winter of 1013–1014 in Rouen, in Normandy. Olav had signed up as a mercenary for King Ethelred (who had just been deposed as king of England by Svein Forkbeard), and his baptism probably came about as a consequence. The queen's brother, Archbishop Robert of Rouen, performed the baptism. Olav Haraldsson conquered Norway in 1015 but met resistance and was eventually thrown out of the country in 1028. When Olav returned at the head of an army, he was defeated and killed in the battle of Stiklastad (at the site of Trondheim) in 1030. His son Magnus in 1035 became the first Norwegian king to have been baptized within the country. Later Norwegian kings promoted Olav as a martyred saint, and he became known as St. Olav, the patron saint of Norway, who had completed the conversion of the country.[47]

The runic inscription on the Kuli stone from northwestern Norway has played an important role in discussions of the Christianization of Norway.[48] Its text is usually interpreted thus: "Thorir and Hallvard raised this stone in memory of . . . twelve winters Christendom had been [*or* had been valid law] in Norway . . ." The inscription has been dated to 1034 because the stone originally was placed next to a bridge that was built with timber felled in that year. If the stone was raised at the same time that the bridge was built, the inscription would point back to some event in 1022. Scholars have taken this to refer to a *thing* in Moster, where Olav Haraldsson is supposed to have issued a Christian law code for Norway, thus formally converting the country.

The interpretation of the Kuli stone, however, is fraught with problems. The connection between the stone and the bridge is far from self-evident, so the date remains uncertain. The importance of King Olav's supposed conversion *thing* in Moster for Norwegian legal history has been played down in recent scholarship.[49] Even more problematic, however, is that the inscription is very worn and hard to read, even using modern micromapping technology. No runologist has been able to read much more than half ("ris . . . umr") of the supposed Old Norse word *kristindómr* (runic *kristintumr*) translated as "Christendom" here. That the text reads *kristindómr* is, thus, no more than a guess. The stone displays a prominent inscribed cross and was surely intended as propaganda for Christianity, but that it would allow an exact date for when Norway was formally Christianized seems an idea based more in wishful thinking than in fact.

SWEDEN

After Ansgar's trips to Birka, the sources for Sweden's conversion are sparse and not very informative. Adam of Bremen states that the Swedish king Erik, who died about 995, was baptized in Denmark but lapsed back into paganism.[50] It is very hard to guess whether this is trustworthy information, especially since Adam borrowed his version of the circumstances of Erik's baptism from what Widukind of Corvey had said about Poppa carrying a hot iron to persuade Harald Bluetooth of Denmark to convert. Erik's son Olof, says Adam, was devoted to Christianity and worked to bring that religion to Sweden.[51] Of Olof's two sons that became Swedish kings, Adam very clearly did not like Emund, whom he called "Emund the Worst." His greatest sin, judging from Adam's text, seems to have been that he brought to Sweden a bishop, Osmund, who had been consecrated in Poland and not in Bremen.[52]

The next hundred years or so are confused with late and unreliable sources giving contradictory information. Describing political turmoil, although not agreeing on the details, these narratives claim that the politics were driven by a great struggle between Christianity and paganism focusing on the king's priestly role in the old sacrifices.[53] There is no reason to accept this account at face value. The authors of the narratives clearly did not know much about this period, so they adapted the few facts they had to the master narrative of mission as a great contest between Christianity and paganism.

What does seem clear is that the Swedish kingdom had not yet come together. This still applied when Cardinal Nicolaus Breakspear visited in 1153 for the purpose of creating an archbishop for a new Swedish church province. He found the country in the throes of violence, so the new archdiocese, in Uppsala, had to wait until 1164.[54]

The accounts of Scandinavian conversion in the narrative sources that underlie the preceding outline have one thing in common: they all portray political violence in Scandinavia as part of an epic struggle between Christianity and paganism. Missionary kings used violence when persuasion did not suffice, and recalcitrant magnates defended their paganism by putting up armed resistance. The point of view of such narratives is often accepted and repeated in modern treatments that fail to take the circumstances of these political conflicts into account. When a young man shows up and tries to take over the power of the magnates, they are likely to fight back no matter what their religion. This is what happened when Olav Tryggvason and Olav Haraldsson showed up in Norway. Medieval chroniclers and saga writers were likely to fit this fight into the preexisting drama of the confrontation of Christianity and paganism, which was part of God's plan for humanity. We know well enough that hostility did not simply follow religious lines. The Christian Svein Forkbeard in 994 fought alongside the pagan Olav Tryggvason against the Christian king of England. In 1000, Svein fought alongside the Christian king Olof Eriksson and the pagan Earl Erik against the Christian Olav Tryggvason.

Medieval historians did not worry too much about falsifying history, as long as they pursued a "higher truth." Svein Forkbeard rebelled against his father, Harald Bluetooth, in the 980s, and Adam of Bremen depicted this conflict as a war of religion in which Svein wanted to reintroduce paganism instead of his father's Christianity. Svein was in fact always a Christian. Adam's story about Svein's apostasy was inspired less by historical events than by stories in the Old Testament and by his wish to downplay the Christianity of Danes.[55]

Adam and other medieval writers describe several similar conflicts between pagan holdouts and fervent Christians in Sweden and Norway. It is very unlikely that those conflicts primarily concerned religion rather than the raw realities of power politics. The leaders who fought might use religion to bring their followers together, or they might use religion as a weapon of propaganda (as we shall see in chapter 10). The wars of religion in the early modern period were not primarily about religion, and neither were the wars of Viking Age Scandinavia.

Bishops

When the kings in Scandinavia were all baptized and their countries had become Christian in the eyes of contemporary reporters, bishoprics still needed to be founded and churches built. The kings and magnates of Scandinavia were expected to donate sufficient endowments for these things, and consequently we can follow the foundation of bishoprics quite closely, for this was the kind of information that tended to be registered and preserved.

Before ordinary bishoprics were set up, bishops without established sees served pagan and recently converted areas. Modern scholars call such bishops missionary bishops, or court bishops, if they stayed close to kings. Ansgar and Gauzbert were missionary bishops before they obtained ordinary bishoprics in Bremen and Osnabrück, respectively.[56] We hear of some other missionary bishops. Adam, for example, tells us about the several bishops whom Olav Tryggvason brought from England to his court and about the bishop Osmund, possibly also an Englishman, who was at the court of the Swedish king Emund in the eleventh century.[57] Adam's comment about missionary bishops is interesting: "I think the reason is that, with Christianity in a rude state, none of the bishops was as yet assigned to a fixed see, but that as each of them pushed out into the farther regions in the effort to establish Christianity, he would strive to preach the Word of God alike to his own and to the others' people. This even now [in the 1070s] seems to be the practice beyond Denmark, throughout Norway and Sweden."[58]

The practice of missionary bishops continued into the late eleventh century, but we hear of bishops with Scandinavian sees as early as 948, when three Danish bishops appear at a church council in Ingelheim. They were bishops of Schleswig (Hedeby), Ribe, and Århus.[59] Scholars have expressed doubts that these men ever left the comfort and safety of Germany. Their archbishop, Adaldag of Hamburg-Bremen, would have appointed them bishops simply because he needed suffragans, and we know that he had none in 937.[60] The archbishop probably consecrated them at the council, where he could get the two co-consecrators he needed according to canon law.

The three Danish bishoprics are mentioned again in 965 and in 988, when a fourth—Odense—was added to the list. There is no real reason to assume that these bishops were not active in their bishoprics. Adam of Bremen recounts that one of the 948 bishops, Liefdag of Ribe, preached in Norway.[61] If this is true, he ought to have been active in Ribe as well, since it is closer to the comfort of Germany. A functioning church needs access to a bishop, who alone is able to perform important sacraments such as confirmation of the faithful, ordination of priests, and consecrations of churches. Thus the three oldest bishoprics in Denmark can count their history back to 948, and Odense was added in 988 at the latest. It is likely that King Svein Forkbeard made an English bishop who was active in Norway the first bishop of Lund after 1000. There was a bishop of Roskilde by 1022.[62]

We have seen how Scandinavian rulers often attempted to bypass the control of the archbishops in Bremen by employing bishops who had been consecrated in Poland or England. The Danish kings strove since at least the 1070s to have the pope recognize the Danish church as independent from Hamburg-Bremen by promoting a Danish bishop to archbishop. These efforts bore fruit in 1103, when Pope Paschal II instituted an archbishopric in Lund with authority over all of Scandinavia.[63]

The bishops in Norway got permanent sees at the earliest in the 1070s, since Adam in 1076 claimed that no fixed bishoprics existed in Norway. At first, there were three bishops, in Trondheim, Bergen (Selja), and Oslo, and Stavanger was added in 1125. When the papal legate Nicolaus Breakspear visited Norway in 1153, he added the diocese of Hamar and instituted an archbishopric in Trondheim. The archbishop was also the metropolitan of the bishops active beyond the Norwegian bishoprics, in the island dependencies of Norway: Iceland (bishops in Skalholt and Holar),

Greenland, the Faeroes, the Orkneys, and the Southern Isles (the Hebrides and the Isle of Man).

The earliest permanent episcopal see in Sweden was Skara, which existed by the middle of the eleventh century. Sigtuna became a bishopric in the 1060s, but its bishop moved to Uppsala about 1140. Uppsala's bishop became an archbishop in 1164, and had four suffragans, at Skara, Linköping, Strängnäs, and Västerås. All of them are mentioned in a list of bishops from the 1120s, in addition to at least one other bishopric, which soon disappeared. The list is, however, difficult to interpret.

We have traced the institutional conversion of Scandinavia from Archbishop Ebo's first visit to Denmark in 823 to the creation of the Uppsala church province in 1164, as it may be reconstructed from written evidence. The story is unavoidably incomplete, due to the lack of sources, but it is also severely distorted by the biases, interests, and perspectives of the people who crafted the sources, often to make a point or promote a cause. A second layer of distortion comes from how conversion was understood by medieval writers and how they told conversion stories, as an almost instantaneous and complete event that immediately turned a pagan person into a fervent Christian (chapter 9). To understand the conversion of Scandinavia, it will be desirable to consider not only the slow seepage of Christian customs independent of missionaries entering the region, but also Scandinavian society at the time of the conversion and what made it receptive to a new religion (chapter 10).

9

Writing Conversion

The real role of Christianity in shaping early-medieval northern Europe has long been obscured by medieval conversion narratives, which lead us astray for two reasons. First, they were often written long after the events, making the real political and social contexts of the conversions impossible for the narrators to grasp. Second, the writers of such narratives were less interested in conveying what actually happened than in extolling the heroism of individual converters, supporting the institutions they represented, and, ultimately, praising God himself. Thus the conversions tend to be quick and immediately complete. The authors of the narratives were trained to think of history as the fulfillment of God's plan for his creation. Any history in the Middle Ages was the history of human salvation. Viewed from that perspective, Olav Tryggvason's essentially political contest with Håkon Sigurdsson of Lade, for example, became an epic struggle between Christianity and paganism, between an idealized missionary king and a benighted representative of the power of demons. To tell such a story, authors did not need to worry too much about actual events and other details. Rather, they simply had to follow the examples set by St. Augustine, the standard historians of the time, and the biographies of earlier missionary saints such as St. Martin of Tours, St. Willibrord of Utrecht, and St. Boniface of Mainz.[1]

We shall look closely at several narrative sources, most of which tell the heroic story of Olav Tryggvason converting masses of people in Norway. One source, however, portrays him as practically a pagan, and we shall see why this is so. The result of these close readings is essentially negative: the sources distort the story so much that they cannot be used for understanding conversion, although they may perhaps be employed to establish individual details in counterpoint with other sources. The stories they tell are more inspired by hagiographical tropes or political considerations than by actual events. Their narrators portray conversion as an instantaneous event, while modern scholars look on conversion (in the sense of Christianization) as a slow process. Neither individuals nor groups are likely to change everything they believe and all their religious practices overnight; Christianization is, rather, a long, drawn-out process that may last generations, as we shall see.

Olav Tryggvason as Convert and Converter

First, I would like to use the Norwegian king Olav Tryggvason (died 1000) as a case study, looking at him from four different angles. We shall see what may be known with certainty about Olav, on the basis of contemporary or near-contemporary sources. Then we shall examine the German chronicler Adam of Bremen's treatment of Olav, and twelfth-century Scandinavian narratives, which construct their stories about Olav with the help of Christian commonplaces. Finally, we shall discuss how conversion is portrayed in the different narratives about Olav.[2]

THE HISTORICAL OLAV

The contemporary or near-contemporary sources for the life and works of Olav Tryggvason are sparse. They amount to some skaldic poetry and a few notices in the *Anglo-Saxon Chronicle*. Nevertheless, on this basis it is possible for a modern historian to write a skeleton history of Olav's life.

After harrying as a Viking, Olav and the Danish king Svein collected a danegeld in 994. As a part of the peace settlement with King Ethelred, Olav was baptized in Andover.[3] He returned to Norway, where he defeated several chieftains and ruled at least parts of the country. In Norway he gained a reputation for destroying pagan sacrificial altars. According to his skalds, he was a *hörgbrjótr*, a breaker of *horgs*, stone altars for sacrifices in open air.[4] He also sponsored the baptism of one of his poets. A few years after his first conquests in Norway, a coalition of two kings and an earl defeated and killed Olav in a great sea battle at Svöldr.

The earliest narrative source to treat Olav Tryggvason is the *Deeds of the Archbishops of Hamburg-Bremen*, which Adam of Bremen wrote in the 1070s. His purpose in writing this history is very clearly to extol and praise the archbishops for whom he worked. His book contains an argument about how much saintly work his church had put into evangelizing and converting Scandinavia. Adam wrote it at a nervous time for the Hamburg-Bremen church. The king of Denmark was trying to persuade the pope to establish a Scandinavian archbishopric, a plan that came to fruition some thirty years after Adam wrote, in 1103 (as we saw in chapter 8). Adam's book may be seen as an extended argument that the church of Scandinavia should continue to be subjected to the archbishop in Bremen. Those archbishops had converted Scandinavia to Christianity, Adam implicitly argued, so they should be in charge of the region.

This background explains Adam's stand on Olav Tryggvason. Adam is very harsh when treating the Norwegian king: "Some relate that Olav had been a Christian, some that he had forsaken Christianity; all, however, affirm that he was skilled in divination, was an observer of the lots, and had placed all his hope in the prognostication of birds. . . . He was also given to the practice of the magic art and supported as his household companions all the magicians, with whom the land was overrun, and, deceived by their error, he perished."[5] Adam portrays Olav as a lapsed Christian; just a couple of pages earlier he says that Olav was baptized and associated with English bishops working in Norway. Adam's portrayal stands in stark contrast to the accounts of Scandinavian sources, which display little doubt about Olav's Christian zeal.

Why was Adam so negative toward Olav? His text gives us a clue, when he says that "certain bishops and priests of England left their home for the sake of doing mission work" in Norway. He says, incorrectly (unless Olav, against the precepts of canon law, was baptized more than once), that one of them baptized Olav. Adam's problem was that these bishops were neither sent out nor sanctioned by the church of Hamburg-Bremen, having received their episcopal consecration in the British Isles. Adam protested piously that "the mother church at Hamburg did not begrudge even strangers that they bestowed grace on her children."[6] Yet, he resented the involvement of other churches in a region that Hamburg-Bremen thought of as its own.[7] The fact that other churches also provided for the Christianity of Scandinavia weakened Adam's argument that his church, and only his church, should keep the ecclesiastical supervision over the region. The best way for Adam to get around the problem was to argue that those other churches did not do a very good job, and he consequently portrayed Olav as a lukewarm Christian. When English clergy were in charge, the results were poor, Adam implies. Only Hamburg-Bremen was able to do a proper job of nurturing Scandinavian Christianity.[8]

Against this background, we cannot take at face value Adam's statements about Christianity in Norway under Olav Tryggvason.

OLAV TRYGGVASON IN TWELFTH-CENTURY NARRATIVES

Scandinavian writers of the twelfth and thirteenth centuries, in contrast to Adam, harbor no doubts about Olav's religion. The most famous narrative is that contained in the *Saga of Olav Tryggvason*, in *Heimskringla* (usually attributed to Snorri Sturluson), from the early thirteenth century. Its author worked out Olav's story with great literary skill. For exactly this reason, this version is practically useless for reconstructing Olav's history.[9] It still, however, influences modern accounts of the conversion of Norway.

When he wrote his account of Olav, the author of the *Heimskringla* used four narrative sources that are preserved for us to read. One of them is the saga that the Icelandic monk Oddr Snorrason wrote in the 1180s. The saga is a substantial work, spanning over 120 pages in modern English translation.[10] The other three are the so-called synoptic histories of Norway from the second half of the twelfth century (or later): *Ancient History of the Norwegian Kings* by Theodoricus monachus, the anonymous *Historia Norwegie*, and the likewise anonymous *Ágrip*.[11] Each of them devotes a few pages to Olav Tryggvason, telling, in general, the same story that Oddr tells. The exact relationship among these four narratives remains uncertain, despite more than a century of research.[12] All of them used an earlier, briefer narrative about King Olav, which Ari Thorgilsson included in the *Íslendingabók* from the early twelfth century, but they must have had other, no longer extant sources as well.[13] Ari focused mostly on Olav's contribution to the conversion of Iceland.

Common to all five accounts is that they celebrate Olav Tryggvason as a saintlike missionary king, far from the lukewarm Christian of Adam's text. None of the authors was a simple transmitter of historical traditions. They were all artful and conscious narrators, who carefully shaped the stories they told in order to emphasize Olav's work of conversion. They used many sources in molding Olav's story, including sources that have nothing to do with Olav.

One of their sources was the life of Christ. In the twelfth-century histories, Olav was born fatherless, just as Christ was. Olav's enemy Earl Håkon "comes across like another Herod" in trying to find and kill the child Olav (in the *Historia Norwegie*).[14] When Olav was twelve years old, he first caught public notice by avenging his foster father, just as Jesus entered public life at the same age by arguing in the temple. After his defeat in 1000, nobody could find Olav's body, just as Christ's body had disappeared from his grave on Easter Sunday. The *Historia* speculates that angels might have brought him ashore, while *Ágrip* states that he disappeared in a flash of light. Oddr is more earthbound when he prosaically suggests that Olav stripped off his byrnie and swam ashore. Several authors report rumors that he was seen alive later, like Christ was after his resurrection.[15]

In other passages, the narratives let Olav Tryggvason play the role of John the Baptist in relation to the "Christ" of Olav Haraldsson, who would posthumously be known as St. Olav. Both Oddr and Theodoricus state (wrongly) that the older Olav baptized the younger Olav, with Oddr explicitly comparing this to the baptism of Christ. He also characterizes Olav Tryggvason as a forerunner of his namesake in converting Norway, saying that Olav Tryggvason Christianized only the coastal regions, while St. Olav completed the work by converting the inland regions.[16] In fact, Olav Haraldsson was baptized as a teenager in Normandy, according to the more reliable testimony of the Norman chronicler William of Jumièges.[17] Theodoricus was aware of William's text. Oddr's reference to John the Baptist is a clear example of how Scandinavian authors used Christian tropes when they wrote their narratives, even when they knew the facts. Oddr did not say that Olav Tryggvason baptized Olav Haraldsson because he had access to information to that effect. He said it because he wanted to establish the former as a pioneer who laid the ground work for St. Olav's missionary works and hence for the Christianization of Norway. There was no better way to accomplish this than to draw a parallel to John the Baptist and Christ.

CONVERSION IN THE NARRATIVES

All four narrative sources focus on Olav's conversion of Norway to Christianity. Each author emphasizes that he was a missionary king who preached with his tongue and his sword to persuade the Norwegians to accept Christ as their savior.

Their accounts of Olav's missionary efforts are, nevertheless, oddly faceless and vague. The *Saga of Olav Tryggvason*, in particular, recounts many individual episodes in Olav's converting mission, but they are all stereotypes. Tropes from the large medieval literature on the encounter between missionary and pagan appear to have inspired them more than anything that might actually have happened in Norway at the end of the first millennium. The narratives do not in fact tell us anything specific about conversion, only that Olav was a converting king.

The *Saga* often tells of the king's converting a lot of people at the same time through his preaching. During the second year of his reign, for example, he summoned a great assembly to Stad. Olav preached to "a countless throng . . . , both men and women, young people and old":

> People say that when the king preached the Lord's name, there was such power in his speech that those who came with hardened hearts and resisted accepting the faith had their hearts so wonderfully softened by the sweetness of his words and the eloquence they heard from his mouth that they gratefully accepted his message. . . .
>
> A multitude of people who accepted the true faith were now baptized and spent some days with the king and bishop. They strengthened them in the holy faith and instructed them in the Christian institutions, urging them to build churches in every district.[18]

Oddr tells us how Olav was able to preach so persuasively: St. Martin of Tours put words in his mouth. The saint had promised to do so once when he had visited Olav in a vision. We may understand Oddr's words about St. Martin's putting words into Olav's mouth as an allegory of the relationship between Martin's biographers and Olav's.

The account is also otherwise full of commonplaces and tropes. It does not contain any specific details (beyond the name of the place to where Olav had summoned the people). We find out, however, that Olav softened with the sweetness of his words the hard hearts of his countrymen, who then accepted the true faith and were truly converted. According to Oddr, the Norwegians did not grudgingly accept baptism; they embraced their new faith with enthusiasm and were eager to learn more. In this, they were much like the Israelites when they heard St. Peter preach at the first Pentecost in Jerusalem: "So those who received his word were baptized, and there were added that day about three thousand souls" (Acts 2:41). All of these details in Oddr's work are hagiographical commonplaces.

The entire episode has all the hallmarks of being fabricated. This is how a missionary should behave: he preaches so eloquently (with miraculous help) that his words convert the pagans, just as so many, starting with St. Peter, had done before Olav.

The *Historia Norwegie* is even less informative about Olav's missionary methods: "In the meantime Olav brought all those of his compatriots who lived along the seaboard into union with the King of Kings, and if the bishop was unable to achieve this with his spiritual sword, the king, applying his earthly weapon, led captive into Christ's empire the noble and ignoble, the babe of the breast and the greybeard."[19]

Theodoricus monachus explains what the *Historia* means by "earthly weapon": Olav used "threats and terror" to convert if "prayer and preaching" did not have the desired effect.[20] Theodoricus also explains the theological basis for using violence in conversion by referring to the words of Christ in the Gospel: "Compel them to come in, that my house may be filled" (Luke 14:23).

Again, the narrative sources actually say nothing beyond clichés and commonplaces about how the conversion happened. Oddr's *Saga* also contains the most famous commonplace of missionary narratives, when the king destroys a statue of a pagan god in Mærin, in the Trondheim region: "King Olav went up to Thor where he was sitting, raised the ax, and brought it down on Thor's ear so that he collapsed forward on the floor."[21] Missionaries and conversion kings from Martin of Tours to Boniface to Charlemagne chopped down pagan idols or holy trees, according to their hagiographers.[22] This was a way for them to prove the fearlessness and steadfastness of faith of the missionary. Olav's deed caused mass conversion, as such deeds usually do in hagiographic texts. Six hundred people were baptized that day, according to Oddr's *Saga*.

That the twelfth-century narratives about Olav Tryggvason contain hagiographical commonplaces and a great deal of wishful thinking has long been well known, and modern historians do not retell stories like the one about Olav converting six hundred people by chopping up Thor's statue, or the one about St. Martin preaching through Olav to convert masses at the Stad assembly. Still, in textbooks and general histories of the conversion of Norway, Olav plays an important role. He and Olav Haraldsson are the two "Christianizing kings" in Norwegian history.[23] Their planting of the seed of Christian faith in Norway did bear fruit. There is some truth to this, but Olav's conversion work was not so much about faith as about politics, as we shall see in chapter 10. He did not preach primarily to save souls; he built up a religious network that also functioned as a network of political loyalties. The network was strong because it was supernaturally sanctioned.

In portraying the two Olavs as turning points in the conversion of Norway, modern historians continue to propagate the basic storyline of twelfth-century historians. If we do not accept Oddr's story about the six hundred instant conversions in Mærin, why do we accept his fundamental agenda of portraying Olav Tryggvason as pivotal in the conversion of Norway? After all, Oddr and the other narrators with a similar agenda wrote their histories more than 150 years after Olav's death. If we were to use only the *Anglo-Saxon Chronicle* and skaldic poetry as sources (as I did above), Olav would still emerge as a baptized king who destroyed pagan sacred places. But this would not be a sufficient basis for portraying Olav as a great converting king. If we were to add the testimony of Adam of Bremen, who wrote within eighty years of

Olav's death, we would certainly not be able to portray Olav at all as a great converting king: Adam suggests that he might have lapsed from Christianity, even though (or perhaps because) he associated with English bishops.

What does emerge from the contemporary sources is that Olav conquered large tracts of Norway, and he was certainly pivotal in the story of unifying or creating the kingdom of Norway. This might have been enough for his twelfth-century historians, who knew from skaldic poetry that he was a breaker of horgs, to conclude that he strove to conquer Norway because he wanted to save the souls of his countrymen. Modern historians are realistic enough not to accept that this was what made Olav fight to conquer the country, but they accept him as a conversion king. This is most likely so, but mostly in respect to the second, institutional strain of conversion, not the Christianization of Norway. Olav broke down pagan horgs, had his followers baptized, and brought bishops and other clerics to Norway. As we shall see in chapter 10, he worked to make the Christian church an institution in Norway in order to extend the group of people who were loyal to him. The story of Christianization is a quite different one.

Conversion as Process

In medieval narratives like the *Saga of Olav Tryggvason* and the *Life of Ansgar*, conversion is usually a clear-cut event. The *Life of Ansgar*, for example, states that "a multitude of people were converted to faith in the Lord" after baptism had cured some dying persons.[24] The *Saga of Olav Tryggvason* is similarly uncomplicated: "A multitude of people who accepted the true faith [after hearing Olav's preaching] were now baptized."[25] Conversion is portrayed as an instantaneous and complete change, as if from black to white. Pagans were inspired to this sudden transformation through the miraculous deeds or the persuasive preaching of a missionary. This is so because most narratives, as we have seen, were written to praise the saintly virtues of individuals, such as Olav Tryggvason and Ansgar. To make that point, it would be counterproductive to introduce any shades of gray into the picture. Medieval people, who were used to stories about God's omnipotence and mysterious ways, would perhaps find these particular stories miraculous but certainly not impossible. As historians, we must approach them differently.[26] In real life, conversion is a much messier business than how our medieval narrators portray it, with many shades of gray. People seldom, if ever, change overnight what they believe, how they perform rituals, or how they dress, all of which may be part of their religion.

In Scandinavia, conversion—change in what people believed and how they acted—was a slow process that happened over centuries, during which the various aspects of Christianity slowly seeped into the region. Missionaries like Ansgar and Olav Tryggvason may have brought Christianity as a complete package of beliefs, rituals, and other practices. Traders, mercenaries, and other travelers, in contrast, brought bits and pieces, including artifacts, symbols, and ideas. They had done so as long as Scandinavia had interacted with Christian Europe, which is to say as long as Christian Europe had existed, perhaps since the conversion of Constantine or even longer. Clerics and conversion kings are not necessary for a religion to spread. It may spread with mercenary soldiers, merchants, and other travelers.

Even when missionaries brought Christianity in all its aspects, Scandinavians did not necessarily embrace it all at once. They appropriated what appealed to them, often adapting it to their particular circumstances.[27] In this view, the conversion of Scandinavia began long before Ebo's first visit in 823, and it continued long afterward. The visits of missionaries and the efforts of converting kings were not the radical breaks with the past that their hagiographers wanted them to appear as.

Pre-Viking Scandinavia was not isolated and cut off from the rest of Europe, but rather the border between Scandinavia and Christian countries was porous. People moved across that border and brought with them ideas, fashions, and practices. Archeological evidence—for example, from burials—shows how Scandinavians slowly assimilated specific Christian ideas, symbols, and artifacts. By closely looking at texts in which the authors, exceptionally, allow us to glimpse the messy reality behind their usually tidy conversion accounts, we observe the piecemeal acceptance of Christianity.

The Porous Border

Archeology teaches us that goods were moved between Scandinavia and the rest of Europe already well before the Viking Age.[28] The presence of European artifacts in Scandinavia, and vice versa, is prima facie evidence of cultural contacts. This is not a controversial argument since few, if any, would argue that Scandinavia was entirely cut off from the Roman Empire, for example. In this section, I will focus on the Scandinavian export of fur and reindeer antlers, and on the import of Roman goods. I will then show, in the following sections, that these contacts allowed Christian ideas, symbols, and practices to seep into Scandinavia quite independently of the work of missionaries.

Fur is a constant among the export goods of the north. The colder the climate in which the animal lived, the better the quality of the fur is. The Swedes were famous in sixth-century Constantinople for selling beautiful fur, "through many intermediaries."[29] The fur trade continued throughout the Viking Age and beyond, as discussed above, in chapter 7. And reindeer antlers, used for many purposes, but especially to make combs, were another article exported from Scandinavia. Reindeer-antler combs from the seventh century have been found on the Orkney Islands. Since reindeer never lived on the Orkneys or anywhere else in the British Isles, the antlers must have been brought from elsewhere, almost certainly from Norway.[30] This not only demonstrates cultural contacts between Scandinavia and the British Isles before the Viking Age; it also demonstrates that Scandinavians or Orkadians, or perhaps both, were able to cross the North Sea already at that early date.

Pre-Viking Scandinavia had strong and multifarious connections to the Roman Empire. The most important evidence for this is the thousands of Roman artifacts and coins found in the north.[31] The artifacts range from quite common terra sigillata pottery to luxurious and ceremonial glass drinking horns; from Roman swords to specially issued gold solidi meant to be hung as an ornament in a chain around the neck. Such goods could reach Scandinavia in different ways. The late Roman army was largely made up of barbarian mercenaries from outside the Roman Empire; retired or deserting Scandinavian soldiers surely brought some items home with them. Archeologists have in fact suggested that some Scandinavian graves contain the bodies of such soldiers. A former Roman soldier who returned home to Scandinavia might have been able to speak Latin and might even have been a Christian.[32]

Some articles might reach Scandinavia through trade, perhaps especially every-day objects, such as glass beads or terra sigillata pottery and money in the form of silver pennies. Such objects have been found in large quantities in Scandinavia. People received these things in exchange for fur or other northern exports. For example, people living on the Swedish island of Öland appear to have produced leather for the Roman market. Archeologists conclude this from the contents of graves on Öland: women's graves often contain a full set of saddlers' working tools, such as curved and straight knives, awls, and curved needles. Much gold has been found on the island, including some 350 freshly minted East Roman gold coins, so archeologists conclude that the Ölanders must have produced some kind of lucrative item, and leather is a good guess. Roman soldiers needed a great deal of leather, for their clothes, boots, and tents.[33]

Some of the most luxurious articles found in the soil of the north probably reached Scandinavia as diplomatic gifts. The Romans were in the habit of keeping barbarian chieftains happy by giving them fancy gifts. A famous example are the two silver cups that have been found in a very rich grave in Hoby, on the Danish island of Lolland (see fig. 21). The silver cups, which depict scenes from Homer's *Iliad*, are of very high quality. A silversmith named

Fig. 21 The former consul Gaius Silius Aulus Caecina Largus took up residence in Trier (today in western Germany) in 14 C.E. as military commander of the Roman province Germania superior. He probably brought with him these exquisite silver cups, decorated with scenes from Homer's *Iliad* and marked with the name "Silius." The cups somehow came to be deposited in a grave in Denmark, illustrating how the borders between the Roman Empire and the "barbarian" lands to its north were porous and did not prevent Mediterranean artifacts and cultural ideas from traveling to Scandinavia. Photo: Lennart Larsen, by courtesy of Nationalmuseet, Copenhagen.

Cheirisophos manufactured and signed them in southern Italy during the reign of Augustus. The name of the original owner is inscribed on the bottom of the cups: Silius. He is probably Gaius Silius Aulus Caecina Largus, a former consul appointed by Emperor Augustus in 14 C.E. as military commander in Germania superior, with his headquarters at Trier. Scholars assume that Silius gave the cups as diplomatic gifts to some barbarian chieftain whom he wanted to befriend. He may also have given them to a barbarian with a command in the Roman army, who then brought them back home after retirement. The man buried with the cups in Hoby might not have been the recipient; he might have inherited, bought, or stolen them, or even received them as a gift at second or third hand.[34]

With their illustrations from the *Iliad*, the Hoby cups carried an ideology from the shores of the Mediterranean to the shores of the Baltic Sea. This does not mean that those ideas were necessarily understood "correctly" by Scandinavians admiring the cups. Occasionally, however, archeological finds permit us to glimpse non-Christian Greco-Roman religious ideas that have traveled to the north. Several Scandinavian graves, for example, contain gold objects that appear to have been put in the mouth of the dead person. One of them is the exceptionally rich woman's grave in Himlingøje, on Seeland, in Denmark. She was buried with a piece of gold in her mouth and a Roman coin (struck for Emperor Titus) at her side. Archeologists have interpreted this as Charon's wages, which Romans and Greeks usually put into the mouth of their dead. Charon would then ferry them over the Styx and Acheron Rivers to the land of the dead. Since coins did not circulate as money in Scandinavia, other valuables were used instead.[35] If this interpretation is correct, the finds demonstrate that Greco-Roman religious practices traveled to Scandinavia. Christian practices later traveled a similar route.

Religious Ambiguities in Archeology

All over northern Europe, archeologists have found early medieval graves that they cannot confidently categorize as either Christian or pagan. I shall argue that it is meaningless to ask whether such graves are Christian or pagan, as they simply represent different stages in the assimilation of Christian practices.

Archeologists look at six or more criteria to determine whether a grave is Christian or pagan. First, Christian burials were almost without exception inhumations, that is, the body was not burned before it was buried. Cremation was taboo among early medieval Christians. For instance, around 780 Charlemagne legislated the death penalty for those burning their dead.[36] He did so because cremation was intimately associated with paganism. This does not necessarily mean, however, that every inhumation is Christian, for pagans also sometimes buried their dead without burning them. This is testimony to shifting fashions, some of which may in fact have been influenced by Christian practices. Archeologists have discovered Scandinavian inhumations from as early as the sixth century.[37] Among the several buried chieftains in the great grave fields of Vendel and Valsgärde, in central Sweden, some were cremated, some were not.[38] This seems to have had little to do with their religion, since these persons according to all other criteria were pagan.

A second criterion for distinguishing pagan from Christian burials is that Christian inhumations tend to be oriented with the head toward the west. Again, pagans also could arrange the bodies of their dead in this way, and again we might question Christian influence. Scandinavian inhumations also begin to be oriented in this way in the ninth century.[39]

The third criterion for distinguishing pagan from Christian burials is the presence of grave goods. Although pagans often were buried with all kinds of things that were thought to be useful after death, Christians were not to be buried with anything more than simple clothing. In practice, this means that

Christian bodies might be found with only neck pendants and metal pieces that were included in their dress (especially belt details and the brooches holding the female dress together). Rich pagans, in contrast, might be buried with horses, domestic animals, weapons, furniture, cooking utensils, food, carts, ships, and even human servants. Richly furnished pagan inhumations have been found all over Scandinavia, most famously perhaps in Oseberg in Norway, Vendel in Sweden, and Jelling in Denmark.[40]

The remaining criteria are less important, but I mention them because they have played a role in the discussion of conversion: Christians were as a rule not buried under mounds;[41] wax candles, which have been found in two Danish graves (Jelling and Mammen), might suggest a Christian burial;[42] and Christian graves may be found very close to each other, even overlapping, because it was important to bury everyone within a limited consecrated area. Such cemeteries have been found in Birka and in Såntorp, in Sweden.[43]

It is often impossible to determine whether an individual grave is pagan or Christian because the different criteria point in different directions. An example is the Mammen man who was buried in 971 or soon thereafter in a richly furnished grave in Jutland. The grave should be pagan, for it is situated under a mound, and the dead man is accompanied by rich grave goods, including the famous Mammen axe (see chapter 5). The grave also contains, however, a wax candle, which suggests to many interpreters that the man was Christian. The accepted explanation is that the man was a chieftain and as such needed to be buried in a way that signaled his rank (hence the axe and the mound), but that he was an early Christian, who died before there were any established Christian cemeteries in the region, so his grave was instead sanctified with the wax candle.[44]

I suggest that instead of trying to find out whether the Mammen man was a Christian or a pagan, we would do well to free ourselves of the either-or categories we have inherited from medieval writers.[45] Religion was more fluid than that, with medieval people usually accepting one or a few things at a time, instead of an entire package of beliefs and practices when they "converted." The people who arranged the funeral of the Mammen man saw no contradiction in using the old traditions of grave goods and mound alongside the new tradition of the wax candle. It must always remain unclear whether the candle to them represented Christianity or just a newly fashionable custom that they may or may not have known was inspired by Christianity.

One may go through report after report of archeological investigations, of burials and other sites, noting many similar ambiguities. But they are ambiguous only in the eyes of those who insist on posing the either-or question of pagan or Christian. A more fruitful approach is to take the purported ambiguities as evidence of a religious culture that drew inspiration from many different sources. Seen from this perspective, the archeological evidence sketches a picture of how Christian practices and symbols spread through Scandinavia, in the process often causing a countermovement that we may call pagan. In the archeological material, we can discern only symbols and (to some degree) practices. We may guess at the ideas and beliefs that gave rise to and accompanied them.

It is particularly instructive to study the Viking Age use of two religiously loaded symbols: the cross and the hammer. The cross was already at that time a preeminent symbol of Christian faith in the redemption of humankind through the death of the savior.[46] The hammer Mjöllnir was the symbol of Thor, the pagan god of war and lightning (which he brought forth with help of the hammer).[47]

European Christians used the cross in many contexts. Scandinavian traders, raiders, and other travelers would have seen crosses as pendants around people's necks, as freestanding stone crosses on the British Isles, and as decorations on buildings. They might also have seen people crossing themselves. The use of the cross spread to the north long before Christian religion in any organized sense came there, as early as the sixth century. Some fifty miniature crosses of silver and four hundred of iron have survived from the Scandinavian Viking Age.[48]

The spread of the cross seems also to have inspired the use of consciously pagan symbols, especially Thor's hammer, Mjöllnir, as a kind of anti-cross. When worn as pendants or attached to clothes, the hammer would hang upside down as compared to the cross. Their superficial similarities clearly helped promote the use of the hammer, as is evident from the close parallels in size, use, and form of many cross and hammer images from the Viking Age.[49] Some people had no qualms about using both cross and hammer imagery at the same time. A women buried in the cemetery of Thumby-Bienebek, close to Hedeby, wore a cross pendant around her neck. She was placed, however, in a wagon decorated with hammers for her funeral.[50]

Many hammer pendants have survived from the Viking Age. One of them, found in western Sweden, is decorated with images of both hammers and crosses.[51] The artisan who made this pendant drew on the symbolic language of both religions. Another artisan possessed a soapstone mold, found in Jutland, in Denmark, with which he was able to make both hammers and crosses.[52] Some graves in Sweden, Finland, and Russia contain cross pendants that hung around the neck of the corpse alongside pagan talismans.[53] When his father, Gorm, died in 958, King Harald Bluetooth of Denmark gave him a stately, old-fashioned pagan burial in a great mound. The old king was accompanied in death by typical pagan grave goods, including furniture and a horse as well as a wooden cross, which archeologists interpret as a Christian symbol.[54]

Other evidence points in the same direction, for example, some runic inscriptions. The famous inscription in Ramsunda, just outside Eskilstuna, in central Sweden, includes both pagan and Christian features. It depicts in great detail the pagan legend of Sigurd Fafnisbani, the young hero of the Völsunga saga who decapitated the smith Regin, then killed the dragon Fafnir, grilled his heart, and ate it. All this, and more, is depicted in the carving while its runic inscription is a memorial for the soul of Holmgeir. The idea of the soul, however, is Christian. Without the images, the text would lead us to conclude that Holmgeir was a Christian. Without the word "soul" in the inscription, the images would lead us to conclude that he was a pagan.[55] As the inscription has come down to us, we must conclude that Holmgeir's heirs did not see any contradiction in the mixed message of their inscription, and it is wise to follow their lead.

Religious Ambiguities in Written Sources

The writers who produced almost all the existing written sources about Scandinavian conversion were Christians. As we saw earlier in this chapter, they had no interest in portraying conversion as anything less than an instantaneous and complete shift, as if from black to white. Despite themselves, however, the writers occasionally reveal something about the gradual and slow process of conversion.

In the twelfth-century *Íslendingabók*, Ari Thorgilsson was unusually open about the compromises reached when the Icelandic Althing famously decided in 999 or 1000 that Iceland would accept Christianity. All Icelanders were baptized and could thus be called Christian, but no one would object if they continued to sacrifice to the gods in secret, to eat horse meat, or to expose unwanted children. These three practices were against Christian law.

When the monk Widukind of Corvey wrote his history of Saxony in the late 960s, he reported about the practically contemporary conversion of Denmark. His account contains several hints relevant to our discussion. When opening the subject, Widukind wrote, "The Danes were Christians of old, but they nevertheless served their idols in pagan rites."[56]

The Danes observed the pagan practice of sacrifice but must also have observed some Christian practices, which allowed Widukind to characterize them as Christians. Perhaps they had been baptized, like the Icelanders in 999 or 1000. They at least believed that Christ was a god, or so Widukind claims in the continuation of the story, which focuses on a quarrel at a banquet attended by King Harald. This was the man who had recently buried his father in an ostentatiously and self-consciously pagan mound. The quarrel concerned which gods were most powerful: "The Danes asserted that Christ certainly was a god, but that other gods were greater than he, since they in fact made themselves known to mortals through greater signs and portents." If Widukind is correct, his statement suggests that the Danes had accepted one feature of Christian belief but not all. This is parallel to archeological finds that show that early medieval Scandinavians had accepted some Christian practices but not all.

There was a cleric present at the banquet, a man called Poppa, who bore witness to "the only true god," and expressed the belief that idols are demons and not gods. The king asked him to prove his faith by carrying a glowing-hot piece of iron. Poppa passed the ordeal, and King Harald "was converted" and ordered his people to stop worshiping idols. He also from then on "held the priests and other servants of God in appropriate respect."

Two things are notable in this account. First, a cleric is present at the banquet. The Danes might have sacrificed to their pagan gods, and King Harald might have just buried his father as a pagan, but whoever hosted the banquet (most likely Harald himself) wanted a Christian cleric there. That cleric, who came from Germany, represented the glory and prestige of that Christian country and its ruler Emperor Otto the Great.

The second observation is that Widukind does not state that King Harald was baptized after his conversion. We should probably not read too much into this, but baptism following conversion is one of the stereotypes of conversion narratives, as we saw earlier in this chapter. Widukind's silence on baptism may suggest that Harald was already baptized, which would have been a reason for Widukind's saying that the Danes were already Christian.

Widukind lets us glimpse some of the ambiguities inherent in the process of conversion. The Danes were Christians who sacrificed to pagan gods. A cleric was in the presence of the king, who needed to be converted but did not appear to need baptism. If we read the story as it is written, the culmination of the process is when the king orders that no god other than Christ will be worshiped and that the idols should be rejected. It seems, then, that to Widukind's mind, the prohibition of any cult not directed to the Christian god was the essential event in conversion. Similarly, in Ari's account of Iceland's conversion, the process culminates in everyone getting baptized and public sacrifice being outlawed. Thus to Widukind and Ari, conversion was when the ruler or ruling body outlawed non-Christian religious practices and welcomed Christian clergy. In other words, they subscribed to the second, institutional strain of conversion. Like most medieval narrators of conversion, they were not interested in what people actually believed. It is easy, and probably correct, to go a step further and conclude that converters like Harald did not care much what people believed either, as long as they did not publicly sacrifice.

Medieval narrators of conversion focused on the institutional side of the process, and modern historians have too long followed their lead. We have examined how medieval stories of conversion are constructed and then sketched a long process of assimilation, in which Scandinavians adopted, one by one and over time, individual Christian practices. We may study the process in the archeological record. It began in the late Roman period and continued for centuries. Practices reflect beliefs, but beliefs are usually not directly visible in the archeological record. When a person adopts one or a few Christian practices, we cannot conclude that he or she also accepted Christian doctrines in such a way that we may meaningfully call him or her a Christian. In fact, the question "Christian or pagan?" is nonsensical for this time. Early medieval Scandinavians clearly drew on what we would call pagan traditions as well as on Christian traditions when they decided what to believe, how to act, and how to bury their dead. Pious medieval historians wanted to draw a clear line between pagan and Christian, and many have followed in their footsteps.

IO

The Gift of Christianity

Just as Scandinavian chieftains sought out prestigious trade goods, they also pursued prestigious ideology, and in Viking Age Europe, no ideology was more prestigious than the Christian religion. It was the religion associated with truly powerful European rulers, including the emperors in Constantinople and Aachen. Chieftains brought Christianity to Scandinavia to gain a share in that prestige for themselves—in other words, for the same reason that they brought trade goods. They distributed both the goods and the religion among their followers, to gain new followers and to strengthen the loyalty of those they already had. This was their immediate purpose in bringing Christianity to Scandinavia. They did not, in the first place, introduce Christianity to fulfill Christ's injunction to his followers: "Go ye, therefore, and teach all nations" (Matthew 28:19). If they had any such ambitions, this would surely have been secondary to their urgent political need to create communities of loyal warriors.

I would argue that during the conversion of Scandinavia, few worried particularly much about beliefs. Conversion was about the external facts of community and loyalty. Chieftains used Christian practices, particularly baptism, to build community because Christianity, with its prestigious associations, worked better than other religions.

Religion has been defined as a system of beliefs and practices that creates community.[1] This definition is a good starting point for thinking about the

138

conversion of Scandinavia, since it reminds us that religion is about more than beliefs. Early medieval people, including churchmen, were in fact remarkably cavalier about beliefs. In the enterprise to convert the pagans in Europe, it was apparently enough if the convert promised to believe in Christ. He or she could then be baptized, while instruction in the actual beliefs of Christianity beyond mere basics could wait until godparents and any available clergy might educate them.[2] Insofar as we are aware, the religions that existed in Scandinavia before Christianity had no strictures against accepting Christian baptism or against engaging in any other Christian practices. There was nothing to stop or slow the assimilation of one Christian practice after another in early medieval Scandinavia.

A focus on religious practices rather than beliefs comes across clearly in Ari Thorgilsson's twelfth-century Icelandic account of the island's conversion to Christianity in 999 or 1000.[3] Everyone should be Christian; thus everyone should be baptized, he says. Ari does not worry about what anyone believes as long as they are baptized. One assumes that baptism allowed them to be called Christians. Ari does worry, in contrast, about community and about practices, that is, what people do. Even so, after conversion, the Icelanders were allowed to continue practices that were contrary to Christian law; pagan sacrifices could be carried out, as long as they happened in secret and thus did not openly disturb the community. There is no reason to take seriously the Christian saga-writer's embarrassed comment about these practices coming to an end after a few years. The main point of the text is that Iceland remained one community because all Icelanders became Christians through baptism, although this did not necessarily entail that they in any real way embrace a new system of beliefs. The Icelandic conversion as Ari saw it, and as it may have played out, was not about beliefs. It was all about community and practices. There is no reason to assume that any other Scandinavian conversion was different in this respect.

Building Communities: Pagan or Christian?

The definition of religion with which we began is useful also for emphasizing religion's power to create community. Scandinavian chieftains strove to create communities of fighting men through the exchange of gifts. The idea of using religion for the same purpose cannot have been far off.

Any religion is capable of building community, and northern chieftains clearly used pagan religions for this purpose. Danish king Harald Bluetooth converted to Christianity at some point in the 960s, but before that, he subscribed to a paganism that had been reinvigorated in conscious emulation of Christianity. When his father, King Gorm, died, for example, he had him buried in a mound with traditional pagan paraphernalia, including a horse.[4] In doing this, Harald referred back to an old tradition that had been out of fashion for centuries.

Harald's early religious policies, as they may be reconstructed from the archeology of his residence in Jelling, appear similar to those that Grand Prince Vladimir of Kiev tried before converting to Christianity in 988. Vladimir attempted to build community around a pantheon of pagan gods, as the *Russian Primary Chronicle* tells us.[5] Both rulers sought to draw on the community-building powers of religion, and they used a non-Christian religion in conscious opposition to nearby Christian rulers. Neither fully succeeded until he converted to Christianity. This illustrates my claim that Christianity was more useful than pagan religions for the purposes of early medieval chieftains. This was because Christianity came with the added advantage of being associated with the most powerful rulers of Europe and was thus very prestigious. In the eyes of Scandinavian chieftains aspiring to power, the religion of Emperor Charlemagne, the emperor in Constantinople, and the kings in the British Isles must have been a fine religion indeed. Viking raiders plundering the riches of monasteries, and Scandinavian traders and mercenaries encountering the splendor of churches in Constantinople, Rome, and London, had reasons to think of Christianity as a prosperous and prestigious religion. Similarly, the Christian sacrifice embodied in the Eucharist fills the same function as pagan sacrificial meals, but in a more attractive way, because it includes wine, a rare and expensive drink. A chieftain who was capable of giving you the Christian religion was a chieftain worth supporting.

The Gift of Religion

As we saw in the account of the Icelandic conversion, you might become a Christian by being baptized. Chieftains used this initiation ritual to give Christianity to their followers. Two features of the baptismal ritual, as it had developed by the Viking Age, made baptism particularly useful for chieftains: a baptism required a performer, normally a priest, and godparents. Priests were rare in Scandinavia, so chieftains who had access to Christian clergy could strive to control who was baptized. Also, the institution of godparenthood created a strong and intimate bond between the baptized person and his or her godparents. As the second part of the compound "godparent" suggests, this was a bond almost as strong as a blood relationship. Godparenthood was therefore perfect for reinforcing the relationship between a chieftain and his followers. In this way, it was similar to marriage alliances and sworn blood brotherhoods, which also created a quasi-familial relationship.[6]

We shall now turn to two Norwegian chieftains—by coincidence, both of them were called Olav—to study how this gift of Christianity worked in practice.

We are able to reconstruct a fragment of the Christian spiritual network surrounding the Norwegian chieftain Olav Haraldsson, who as king from 1015 claimed the loyalty of all of Norway. Through his own baptism (as an adult), Olav gained connections with some of the most powerful rulers around the North Sea: the families that ruled England and Normandy. He used baptism to tie his followers closer to himself. We know from preserved sources that Olav was the godfather of at least two of his followers, and one of his followers was the godfather of his son Magnus. Olav's immediate purpose in these baptisms was to reinforce the bond between himself and his followers. In a wider context, the baptisms were steps in the conversion of Norway, but Olav was more concerned with his immediate political goals.

In the early 1010s, Olav raided as a Viking around the Baltic and North Seas. He participated in the expedition to take danegeld from England in 1012. After the Viking army that accomplished this broke up, its leader, Thorkil, with forty-five ships, went into the service of King Ethelred of England as Olav continued to plunder along the coasts of France and Spain. When Danish king Svein Forkbeard attacked and conquered England in 1013, Ethelred and his wife, Emma, took refuge with her family in Normandy. Ethelred was collecting mercenaries for reconquering England, and Olav joined him. During the winter of 1013–1014, Olav was baptized by Archbishop Robert of Rouen.[7] The archbishop was the brother of Duke Richard of Normandy and of King Ethelred's queen, Emma. Olav was in Ethelred's service, and his baptism confirmed that relationship. Being associated with some of the most powerful people on the shores of the North Sea also brought Olav prestige.

Olav passed on some of that prestige to his own followers. He later became the godfather of a man called Eyvind, who lived in Oddernes, in Agder (in southern Norway, close to Kristiansand). We do not know much about him, but he must have been a man of substance, probably a chieftain in his own right, who could command the loyalty of warriors, and certainly rich enough to build a church, which he did. When Olav set out to conquer Norway in 1015, he needed to draw on the help of men like Eyvind and his followers. Eyvind's baptism would have sealed his alliance with Olav. By being his godfather, Olav shared with Eyvind his links to King Ethelred and Duke Richard.

We know about Eyvind's relationship to Olav through a runestone that Eyvind erected next to his church after the death of his godfather: "Eyvind, godson of Olav the Holy, made this church on his property."[8] By building a church, Eyvind passed on Christianity, with its associated prestige, to his own followers, who could participate in Christian rituals (including baptisms) in the church.

Olav Haraldsson was also the godfather of the daughter of one of his retainers, the poet Sigvat Thordarson. We have encountered Sigvat in previous chapters as the recipient of several of Olav's gifts, including a gold-wound sword, a walnut, and golden arm rings. Olav also used baptism to tie Sigvat close to himself. He was the godfather of Tofa Sigvatsdottir. This made Sigvat happy, as he comments in the poem he wrote after Olav's death in 1030: "Lord, help him who lifted my daughter home from heathendom and gave her the name Tofa (your will is dear!); Harald's courageous and wise brother [i.e., Olav Haraldsson] held my child in baptism. I became very happy that morning."[9] Sigvat appears to have been the godfather of Olav's son Magnus Olavsson (who would later become king of Norway), reinforcing the existing bond between him and Olav, and obliging Sigvat to assist Magnus after his father's death.[10]

The sparse sources allow us to know only a fragment of the spiritual network which surrounded Olav Haraldsson. I suggest that it was much larger, just as the network of gift exchange surrounding him surely was much larger than we actually know. What we know suggests that Olav consciously used Christian ritual to reinforce his relationship with his followers. This gave him the reputation of being a missionary king, and it was as such that he became revered as St. Olav after his violent death in Nidaros in 1030. Christian writers who wrote his history long after his death had no particular interest in Olav's immediate political needs, which caused him to sponsor Eyvind and Tofa Sigvatsdottir in baptism. To them, Olav's life fitted more appropriately into the sacred history of human salvation. In the narrative sources, Olav is thus portrayed as more of a missionary than a politician. Contemporary sources show him in a very different light, as a warrior chieftain willing to use any means, including religion, to gain a greater following and more power.

THE RELIGIOUS NETWORK OF OLAV TRYGGVASON

The life of Olav Tryggvason is in many respects parallel to that of his younger namesake. This Olav was also baptized during military adventures in western Europe, and he also built up his following by using gift exchange as well as Christian ritual.

With King Svein Forkbeard of Denmark, Olav had raided in England. In 994, they made peace with King Ethelred, who paid them a danegeld of sixteen thousand pounds. Svein was already a Christian, but Ethelred sent for the pagan Olav and brought him to Andover. There, Bishop Aelfheah baptized him, and King Ethelred "received him at the bishop's hands," that is, he stood as his godfather.[11] Through this baptism, Olav tapped into the same spiritual network that Olav Haraldsson would tap into later. In 994, Olav Tryggvason earned two kinds of capital that he could spend to gain followers: silver and Christianity. By distributing them to his (potential) followers, he secured enough warriors to go back to Norway and successfully start carving out a kingdom for himself. He defeated Earl Håkon Sigurdsson, who had previously dominated Norway. According to Einar Helgason's great praise poem *Vellekla*, Håkon exactly represented the type of generous Scandinavian chieftain who built up his support through gift exchange and pagan religion. "The generous chieftain" had conquered the lands of sixteen earls and ruled over seven *fylker* ("regions, counties"), which amounted to all of Norway north of "Viken" (the Oslo fjord).[12] Einar tells us that the gods looked propitiously on Håkon's sacrifices, so that the earth became fertile again. "The generous man allows the warrior to crowd the temples again."[13] Here, Einar explicitly testifies to the connection between religion and community (and the chieftain's generosity): the crowd in the temple are the warriors who feel bound to the generous chieftain. Håkon tried to use pagan religions in the same way that Grand Prince Vladimir and King Harald Bluetooth did before their conversion. He had as little success as they.

In 995, Earl Håkon faced an enemy who used the same techniques to secure a following of warriors, but Olav was better at it. Thanks to the danegeld he had collected in England, he had more wealth to distribute among his warriors, and thanks to his baptism at the hands of King Ethelred, he had a more prestigious religion to offer. Olav won the contest over the earl and went on to rule all of Norway as king, until he fell in 1000 at the famous battle of Svöldr, fighting Earl Håkon's son Eirik and the kings of Sweden and Denmark.

We know of one of Earl Håkon's followers who went over to Olav's side, although we do not know whether this happened before, during, or after Olav's definitive victory. This was the poet Hallfred Ottarson, with whom this book begins. He received the expected gifts from Olav Tryggvason: a sword and gold.[14] Olav was also Hallfred's godfather in baptism.[15] In other words, Olav's new supporter Hallfred received his full share in the returns from the English adventure of 994: wealth and religion.

After gaining power in Norway, Olav worked against pagan rituals. He broke down temples and prohibited sacrifices, according to contemporary skaldic poetry.[16] In doing so, he carried out the mission of a Christian king, but he also looked out for his political advantage. I would suggest that the latter motivation was the more important to him. Olav and Håkon had used two different religions to build their communities of warriors; it was an urgent need for Olav to annihilate the religion of his enemy and propagate his own religion. Thus, it was impossible for Hallfred, as he himself stated, to remain a pagan after joining the retinue of King Olav. This had little to do with religious conviction and everything to do with political realities.

I I

Kings of God's Grace

A new kind of regime turned up in Scandinavia, starting in Denmark, in the late tenth century. This was the European-style kingdom, which did not rely on personal relationships among a small group of warriors reinforced by gift exchange. Instead it relied on formalized power relationships reinforced with a suitable ideology (some of which the church provided). The growth of the high-medieval kingdom was a slow process, which began when Harald Bluetooth first garrisoned soldiers throughout the Denmark that he "had won for himself," and thus he became able to control the territory. He made himself the lone ruler in Denmark, and we can for the first time rightly talk of a king *of* Denmark rather than a king *in* Denmark or a king of the Danes.

Christianity played a key role in this process, for the second kind of conversion, the institutional, political conversion, was a way for kings to develop states in which they alone had power. They accomplished this by, among other things, monopolizing and controlling religion. Christianity was suitable for this end, as Christian rituals demand specially authorized people and buildings, while Scandinavian pre-Christian religion did not. Only bishops could ordain priests and deacons and consecrate churches, and early medieval bishops in Scandinavia were the faithful servants of their kings, who became the virtual heads of their "national" churches after the conversion.

Christianity worked very differently from paganism, which explains the often-observed coincidence of the creation of stable kingdoms and the official conversion of those kingdoms to Christianity. In each of the Scandinavian kingdoms, unification goes hand in hand with conversion. By officially accepting and imposing Christianity, kings achieved two goals. First, they removed the ability of their competitors to use religion to build networks of friendship and spiritual relationships. The competitors were unable to use paganism for that purpose, since public pagan rites were outlawed, as well as Christianity, since the kings controlled the bishops and thus access to the rituals of that religion. Second, they acquired all the advantages of Christianity, including its legitimizing power, the administrative know-how of its clergy, and its prestigious international connections.

The conversion of Scandinavia came about because it created a mutually beneficial symbiosis between clergy and kings, not because of the persistent efforts of Christian missionaries. Medieval history-writers like Widukind of Corvey, Adam of Bremen, and Oddr Snorrason may have propagated the traditional explanatory model of clerical and missionary persuasion leading to personal convictions in kings and others, but Scandinavian kings, not foreign missionaries, converted Scandinavia.

Pagan rituals did not, as far as we know, need specially designated ritual experts or spaces. Thus, any chieftain could use pagan cult to create community, while it was impossible for just anyone to use Christianity in this way, since it was a monopoly cult. This is why the converting kings of Scandinavia were so keen to outlaw pagan cults at the conversion and from early on to control the Christian church in their territory.

Paganism

It is difficult to describe the pagan rites of pre-Christian Scandinavia, for we know very little about them with any certainty.[1] All the evidence suggests, however, that pagan rites were very widespread and that they required neither special buildings nor any specially appointed clergy. Historians of religions usually reckon that pagan rites could be carried out almost everywhere by almost anyone. Heads of families surely performed some rites in the household, and chieftains seem to have performed more-important sacrifices in the outdoors. Such sacrifices were more important because important people carried them out, not because of some strict hierarchy among different cultic places (as in Christianity).[2] Evidence from written sources, from archeological excavations, and from place names largely bear out this sketch of pre-Christian religion in Scandinavia.

Some sources written by Christians have a great deal to report about pagan sacrifices, but in almost every case, those reports are based either on hearsay or on the imagination of the writer. Stories of sacrifices in the Old Testament have also influenced what medieval writers claim about Scandinavian pagan sacrifices. The Icelandic sagas of the thirteenth and later centuries tell many gloriously composed stories about paganism and pagan rites, sometimes on the basis of misunderstood skaldic poetry. Their authors were so far removed from any actual pagans that there is no reason to take as fact what they say.[3] Snorri Sturluson in his *Prose Edda* surveys the northern pantheon, which thus is quite well known (if we throw caution to the winds and trust Snorri, which is probably not a good idea). Alas, this does not help very much, for however well we know the names and adventures of the pagan gods, that does not tell us much about how religion functioned on the ground in Scandinavia and, particularly, how religion worked as a political tool.

In addition to the Icelandic sagas, a couple of earlier narrative sources talk about pagan rituals, and are equally unreliable. For example, the German chronicler Thietmar of Merseburg, when he discussed "Northmen and Danes" about 1015, said,

> But since I have heard remarkable things about their old sacrifices, I will not allow these to pass by unmentioned. There is a place in this country, the capital of this kingdom called Lejre in the region which is called Seeland; here all of them come together every ninth year during the month of January, after the day when we celebrate the Epiphany of the Lord, and there they sacrifice to their gods ninety-nine persons and as many horses, together with dogs and hens (instead of hawks), believing with certainty (as I said) that this will serve them well among the inhabitants of the lower world and that it will placate them for their committed crimes.[4]

Thietmar indicates that this is hearsay, and it is hard to escape the impression that the text at least in its details reflects clerical fears and imagination rather than any trustworthy information that the writer had. Since Thietmar wrote about fifty years after King Harald Bluetooth had outlawed pagan sacrifices, the distance in time to when these sacrifices supposedly took place is too great for us to take the account seriously. It should also be noted that many years of excavations at Lejre have revealed no traces of sacrifices on such grand a scale, although they have uncovered weapons and animal bones that may reasonably be interpreted as remnants of more modest pagan rites.[5]

In contrast with Thietmar, who reported on things that happened long before his time, Adam of Bremen purported to describe a pagan temple in Uppsala, in

Sweden, that actually still existed when he was writing in the 1070s. He gave a detailed description of the temple and the sacrifices that took place there:

> It is customary also to solemnize in Uppsala, at nine-year intervals, a general feast of all the provinces of Sweden. . . . The sacrifice is of this nature: of every living thing that is male, they offer nine heads, with the blood of which it is customary to placate gods of this sort. The bodies they hang in the sacred grove that adjoins the temple. Now this grove is so sacred in the eyes of the heathen that each and every tree in it is believed divine because of the death or putrefaction of the victims. Even dogs and horses hang there with men. A Christian seventy-two years old told me that he had seen their bodies suspended promiscuously. Furthermore, the incantations customarily chanted in the ritual of a sacrifice of this kind are manifold and unseemly; therefore, it is better to keep silence about them.[6]

Adam cites an eyewitness, not to the sacrifices but at least to the hanging bodies. Still, it is suspicious that he, like Thietmar, says the sacrifices happen every ninth year. Either this was a pervasive tradition in Scandinavia, or Adam had read Thietmar and borrowed that detail from him.[7]

Even more suspicious is that archeologists have been unable to find any remnants of the Uppsala temple where it ought to have been situated. They have found a chieftain's hall close to the location of the present church in Old Uppsala (as the place is called today), but no temple.[8] Another oddity is that hundreds of eleventh-century runestones from the region around Uppsala carry many Christian characteristics that are hard to reconcile with the idea of an avowedly pagan temple in their midst.[9] The conclusion seems unavoidable: Adam simply made up the temple in Uppsala on the basis of his imagination and borrowings from earlier literature. Adam placed the temple in Uppsala because the Christian rulers of that part of Sweden refused to acknowledge the authority of the archbishop of Hamburg-Bremen. The current Swedish king, Emund, had recently obtained a bishop, Osmund, from Poland rather than from Bremen. When King Svein of Denmark similarly recruited his bishops from England rather than from Bremen, Adam also accused him of being almost a pagan. Thus we cannot trust either Thietmar or Adam to give a fair representation of pre-Christian rituals in Sweden.[10]

A single report of pagan rituals in Scandinavia survives from someone who claims to actually have been present, although this witness was not allowed to observe the actual sacrifices.[11] The skald Sigvat Thordarson wrote in the poem *Austrfararvísur* ("Songs of a traveler to the east") about a diplomatic trip he made to Sweden on behalf of his king, Olav Haraldsson of Norway. Sigvat portrays the hardships of the overland trip through the dark backwoods of Sweden. At one point, he and his companions were looking for night quarters.

They arrived at a farmstead, where they found the door closed. When Sigvat popped his head in, he was told to go away:

> "No farther can you enter,
> You wretch!" said the woman
> "Here we are heathens
> And I fear the wrath of Odin."
> She shoved me out like a wolf,
> That arrogant termagant,
> Said she was holding sacrifice
> To elves there in her house.[12]

In other words, the inhabitants of the farm were in the midst of a sacrifice and did not want to let in any outsiders. Sigvat and his companions had to look for shelter elsewhere. The point of the story for us is that the sacrifices to elves (a kind of lower rank of pagan deities,[13] which Sigvat probably mentioned to denigrate the unfriendly woman) show pagan rites being carried out at what appears to have been living quarters (otherwise why would Sigvat have sought to stay there overnight?), with a woman as a participant or at least a doorkeeper. On this evidence, pagan religious rituals did not require any especially dedicated buildings.

Archeology provides more knowledge of pre-Christian cult in Scandinavia. Among the most exciting recent discoveries are the remnants of animal sacrifices under the medieval church in Frösö, which is centrally located on an island in the northern Swedish province of Jämtland. Around the burned stump of a tree (a birch) are the bones from several animals, including at least five bears. This site is clear evidence of sacrifices on a grand scale, which apparently took place in the open air at a tree.[14] Unlike the "private" sacrifices that Sigvat encountered, the Frösö sacrifices probably involved the entire community. The Frösö find shows that pagan rituals were organized on the regional level, which would have served the needs of a local chieftain very well, if he were able to control the rites.

The archeological discovery of a pagan temple or cult house in Uppåkra, in Scania, in southern Sweden, demonstrates that such buildings existed. This temple was first constructed around 200 C.E. It was rebuilt at least seven times, without ever changing the basic layout of the building, until it was demolished in the ninth century. A beautiful beaker and a glass bowl—expensive and exotic artifacts—found there suggest that the building was the site of lavish feasts, or at least drinks. More than 110 gold-foil figures (*guldgubbar*) strengthen the impression of a cult place. The discovery of many hundreds of deliberately destroyed weapons outside the building suggests weapon sacrifices. Animal and human bones suggest other sacrifices.[15] Again, the site testifies to pagan rites organized on the local level, most likely by a chieftain.

Place-name evidence further strengthens the impression of pagan ritual as a widespread phenomenon. Many northern place names contain either the name of a pagan deity or a noun denoting a place where rituals were carried out. Some names contain both. The place where the skulls of sacrificed bears were found, Frösö, carries such a name. It is a compound of two words, the first being the name of either of the gods of fertility, Freya or Freyr, while the second is the common Swedish word for "island." In Sweden, there are at least eighty places whose names begin with the name of a god and end with a derivation of Old Norse *vé*, which means "holy place."[16] Odensvi is a place name compounded of the name of the main god, Oden, and *vé*. One supposes that rites to Oden were carried out here. Place names ending with *vé* are more unusual in Denmark and Norway, but place names containing the word *hof*, which has been defined as "a farm where cult meetings were regularly held for more people than those living on the farm," are common in Norway. Twenty-two Norwegian place names are compounded with the name of a god and *hof*, while eighty-five places are simply called *Hov*, and forty-one combine *hof* with something other than the name of a deity.[17] Sigvat called the place where he was refused night quarters "hof," but it is uncertain if this should be interpreted as a place name or a common noun. *Hof* and *vé* are only the most interesting of the many place-name elements that have been interpreted as evidence of pagan cult.

The interpretation of individual place names may be debatable, but the strong impression that comes across from the place-name evidence as a whole is that the cults of pagan deities were widespread. We have no reason to assume that every place with a cult received a name to reflect that cult, so pagan rituals must have been carried out at very many places indeed. There is no evidence that pagan religion was organized above the local level, or that there was a specially designated pagan clergy akin to the Christian clergy. The consistent impression given by written, archeological, and place-name evidence is that pagan ritual was decentralized, nonhierarchical, and easily accessible by most. There was, thus, no way for a chieftain to monopolize pagan religion. Christianity, on the other hand, made such a monopoly possible.

Paganism Outlawed

Against the background of what is known about pagan rites sketched above, the campaigns, sometimes ferocious, against pagan religion are easy to understand. Christian kings fought against the old religion as a part of their struggle for political supremacy, and their reasons for making Christianity the only religion were political.[18] When they succeeded, they in effect controlled religion in their lands, for they sponsored and controlled the church. The great struggles between church and state were still in the future, especially in newly converted areas like Scandinavia. When kings had succeeded in rooting out other religions, no competing chieftains or would-be kings were any longer able to create competing networks of personal relationships using religion. The kings controlled religion in all their territory and with it the means to enhance personal relationships with religious overtones and to institutionalize such relationships in order to reach broad swaths of the population.

A key moment in the conversion process was when kings outlawed religions other than Christianity.[19] Medieval Christian writers reported with joy on such events. For them, it was the fulfillment of the vision that Christianity was the one true religion, but for the kings, the prohibition also and more importantly served political ends.

In Denmark, Harald Bluetooth prohibited pagan rites in the mid-960s, according to the testimony of Widukind of Corvey: "Thereafter the king, who had been converted, decided that Christ would be the only god to be worshiped, and he ordered that his people should reject the idols."[20] Olav Tryggvason of Norway followed suit in the 990s, when the skalds characterized him as *hörgbrjotr* and *végrimmr*: a breaker of pagan altars who was cruel to (pagan) sacred places.[21] The later narratives in the sagas expand these characterizations in much more detail: with his axe, Olav chopped up wooden images of pagan gods, and he tortured those who refused to convert (see chapter 8). This tells us more about the imagination of the authors of the narratives than about history.

The most fine-grained account of legislation to outlaw paganism comes from Iceland. In the early twelfth century, Ari Thorgilsson wrote the story of the conversion that had happened in 999 or 1000. His narrative culminates in the judgment of the law-speaker at the Althing, which Ari summarizes as follows: "It was then proclaimed in the laws that all people should be Christian, and that those in this country who had not yet been baptized should receive baptism; but the old laws should stand as regards to the exposure of children and the eating of horse-flesh. People had the right to sacrifice in secret, if they wished, but it would be punishable by the lesser outlawry if witnesses were produced. And a few years later, these heathen provisions were abolished, like the others."[22]

The emphasis is firmly on the community. Everyone should be baptized, so that they may be called Christians, but pagan sacrifices were acceptable, as long as they happened in secret. Two other practices, the exposure of unwanted children and the eating of horse meat, were apparently seen as indispensable.[23]

The Icelandic prohibition of public sacrifices and simultaneous tolerance of private sacrifices is key to understanding conversion. Clearly this was, in the first place, about politics, not religion. If the prohibition had been motivated by only religious considerations, private sacrifices would also have been outlawed, for they break the Christian God's laws just as much as public sacrifices. The public celebration of pagan rites was a very political act. It concentrated the community at one place at one moment in time, boosting the standing of the persons who performed or sponsored the rites. The people celebrating the sacrifices used this for their political purposes, to build up a following. This is what the prohibition of public sacrifices was intended to prevent.

The celebration of Christian rituals was much easier to control, since there were only so many properly ordained priests. Our sources are patchy, but everything points to there being rather few clerics in Scandinavia after the conversion.[24] By making all public expression of religion Christian, the kings and other rulers could control public rites, for they controlled the clergy. In Iceland, it was the chieftains who thus monopolized religion for their group, making it more difficult for new men to join their ranks.[25] In continental Scandinavia, the kings similarly removed an important means by which their opponents might gain support.

Kings and Their Churches

The perspective here sketched makes possible new readings of long-known sources, for example, Harald Bluetooth's large runestone at Jelling. The runestone is emphatically about power, specifically Harald's power. In addition to the stereotypical pious remembrance of his parents, he announces his conquest of Denmark and Norway and his conversion of Denmark. Harald's main purpose when creating the inscription was to proclaim, and thereby solidify, his political successes. The memorial to his parents was simply the traditional form this took: "King Harald had this monument made in memory of his father Gorm and in memory of his mother Thyre; that Harald who won for himself all Denmark and Norway and made the Danes Christian."[26] It was Harald *personally* who made the Danes Christian, he claims. Thus he signals his role as the de facto head of the church in Denmark. The magnificent carving of the crucified Christ just above the text reinforces the message. Harald is now in charge of Denmark and he is in charge of religion there (pagan rites having been outlawed, according to Widukind's testimony).

That message comes across loud and clear. It was an act of power in itself to have the inscription made.

The eleventh-century runestone in the northern Swedish province of Jämtland should be seen in the same light (see fig. 22). Its inscription includes

Fig. 22 In the eleventh century, Östman Gudfastsson raised a runestone to boast that he had Christianized the Jämtland region in Sweden. The stone was placed not far from a site where pagan sacrifices of bears had been carried out around (and in?) a birch tree, which was destroyed at about the same time as Östman erected his runestone. Photo: Bengt A. Lundberg, by courtesy of Riksantikvarieämbetet, Stockholm.

a simple cross, and the text claims that a man called Östman Christianized the province: "Östman, Gudfast's son, had this stone raised and this bridge made and he had all of Jämtland Christianized."[27] His claim to have Christianized the entire province should be interpreted as a claim to be the head of its church and hence to have power over the province. Jämtland is only a small region, and we should probably think of Östman as a chieftain rather than a king (although who knows what he thought of himself).[28] He is an example of a locally powerful man, the kind of man who would surely have aspired to subdue his neighbors and become king.

Östman's runestone stands today only a couple of kilometers from the church of Fröső, under which archeologists have found the pagan sacrificial site mentioned earlier in this chapter. Because of this proximity, it is tempting to conclude that Östman closed down the pagan site and introduced Christian rites instead at the same place, leading to the construction of a church.

We do not know exactly who Östman was or the circumstances of his Christianization of Jämtland, but we may imagine that he was a chieftain who had been performing sacrifices of bears at the birch on Fröső. As such, he could easily be replaced by any other chieftain who had the military resources to take over. Converting to Christianity meant that only an ordained priest could perform the rites. Östman could keep the priest within his control, or perhaps he himself was ordained (as many Icelandic chieftains were).[29] Now it would be more difficult for another chieftain to take over, unless that competitor would revert to paganism. One imagines that Östman would have made sure that everyone was aware of the superiority of Christianity, as he did on his runestone, which also made clear to everyone that he had brought that religion to Jämtland. We may imagine King Harald of Denmark reasoning along similar lines when he decided to "make the Danes Christian" and to have his runestone inscribed.

The one obstacle to the king's use of his church was that the pope had formally subjected the Scandinavian church to the supervision of the archbishop of Hamburg-Bremen, and hence to the German national church. This meant that the German emperor (who was still firmly at the head of the German church) could claim to supervise Christianity in Scandinavia. This galled the Scandinavian kings. They found many ways around the archbishop's lawful authority, as his history writer Adam of Bremen lets us know in no uncertain terms. Harald Bluetooth's son Svein Forkbeard expelled most of the Bremen-appointed bishops in his kingdom and instead brought bishops from England. In response, Adam portrayed him as a pagan. Norwegian kings and chieftains also usually brought bishops from England rather than from Bremen. King Emund the Worst (*pessimus*) of Sweden bypassed Bremen by getting a bishop consecrated in Poland, with which he was allied.[30] The archbishops of Hamburg-Bremen fought back, quite literally. Archbishop Unwan (1013–1029) captured Gerbrand, who was one of King Cnut's bishops, while he was on his way from England to Denmark. Gerbrand was forced to submit and swear fidelity to Unwan, who sent a scolding message to King Cnut.[31] The eventual outcome was that each Scandinavian country between 1103 and 1164 became its own church province with its own archbishop directly subordinated to the pope. Much of the time, Scandinavian kings succeeded in holding their own against the Bremen church, certainly insofar as using their local churches for their own political purposes. Individual churchmen in Scandinavia were too dependent on the king to be able to oppose him, at least before the twelfth century. Each king strove to control his church and use it as a means in his pursuit of power.

Iceland might appear to be a counterexample to this, since it converted without becoming a kingdom. The decision, rather, came about at the meeting of the chieftains of the island at the Althing in 999 or 1000. This parliamentary gathering is often portrayed in modern literature in the same way that Ari Thorgilsson imagined it in the early twelfth century. The community of Iceland was in danger of being broken apart because some Icelanders were Christians and some were pagans. Mediators came together at the Althing and brokered a compromise that allowed the continuing existence of a peaceful community—the same kind of solution that the Icelanders liked to apply to feuds.[32]

There is much to recommend this interpretation, but it overlooks the pressure that Olav Tryggvason in Norway had applied to the island, trying to persuade it to convert to Christianity. The king sent as his agents several missionaries. If the Icelanders had accepted Christianity from these clerics, and through them from King Olav, they would have become subject to him. The decision of the Althing was, thus, a way for the Icelanders to bypass King Olav and his missionaries. That decision neutralized at least a part of the threat from the king; the Icelanders got their own church and accepted Christianity in a way that did not make them dependent on Olav.

Ari emphasized this independence by providing a list of twelve bishops who served in Iceland in the years following the conversion.[33] It is clear from Ari's description that many of them were wandering missionary bishops who did not necessarily have any strong ties of loyalty to any particular ruler. Such bishops might have been more common in Scandinavia during the conversion period than the sources otherwise lead us to expect. Interestingly, Ari characterized three of them—Peter, Abraham, and Stephen—as Armenian bishops.[34] It is easy to imagine them as adventurers or captives arriving in Scandinavia via the trade routes of eastern Europe. We know more about Bishop Bernhard, another wandering bishop active in Iceland, than about the others. He was an Englishman who served in the retinue of Norwegian king Olav Haraldsson, then came to Iceland, and finally became bishop in Scania, serving King Cnut the Great of Denmark and England.[35] Hrodolfr was also among King Olav's English bishops, but he was probably sent to Iceland not by the king but by Archbishop Libentius of Hamburg-Bremen. Later he returned to England and became abbot of the monastery of Abingdon. By using such itinerant bishops, the people of Iceland were able to maintain their independence from the king of Norway. The bishops provided such consecrations as only bishops could supply. They consecrated the churches of the island, which long remained as *Eigenkirchen* (proprietary churches) in the control of individual chieftains. They also ordained many chieftains as priests.[36]

When the time came for Iceland to get a resident bishop, the local magnate Isleif Gizursson, who was the son of one of the heroes of the 1000 conversion, traveled to Bremen in 1056 to be consecrated, just as he had gone to Herford in Germany to be educated.[37] In keeping with canon law, the metropolitan of the province consecrated the new bishop. Thus Iceland received its own church under the archbishop of Hamburg-Bremen and for the time being remained independent of Norway.

The sparse source material from the conversion period strongly suggests that kings from the beginning were the virtual heads of their "national" churches. This impression is reinforced when the source material starts to flow more abundantly in the eleventh and twelfth centuries. Kings appointed bishops in all of the Scandinavian kingdoms, and bishops frequently swore oaths of fealty to their kings.[38] Adam's account of what happened to the "diocese of Scania" after the death of Bishop Avoco, at some point between 1043 and 1059,[39] illustrates the king's power over the church: "But lately, on the death of Avoco, King Svein divided the diocese of Scania into two bishoprics, giving one of them [at Lund] to Henry, the other [at Dalby] to Egino. The archbishop [of Hamburg-Bremen], in fact, consecrated the latter; Henry had previously been bishop in the Orkneys and, it is related, the keeper of King Cnut's treasure in England. . . . About him it is even stated that, reveling in the pestiferous practice of drinking his belly full, he at last suffocated and burst."[40]

The point is that Adam admits that it was the king who divided the bishopric into two, and it was he who decided who the bishops were going to be. According to canon law, only the pope was able to divide bishoprics, and only the pope was able to move a bishop from one bishopric to another.[41] In this case, however, the pope was too distant to worry about these developments. The archbishop of Hamburg-Bremen, who should have consecrated all his subordinate bishops, was powerless. Egino was clearly his candidate, but the king's power was too great for him to be able to do anything about Henry. Adam took revenge on Henry by disparaging him as a drinker who finally burst, much as Judas had done (Acts 1:18). From Adam's account, it stands clear that Henry was the king's man, who had served him faithfully before.

Eventually, in the twelfth century, Scandinavian bishops began, however, to object to the kings' rule over the churches. The papal reform movement inspired them to take this stance. The second half of this century saw a series of clashes between kings and churches, as the bishops strove to have canon law strictly applied in Scandinavia. This threatened the kings' positions as heads of their churches, so they fought back, with the result that each of the three Scandinavian archbishops was forced to live in exile at some point during the second half of the twelfth century.[42] Until that point, however, the Scandinavian kings had been the undisputed heads of their respective churches, which helped them remain kings in the face of any opposition.

The Real Kings

Of the three Scandinavian kingdoms, we know the most about how the Danish state came into being. During the first decade of the ninth century, annalists tell of a Danish king named Godfrid who was powerful enough for the Franks to notice him and seek a peace treaty with him. That no stable state existed in Denmark during his reign is evident from what happened after Godfrid was murdered in 810 (by one of his own retainers, claim the *Royal Frankish Annals*): several men, including two of his sons, fought for power, and two of these contenders were killed in 814.[43] For more than a hundred years afterwards, our information about who wielded power in Denmark is fragmentary and confused. It is impossible to construct an unbroken list of kings, although a few stand out as strong rulers.[44] The best interpretation of this state of affairs is that power in Denmark was fluid and constantly contested by chieftains, much as during the decade or so after the death of Godfrid. There were rulers who now and then were able to dominate small or large regions, but they needed constantly to reassert whatever power they had. Many chieftains wanted their own piece of the pie. Against that background, it is not difficult to understand why some chieftains would take their retinues and, instead of fighting strong competitors at home in Scandinavia, sail to Europe, either to find somewhere to settle and wield power, or to get the means to recruit a larger retinue with which to sail home and take power.

The turning point in the formation of a Danish state comes after the middle of the tenth century. King Gorm died in 958, and his son Harald Bluetooth buried him in a huge burial mound. He also inscribed a runic memorial to his parents on a boulder close by. On this boulder, Harald tells us that he "won all of Denmark." Exactly what "Denmark" means here is debatable, but most agree that Harald claimed to have unified an area corresponding to medieval Denmark: Jutland and Scania plus the islands in between. Since the bishoprics instituted at the middle of the century were all on Jutland, historians further conclude that the basis of Harald's power was there and that he was able to assert authority farther east only toward the end of his reign.[45] The inscription implies that Harald's father, Gorm, did not rule over as large an area. If we take Harald's words as the literal truth, Denmark was created in the decades following the death of Gorm. This kingdom was stable enough to pass to Harald's son and grandson, and it was fought over by his great-grandsons.

Harald's kingdom was centralized, and Harald was able to control its different regions. He had constructed around 980 a series of circular forts, so-called trelleborgs. Five of them have been identified: two on Jutland, one on each of the islands of Fyn and Seeland, and one in Scania. The largest, at Aggersborg, in North Jutland, was 240 meters in diameter. The forts were constructed with great accuracy according to a common plan with some local variation. The walls are exactly circular, and the area in the middle was divided into four "blocks," with two wood-paved streets meeting at a right angle. The blocks contained buildings with many distinct uses: dwellings, workshops, storage buildings, stables. Both warriors and women lived and worked in the trelleborgs, which, however, were abandoned soon after being constructed.

The construction of five trelleborgs, spread out over Denmark, in Harald's reign strongly suggests that he was able to command the work of his subjects all over the country. The forts may have served as defenses against threats from the outside, as the one posed by the German emperor Otto II, who had conquered southern Jutland with Hedeby in 974. More importantly, however, they mark Harald's control over the people of Denmark. The forts demonstrated eloquently to all the strength of Harald's rule and, with their garrisons of warriors, must have made people think twice before attempting anything against the king. The trelleborgs secured Harald's rule and made it easier for him to control the resources of Denmark, including whatever fees and taxes that people would have to pay to him.[46]

The same desire to control violence is also visible in the two bridges that were constructed in timber around 980, during Harald's reign. One of them, at Ravning Enge, cuts across the large swampy area around the Vejle River.[47] Both bridges made it possible for Harald to move his army much faster south or north on Jutland. He was thus better able to defend the peninsula against foreign aggression and to control domestic violence and resources in the region.

Harald's building works suggest a new kind of ruler, who strove to control territory and the people inside it. With his garrisons spread out all over Denmark, he sought a monopoly on violence, just as he worked to get a monopoly on religion by outlawing pagan cults in the 960s. Harald comes across as more of a medieval European king who gets his income by collecting taxes and fees from his own people than a Viking chieftain who raises wealth by plundering someone else. In other words, Harald, a chieftain who had outcompeted all other chieftains, founded the medieval kingdom of Denmark.

The archeological material allows us to catch a glimpse of the defeated chieftains. The hall in Slöinge, in Halland, stood until some point in the tenth century. A chieftain had invited his warriors to share drink, food, and sacrifices in the hall for hundreds of years, until the settlement at Slöinge simply vanished, around 1000, without even a simple farm as its successor. Its location had been chosen not for its agricultural value but for its dominant position overlooking the local routes of communication, in other words, because the chieftain who built the hall strove for power. After the hall disappeared, its land became pasture for surrounding farms.[48] The hall was the focus of its chieftain's power and the religious rites he carried out there, but those rites were outlawed by a king who was able to put force behind his words, and the chieftain no longer had much power.

Similarly, halls and other anchors for the power of chieftains disappear all over Scandinavia around the year 1000. The mighty hall in Lejre—the largest in all of northern Europe and arguably a model for Heorot in *Beowulf*—was destroyed at the end of the tenth century, at about the same time that Harald Bluetooth built a church and probably a royal residence in Roskilde, ten kilometers away.[49] The settlement in Uppåkra also lost its importance at about the same time, just as the king founded the town of Lund, with a church and a mint, some four kilometers to the north.[50]

What happened to the chieftains themselves, at Slöinge, Uppåkra, and elsewhere? Were they, like Finn, "slain, the king among his host," when "the hall was stained with the lifeblood of foes."[51] Surely some of them were, while others chose to accommodate and submit to their conquerors. Is it too daring to assume that some of the medieval aristocracy descended from the chieftains who did not become kings? Such an argument could be made for Earl Thorkell, who served King Cnut in both England and Denmark and whose own power base seems to have been in Scania. The sources are murky, but it has been argued that he belonged to the family of the earls of Scania, who may have been the chieftains residing in Uppåkra. They were at any rate powerful chieftains and may have been the main opponents of Cnut's grandfather, Harald Bluetooth, when he "won for himself all of Danmark."

Thorkell was certainly independent minded, and his relationship with Cnut was not without friction.[52]

The pattern seems clear. King Harald took over all of medieval Denmark, and there was no longer any place for powerful chieftains or pagan rituals. The places where the old chieftains had sacrificed and feasted with their followers and traded in exotic goods declined, and many of their functions were taken over by royal and Christian towns, which were really a new ingredient in the political and economic landscape of Scandinavia. Hedeby, Birka, Lejre, Uppåkra, and Slöinge disappeared, while the royal foundations Schleswig, Sigtuna, Roskilde, and Lund appeared.[53]

The kingdom of Denmark was not created overnight, and Harald took only the first steps toward medieval kingship. Beyond his construction works and town foundations, the sources tell us practically nothing about how he and his immediate successors organized the administration of their kingdom. Harald's grandson Cnut was king both of Denmark and the much more sophisticated England, and this likely means that Denmark acquired some English governance structures.[54] Be that as it may, only much later do the sources allow us to glimpse how Denmark was organized. A royal functionary called *stabularius* (constable or marshal) appears in the sources from 1085; a chamberlain (treasurer) is mentioned in the early twelfth century; and clerics functioned as royal notaries certainly by the middle of the twelfth century but most likely much earlier.[55] This shows a specialized central administration coming into being. In other words, Denmark was becoming a typical medieval European kingdom.

By introducing a monopolizing, hierarchical religion, kings changed the way in which their societies functioned. They also monopolized power in a hierarchical organization with assistance from Christian clerics, who, with their literacy, numeracy, and knowledge of how more-sophisticated states were run, were important as royal administrators and councillors. The clerics helped the kings create a government that relied on law and written documents, that obliged the king's subjects to provide manpower for the defense of the country (also against any competitors of the king), and that enforced the king's law and the judgments of his courts. The church also provided the ideological backbone of kingship: clergy taught that the king ruled with God's approval and was divinely appointed to promote Christianity. Just as there could be only one God and one church, there could be only one king.

12

Scandinavia in European History

Historians of medieval Europe often treat the expansion of European Christian culture during the early and high Middle Ages as a protocolonial endeavor.[1] If conquerors and colonizers did not go out into the barbarian world to conquer and colonize, then at least missionaries played a key role in bringing Christianity to the heathens and in thus pulling them into the sphere of European civilization. In understanding the missionaries as driving agents and the pagans as passive recipients, many scholars have fallen prey to two strong story lines that insist on this distribution of roles. One is the story told by medieval historians and biographers of missionaries. The other is the traditional Christian understanding of mission, the heyday of which was perhaps during the colonial endeavors of the nineteenth century.[2] The story of Scandinavian conversion is usually told as the exploits of a series of missionary heroes. As historians, we need to free ourselves of this master narrative. It is not enough to put the medieval sources through the acid bath of historical criticism, burning away detail after detail; their cumulative story line needs to be put aside.

Much of central Europe was conquered or colonized by Christians, and the expansion on many of Europe's frontiers came as the result of conquest, colonization, and mission, but this model does not apply to the northern frontier. Scandinavia was a special case, a status that the region shares with a few other European areas.[3] In Scandinavia the driving force behind the conversion came from the inside. Powerful Scandinavians perceived advantages in embracing European culture; they were not forced to accept it. Scandinavians did not convert because missionaries went to them and persuaded them of the truth of Christianity; missionaries came to Scandinavia because leaders there perceived a need for them and the religion they brought. They wanted the missionaries to come and, thus, sent for them, as did Swedish king Björn in the late 820s, or they brought clerics with them from their foreign travels, as did Olav Tryggvason in the 990s and Olav Haraldsson twenty years later. To explore the conversion of Scandinavia, this book insists on a broad perspective on society, politics, and economy, because the decision to adopt Christianity cannot be understood solely from the narrow perspective of missionary or religious history. It must be considered in the context of the political, economic, and cultural aspirations and needs of Scandinavians. By applying such a broad perspective, it is possible to interpret religion in general and conversion in particular as constituents of the political economy of Scandinavia, as tools in the toolbox of Scandinavian political leaders. The book draws parallels between religious and material culture and examines how the rituals and practices of Christianity could function like the exotic, expensive, and otherwise desirable trade goods that chieftains used to create essential (to them) relationships with their followers. Silver, swords, baptism: they all served as gifts in the gift exchange system of early medieval Scandinavia, and that exchange of gifts greased the wheels of Scandinavian politics.

Against this background, there is no reason to believe that Ebo, Ansgar, Poppa, or Håkon Adalsteinsfostre came to a Scandinavia that entirely lacked Christian practices and ideas. Widukind tells us as much when he says that Poppa went to people who were already Christian. There was not much need for them to bring Christianity as such. The religion, or at least its components, already existed in Scandinavia.

Missionaries did bring something, however, that did not exist before: the *idea* of Christian conversion. In this view, conversion is a momentous change, a choice between mutually exclusive alternatives. It is pointless to accept individual practices (inhumation, pendant crosses, baptism) unless one accepts all Christian practices and beliefs. The convert has to become a new person. The convert must "put off [the] old self" and "put on the new self" (Ephesians 4:22–24). This includes abjuring old gods and old religious practices, and conversion must be complete and preferably instantaneous. This is the viewpoint that medieval narrators expressed when recounting the history of Scandinavian conversion.

The Christian idea of conversion also entailed the creation of an organized church with buildings, clergy, dioceses, rituals, rules, and institutions. That church had to be exclusive; all competing religions had to be thoroughly rooted out. The narrators of conversion would have thought that mission was effective only if it produced such a church. Adam of Bremen was thus, in his own terms, correct in portraying Ansgar's mission as a failure.

Because this was the goal, missionaries sought out Scandinavia's powerful people, the ones with the means to endow churches and help create a structured organization. Ansgar got royal permission to build churches in Hedeby and Ribe, and the kings may well have provided the land.[4] Olav Tryggvason's English bishops persuaded him to set conquered land aside for the needs of the church (although the details escape us). Cathedrals in mainland Scandinavia appear to have been founded by kings, insofar as we are familiar with their foundations.[5]

The chieftains, in turn, were interested in appropriating aspects of Christianity to build communities around themselves. They had, at first, very little interest in adopting Christianity in the exclusive and organized form that the missionaries sought. For the purposes of kings and chieftains, it was sufficient to have access to the prestigious gift-giving capital of Christianity. They used this to create personal relationships with the most important of their followers. This explains why, for example, kings in Sweden and Denmark welcomed Ansgar, although they had no intention of creating the kind of church that he desired.

In the competition for power among chieftains, some came out on top, with the result that the first millennium saw fewer and fewer serious contenders as the centuries passed, until only three remained in the early second millennium. They were the kings of Denmark, Norway, and Sweden, and, not coincidentally, all of them were Christians. They needed Christianity and the church, for they had become so powerful that they were unable to create personal relationships with their followers and subjects because there were too many of them. At that point, Scandinavian kings institutionalized their power. They used the church to help create and legitimize structured kingdoms that were held together by more than gift exchange relationships. The church provided an ideology of kingship that emphasized, among other things, that there could be only one king, just as there was only one God and only one church.

It was at that point that kings began to root out religions other than their own brand of Christianity, as Harald Bluetooth did from the mid-960s, and as the two Norwegian Olavs did around the beginning of the second millennium. This was also the point that later narrators in hindsight saw as the pivotal moment in the long story of making Scandinavia Christian.

At the end of the Scandinavian conversion, three Christian kings governed three Christian kingdoms in Scandinavia. The region had become a part of European civilization—three kingdoms among many in Europe. The northern kingdoms were never particularly large or more than peripheral in the big picture, but they had achieved a kind of normalcy, as the papacy recognized when giving each of them its own archbishop between 1103 and 1164.

Scandinavia became a part of the culture and civilization of Latin Christendom, often thought of simply as "Europe," and as such the region participated in the general European flourishing during the high Middle Ages, when population, productivity, and wealth grew greatly and relatively quickly. That flourishing laid the foundations for European world dominance in the modern period, and the reasons for it are very complex and much discussed. The roots of Europe's growth lay in the essentially agrarian society of the early Middle Ages, where the demands for revenue of lords (secular as well as ecclesiastical) and kings stimulated local markets as well as long-distance trade, agricultural improvements, and social reorganization. Whether Europe saw fundamental social changes clustered closely around the year 1000 ("the feudal revolution"), which would coincide neatly with the conversion of Scandinavian kings, or whether the changes played out more slowly over a longer time period, has been much debated over the past several decades.[6] Much recent research has preferred to see a slow development of European society and economy, with deep roots going back, at least, to the Carolingian era, as exemplified by the surge of trade around the Baltic Sea in the Viking Age.[7]

Europe's growth during the centuries around the year 1000, when the geographical area of western Christendom about doubled, is an important background for establishing the positive feedback loop that made Europe flourish. It is impossible to pinpoint exactly how important the inclusion of Scandinavia into European culture was for achieving the necessary critical mass, but Scandinavia certainly played a significant role in some aspects of the political and economic history of Europe. Scandinavia's entrance into European history during the early Middle Ages changed the way that Europe worked in at least two areas: the Vikings forced European kings to become better at organizing their defenses and, thus, better at appropriating more income from their populations, and Scandinavians brought precious metals into circulation, helping European commerce to take off.

When the Vikings first attacked Europe, they found governments that were poorly equipped to defend their lands against the new threat. The Frankish army was a formidable military force—as many of Charlemagne's neighbors discovered—but it was slow and lumbering, not designed to defend against a suddenly appearing and fast-moving enemy like the Vikings.[8] European rulers were forced to rethink their military strategy. Charlemagne's grandson Charles the Bald, for example, built fortified bridges over rivers in his kingdom, where relatively small garrisons could prevent Viking fleets from sailing upriver and inland. King Alfred the Great organized the *fyrd*, an armed militia that could defend Wessex. This established or reemphasized the right of the king to ask for the services of ordinary inhabitants in his kingdom. Such duty could be and often was commuted into payments in kind or money.

When the Vikings asked for increasingly large tributes, the rulers they negotiated with were forced to collect money from the inhabitants of their kingdoms. When Northmen sailed up the Seine to Melun, Charles the Bald paid them off with four thousand pounds of silver. To get that much silver, the king collected a levy from his entire kingdom, each free mansus paying six pennies and each servile mansus paying half as much. Other taxpayers, including priests, merchants, and free Franks, paid different sums.[9] Similarly, to collect the large sums paid to Vikings as danegeld or as wages for defending England, English kings began to tax their subjects. When Ethelred in 1012 hired the Viking chieftain Thorkell to defend England against other Vikings, he began to collect an annual tax, called *heregeld* or danegeld. That tax continued to be collected by subsequent English kings long after Thorkell left.[10] The emergency situation of large bands of Vikings needing to be paid off thus created the preconditions for imposing taxes that continued to be collected long after the emergency had disappeared. The Vikings helped create stronger states in Europe because they forced European kings to improve their administration, their tax collection mechanisms, and their armed forces. The demands for revenue also served to stimulate productivity and commerce.

Scandinavians also helped start the commercial revolution of medieval Europe. Commerce during the centuries before 800 had been choked by the dearth of liquid wealth, precious metal in the form of coins, which could be used as a means of exchange to facilitate the movement of trade goods. Early medieval Europe had no gold mines and only marginal silver mines, so its stock of precious metals was nearly constant. Much of it was unavailable to commerce, since it was locked up in church treasuries, in the form of reliquaries, chalices, and other holy objects.

The early medieval European economy was caught in the impracticalities of barter systems. For barter to take place, you needed a "double coincidence of wants": two persons whose desires and resources matched each other. If you had walrus ivory and wanted to get a Frankish sword, you needed to find someone who had swords and wanted walrus ivory, something that might be easier said than done. With liquid wealth, the problem was easily solved. You sold your walrus ivory to a merchant for silver coins, each with an established value, and then used that silver to pay another merchant for your Frankish sword. Trade and commerce function much better and certainly more smoothly when an economy has access to liquid wealth.

Scandinavians made liquid wealth available in at least two ways, by bleeding the treasuries of churches and monasteries dry of their inert silver and gold, and by transporting Arab silver into western Europe.

At the beginning of the Viking Age, much gold and silver resided in the treasuries of western European churches and monasteries. Some of that was simply stolen by Vikings, but surely more was melted down and fashioned into coins by European kings to pay off bands of Vikings. Contemporary annals often noted that churches contributed greatly to the payments of tribute, as when Charles the Bald paid ransom for the abbot of St. Denis, and "many church treasuries in Charles's realm were drained dry, at the king's command."[11] Just how dry ecclesiastical treasure-chambers could become is illustrated by a charter from 994, in which Archbishop Sigeric of Canterbury borrowed ninety pounds of silver and two hundred mancuses of gold from another bishop. The archbishop needed the money, which he apparently was unable to find in the treasury of his own cathedral, to pay off a band of Vikings who had threatened to burn Christ Church in Canterbury to the ground.[12]

The Vikings recycled at least some of the wealth they acquired into the economy of Europe; not all of it was brought back to Scandinavia to be made into arm rings, brooches, and other artifacts, or to be deposited in the ground. Several Viking bands set up markets after a successful season of plunder; some bands took up residence in western Europe, and Viking chieftains were at any rate eager to acquire the exotic and otherwise prestigious stuff that was sold in European market towns. All of this would have brought silver and gold back into circulation after having resided as inert capital in treasuries.[13]

Scandinavian trade with the east also had the effect of bringing silver into circulation in western Europe. The trade with Arabs paid off handsomely with silver and gold coins, for the Arabs had recently discovered very rich silver deposits in the mountains of Afghanistan, at the very eastern reaches of the Caliphate. This had made the Arab economy very silver rich, and Scandinavians siphoned off some of that silver in exchange for European trade goods, particularly slaves and fur. This also brought precious metals into circulation in western Europe. The proof for this is that the western penny in the ninth century became a strong and seldom devalued currency, suggesting the steady availability of silver.[14] Viking depredations of ecclesiastical treasuries and the profitability of northern commerce are certainly not the only reasons for the increased availability of liquid wealth on the European market; trade in slaves and other goods through Venice and other ports on the Mediterranean also played an important role, and the Scandinavians may very well have tied also into that slave-trading network.[15]

While an enormous number of Arab coins have been found around the Baltic Sea, very few have actually been found in the core of western Europe. This is not surprising, since the economy of western Europe was monetized. In other words, while silver in Scandinavia was used as an object of exchange according to its weight in precious metal, western Europe used coins with a standardized value imposed by royal authority. In Scandinavia, an Arab dirham had value as silver bullion, while in western Europe Arab coins would be sent to the mint, where the king's moneyer would make European pennies out of their silver content.[16]

The increased availability of liquid wealth in western Europe helped catalyze the general economic upswing that is known as the Commercial Revolution.[17] Beginning slowly in Carolingian times, European trade surged in the high Middle Ages, particularly in the areas around and between the two main trading poles: the cities of northern Italy and those of the Low Countries. The wealth and habits developed at that time would stand behind Europe's economic world domination that lasted until the twentieth century.

Just as Scandinavian history cannot be understood except in the context of all of Europe, so European history cannot be understood without bringing Scandinavia into our purview. The early-medieval political economy worked in the same basic way in the north and in Europe, only the scale was different. Rulers and leaders acquired wealth by plunder and tribute taken outside their own groups. Charlemagne brought his Frankish army outside the boundaries of his kingdom practically every year, just as Viking chieftains took their bands of warriors to wherever they could get plunder or tribute. The difference is one of scale and of organization: Charlemagne ruled an early state, while the Viking chieftains inspired bands of followers.

One of the important mileposts in the history of medieval Europe, in Scandinavia and outside, was when rulers began to collect taxes and other fees from their own people rather than stealing someone else's wealth. This shift did not happened overnight. It clearly had begun in the eleventh century in each of the three Scandinavian kingdoms, but Scandinavian kingdoms continued for centuries after the year 1000 to plunder and take tribute from still unorganized areas, such as the lands east of the Baltic Sea, and from the Sami population of northern Scandinavia.[18]

The new kingdoms required new technologies of power. They needed royal servants rather than the independent-minded magnates who agreed to do what their leader wished because they were closely tied to his person and thus persuaded to follow the leader. Royal judges and collectors of fees may have been aristocratic also under medieval kings, and they sometimes were disconcertingly independent minded, but their relationship to the king was essentially one of paid servant to master, not of less-powerful friend to more-powerful friend. A special place among royal servants was occupied by the clergy, who in fact often fulfilled many of the secular functions of the fledgling states, from royal chancellor and advisor to local tax collector. They were particularly suitable for these kinds of employment since they were literate and often also numerate. When Scandinavian kings "modernized" their kingdoms in these ways, they were following the examples of European rulers and their more advanced kingdoms.[19]

If this book contributes to our understanding of the important role Scandinavia played in European history, it also contributes to our understanding of how stateless societies in Europe functioned. It gives us insights into a world of charismatic warlords and chieftains who were always wary of each other, who may have formed uneasy alliances in order to pillage in western Europe, but who ultimately competed with each other. They were leaders who used whatever resources they could get access to in order to build a following of loyal warriors whose military prowess could help the leaders get more resources and more power. This book tells the story of how Scandinavian society changed as a consequence of chieftains striving for power. Components of the story were known, but the story has never been told in full before. It needs to be told, if we are better to appreciate the complexities of European history.

Abbreviations

DR   Denmark in the "Samnordisk rundatabas"

G   Swedish province of Gotland in the "Samnordisk rundatabas"

JE, JL   Philippus Jaffé, *Regesta pontificum Romanorum* (2nd ed.; Leipzig, 1885–1888)

KLNM   *Kulturhistoriskt lexikon för nordisk medeltid* (Malmö, 1956–1982)

MGH   Monumenta Germaniae Historica

     Epp.   Epistolae [in quarto]

     SS   Scriptores [in folio]

     SS rer. Germ.   Scriptores rerum Germanicarum in usum scholarum separatim editi

     SS rer. Germ. NS   Scriptores rerum Germanicarum: Nova series

     SS rer. Merov.   Scriptores rerum Merovingicarum

N   Norway in the "Samnordisk rundatabas"

Ög   Swedish province of Östergötland in the "Samnordisk rundatabas"

Öl   Swedish province of Öland in the "Samnordisk rundatabas"

RGA   *Reallexikon der germanischen Altertumskunde* (2nd ed.; Berlin 1967–2007)

s.a.   *sub anno*, precedes the year under which a notice is found in an annalistic work

Sö	Swedish province of Södermanland in the "Samnordisk rundatabas"
U	Swedish province of Uppland in the "Samnordisk rundatabas"
Vg	Swedish province of Västergötland in the "Samnordisk rundatabas"
Vs	Swedish province of Västmanland in the "Samnordisk rundatabas"

Notes

Introduction

1. The story of Hallfred as told here is based on his poetry, not on the saga that bears his name. I have filled in a few details from the life of other skalds, as known from their poetry. The poetry is edited in Finnur Jónsson, *Den norsk-islandske skjaldedigtning* (Copenhagen, 1912), B:1, 147–163. Most of it (as well as Hallfred's saga) is translated in Diana Whaley, *Sagas of Warrior-Poets*, World of the Sagas (London, 2002). See also Dag Strömbäck, *The Conversion of Iceland: A Survey*, trans. Peter G. Foote ([London], 1975); Phillip Pulsiano and Kirsten Wolf, eds., *Medieval Scandinavia: An Encyclopedia* (New York, 1993), 263–264, s.v. "Hallfreðr Óttarson," by Folke Ström; Russell Poole, "The 'Conversion Verses' of Hallfreðr vandræðaskáld," *Maal og minne* (2002); Diana Whaley, "The 'Conversion Verses' in Hallfreðar saga: Authentic Voice of a Reluctant Christian?" in *Old Norse Myths, Literature and Society*, ed. Margaret Clunies Ross (Odense, 2003); Angus A. Somerville and R. Andrew McDonald, *The Viking Age: A Reader* (Toronto, 2010), 408–409.

2. *Anglo-Saxon Chronicle*, s.a. 994, in ed. Susan Irvine, *MS E: A Semi-Diplomatic Edition with Introduction and Indices*, vol. 7, *The Anglo-Saxon Chronicle: A Collaborative Edition*, ed. David Dumville and Simon Keynes (Cambridge, 2004), 61–62; trans. Michael Swanton, *The Anglo-Saxon Chronicle* (London, 1996), 126–129.

3. The story of Håkon being killed by his own slave comes from late sagas and is probably not reliable; see Oddr Snorrason, *Ólafs saga Tryggvasonar* 19/21, in ed. Ólafur Halldórsson, *Færeyinga saga: Ólafs saga Tryggvasonar eptir Odd munk Snorrason*,

Íslenzk fornrit 25 (Reykjavik, 2006), 202; trans. Oddr Snorrason, *The Saga of Olaf Tryggvason*, trans. Theodore M. Andersson (Ithaca, N.Y., 2003), 71. The saga is preserved in somewhat different form in two main manuscripts. The numbering of chapters differs between the texts. Ólafur prints the two texts in parallel, the Stockholm text at the top of the page, and the Arnemagnean text at the bottom. I give both chapter numbers in that order, neither of which corresponds to the chapter numbering in Andersson's translation (which was based on an earlier edition).

4. Hallfreðr Óttárson, Lausavisa 19, ed. Finnur, *Skjaldedigtning*, B:1, 159; trans. Whaley, *Sagas of Warrior-Poets*, 85.

5. Alcuin, *Vita Willibrordi* 9, in Carolus de Smedt, Franciscus van Ortroy, Hippolytus Delahaye, Albertus Poncelet, and Paulus Peeters, eds., *Acta sanctorum*, Novembris 3 (Brussels, 1910), 441; ed. W. Levison, MGH SS rer. Merov. 7.123–124; trans. Charles H. Talbot, *The Anglo-Saxon Missionaries in Germany; being the Lives of SS. Willibrord, Boniface, Sturm, Leoba, and Lebuin, together with the Hodoeporicon of St. Willibald and a selection from the correspondence of St. Boniface* (New York, 1954), 9. Cf. also Alcuin's versified *Vita metrica* of Willibrord, c. 7.

6. Widukind, *Res gestae Saxonicae* 3.65, ed. Paul Hirsch and Hans-Eberhard Lohmann, *Die Sachsengeschichte des Widukind von Corvey*, MGH SS rer. Germ. (Hanover, 1935), 140–141.

7. Adam of Bremen, *Gesta Hammaburgensis ecclesiae pontificum*, praefatio, in *Hamburgische Kirchengeschichte*, ed. Bernhard Schmeidler, MGH SS rer. Germ. (Hanover, 1917), 2; trans. Adam of Bremen, *History of the Archbishops of Hamburg-Bremen*, trans. with an introduction and notes by Francis J. Tschan, with a new introduction and selected bibliography by Timothy Reuter, Records of Western Civilization (New York, 2002), 4.

8. Gregory I, *Moralia super Iob* 29.13.

9. Cf. Philip Grierson, "Commerce in the Dark Ages: A Critique of the Evidence," *Transactions of the Royal Historical Society, Fifth Series* 9 (1959), 129.

10. Stefan Brink, ed., in collaboration with Neil Price, *The Viking World*, Routledge Worlds (London, 2008).

11. JE 2553; *Regesta pontificum Romanorum: Germania pontificia* 6 (Göttingen, 1981), 24 n. 6; ed. Karolus Hampe, MGH Epp. 5 (Berlin, 1899), 68–70 n. 11.

12. Rimbert, *Vita Anskarii* 13, ed. G. Waitz, *Vita Anskarii auctore Rimberto: Accedit Vita Rimberti*, MGH SS rer. Germ. (Hanover, 1884), 35; trans. Rimbert, *Anskar, the Apostle of the North 801–865*, trans. Charles H. Robinson, Lives of Early and Mediæval Missionaries ([London], 1921), 54. Robinson's translation partially reprinted with revisions in Somerville and McDonald, *Viking Age*, 42–74.

13. For Rimbert's use of the expression with regard to Ansgar, see *Vita Anskarii* 3, ed. Waitz, 21; trans. Robinson, 30.

14. C. Patrick Wormald, "Viking Studies: Whence and Whither?" in *The Vikings*, ed. R. T. Farrell (London, 1980), 146; Jørgen Jensen, *The Prehistory of Denmark* (London, 1982), 255–274; Chris Wickham, *Framing the Early Middle Ages: Europe and the Mediterranean, 400–800* (Oxford, 2005), 364–376. Wickham's informed speculation about what might have happened in England when Roman power broke down there is stimulating (330–331).

Chapter 1 The Dynamic Eighth Century

1. Einhard, *Vita Karoli magni* 25, ed. G. Waitz, *Einhardi Vita Karoli magni*, MGH SS rer. Germ. (6th ed.; Hanover, 1911), 30; trans. Paul Edward Dutton, *Carolingian Civilization: A Reader* (Peterborough, Ont., 1993), 37. About poetry at the Frankish court, see Peter Godman, *Poets and Emperors: Frankish Politics and Carolingian Poetry* (Oxford, 1987).

2. MGH Poetae 1, ed. Ernst Dümmler (Berlin, 1881), 50–51; Karl Neff, *Die Gedichte des Paulus Diaconus: Kritische und erklärende Ausgabe*, Quellen und Untersuchungen zur lateinischen Philologie des Mittelalters 3:2 (Munich, 1908), 98–100. About this poetic exchange, see Godman, *Poets and Emperors*, 54–55; Eric Christiansen, *The Norsemen in the Viking Age*, Peoples of Europe (Oxford, 2002), 118.

3. The poems must have been written while Paul the Deacon resided at Charlemagne's court during the 780s. The exact dates are debatable. Walter Goffart, *The Narrators of Barbarian History (A.D. 550–800): Jordanes, Gregory of Tours, Bede, and Paul the Deacon*, 2d ed., Publications in Medieval Studies (Notre Dame, Ind., 2005), 341–342, gives a reasoned argument for dating Paul's sojourn at the court to 781–784 or 785. Neff thought the poems were written in 783; see Neff, *Gedichte des Paulus Diaconus*, 102.

4. MGH Poetae 1.52–53; Neff, *Gedichte des Paulus Diaconus*, 101–105.

5. *Alcuini sive Albini epistolae* 6, ed. Ernst Dümmler, MGH Epp. 4 (Berlin, 1895), 31. Cf. the story told in Altfrid's life of his uncle Liudger (died 805), who was the first bishop of Münster. Liudger is said to have desired to go and teach the Northmen about Christianity, but Charlemagne prevented him from doing so. The life was written after 825, perhaps even after Altfrid had become bishop in 839. The story may just as well be inspired by the recent missions to the north at that time as by Liudger actually expressing any wish to convert Scandinavians. *Altfridi Vita sancti Liudgeri* 1.30, ed. Wilhelm Diekamp, *Die Vitae sancti Liudgeri*, Die Geschichtsquellen des Bisthums Münster 4 (Münster, 1881), 36. About the date, see Diekamp, *Die Vitae sancti Liudgeri*, xx.

6. *Annales regni Francorum*, s.a. 782, ed. Fridericus Kurze, *Annales regni Francorum inde ab a. 741 usque ad a. 829, qui dicuntur Annales Laurissenses maiores et Einhardi*, MGH SS rer. Germ. (Hanover, 1895), 60; trans. Bernhard W. Scholz and Barbara Rogers, *Carolingian Chronicles: Royal Frankish Annals and Nithard's Histories* (Ann Arbor, 1970), 59.

7. *Alcuini sive Albini epistolae* 20, ed. Dümmler, 56–58.

8. *Alcuini sive Albini epistolae* 19, ed. Dümmler, 55. Jeremiah 1:14.

9. Peter Godman, ed. and trans., *Poetry of the Carolingian Renaissance* (Norman, Okla., 1985), 126–139.

10. Alcuin, *Vita Willibrordi* 9. For references, see Introduction, n. 5.

11. *Alcuini sive Albini epistolae* 124, ed. Dümmler, 183; *Beowulf*, line 2064, ed. R. D. Fulk, Robert E. Bjork, and John D. Niles, *Klaeber's Beowulf and the Fight at Finnsburg* (Toronto, 2008), 70; trans. R. M. Liuzza, *Beowulf: A New Verse Translation*, Broadview literary texts (Peterborough, Ont., 2000), 116; John D. Niles, Tom Christensen, and Marijane Osborn, eds., *Beowulf and Lejre*, Medieval and Renaissance

Texts and Studies 323 (Tempe, Ariz., 2007), 237; RGA 22.104–105, s.v. "Ongendus," by Roberta Frank.

12. Einhard, *Vita Karoli Magni*, 12, ed. Waitz, 15.

13. Johann Friedrich Böhmer, Engelbert Mühlbacher, and Johann Lechner, *Die Regesten des Kaiserreichs unter den Karolingern, 751–918*, 2d ed., Regesta imperii (Innsbruck, 1908), no. 829d.

14. Horst Zettel, *Das Bild der Normannen und der Normanneneinfälle in westfränkischen, ostfränkischen und angelsächsischen Quellen des 8. bis 11. Jahrhunderts* (München, 1977), 285; Janet Nelson, "The Frankish Empire," in *The Oxford Illustrated History of the Vikings*, ed. Peter Sawyer (Oxford, 1997), 22–24.

15. See below, ch. 8.

16. Jordanes, *Getica* 3.21, ed. Theodor Mommsen, *Jordanis Romana et Getica*, MGH Auctores antiquissimi 5 (Berlin, 1882), 59; trans. Charles C. Mierow, *Jordanes, The Origin and Deeds of the Goths, in English Version* (Princeton, 1908), 7. Lauritz Weibull, "Upptäckten av den skandinaviska Norden," *Scandia* 7 (1934), repr. in Lauritz Weibull, *Nordisk historia: Forskningar och undersökningar* (Lund, 1948), 1.71–126.

17. Wickham, *Framing the Early Middle Ages*, 364–376, presents an argument for the development of Denmark.

18. Frands Herschend, *Livet i hallen: Tre fallstudier i den yngre järnålderns aristokrati*, Occasional Papers in Archaeology, 14 (Uppsala, 1997); RGA 13.414–425, s.v. "Halle," by F. Herschend; Stig Welinder, *Sveriges historia: 13000 f.Kr.-600 e.Kr.*, Norstedts Sveriges historia (Stockholm, 2009), 410–428.

19. KLNM 7.289–294, s.v. "Högsäte," by Wilhelm Holmqvist, Hilmar Stigum, and E. A. Virtanen.

20. RGA 13.419: Dejbjerg, Dankirke, Helgö, and Borg.

21. *Beowulf*, lines 620–624, ed. Fulk, Bjork, and Niles, 23; trans. Liuzza, 72. Cf. Michael J. Enright, *Lady with a Mead Cup: Ritual, Prophecy, and Lordship in the European Warband from La Tène to the Viking Age* (Blackrock, Ireland, 1996). I think it is defensible to use the English poem *Beowulf* to illustrate early medieval attitudes toward, among other things, gift giving, chieftains, exotica, and loyalty in northern Europe, since it espouses (or imagines) a warrior culture common to the British Isles and Scandinavia. From this perspective, it matters little exactly when one dates the poem, although that date is a long-debated problem; see Roberta Frank, "A Scandal in Toronto: The Dating of 'Beowulf' a Quarter Century On," *Speculum* 82 (2007), and Fulk, Bjork, and Niles, *Klaeber's Beowulf*, clxiii–clxxx.

22. *Beowulf*, lines 2315 and 2324–2328, ed. Fulk, Bjork, and Niles, 80; trans. Liuzza, 124.

23. The idea that many chieftains held power in early medieval Scandinavia is often expressed in the literature; see, e.g., Mats Burström, *Arkeologisk samhällsavgränsning: En studie av vikingatida samhällsterritorier i Smålands inland*, Stockholm Studies in Archaeology 9 (Stockholm, 1991).

24. Since the hall is not mentioned in any medieval source, it is known under the modern name of the place. For a possible mention of this hall, see Lars Lönnroth, "Hövdingahallen i fornnordisk myt och saga: Ett mentalitetshistoriskt bidrag till förståelsen av Slöingefyndet," in *"Gick Grendel att söka det höga huset": Arkeologiska*

källor till aristokratiska miljöer i Skandinavien under yngre järnålder, ed. Johan Callmer and Erik Rosengren (Halmstad, 1997). For the illustration in figs. 1 and 2, see Nicolai Garhøj Larsen, "Virtual Reconstruction: The Viking Hall at Lejre," in *Beowulf and Lejre*, ed. Niles, Christensen, and Osborn.

25. Welinder, *Sveriges historia*, 426.
26. RGA 13.420. Frands Herschend, "Hus på Helgö," *Fornvännen* 90 (1995): 227; Welinder, *Sveriges historia*, 426.
27. *Beowulf*, lines 4–6, ed. Fulk, Bjork, and Niles, 3; trans. Liuzza, 53.
28. Sven B. F. Jansson, *Runes in Sweden* ([Stockholm], 1987), 25–26; Else Roesdahl, *The Vikings*, 2d ed. (London, 1998), 48; Lars Magnar Enoksen, *Runor: Historia, tydning, tolkning* (Lund, 1998), 66.
29. Jensen, *The Prehistory of Denmark*, 265–266; Peter Sawyer, ed., *The Oxford Illustrated History of the Vikings* (Oxford, 1997), 5; Paolo Squatriti, "Digging Ditches in Early Medieval Europe," *Past and Present* (2002); Wickham, *Framing the Early Middle Ages*, 366; RGA 5.236–243, s.v. "Danewerk," by H. H. Andersen; Pulsiano and Wolf, eds., *Medieval Scandinavia*, 120–121. The Frankish major domo Charles Martell had thoroughly defeated the Frisians after a revolt in 734, which might make the 730s an appropriate time to build a defensive work like the Danevirke. Pierre Riché, *The Carolingians: A Family Who Forged Europe*, trans. Michael Idomir Allen, Middle Ages Series (Philadelphia, 1993), 40.
30. Herschend, "Hus på Helgö."

Chapter 2 The Raids of the Vikings

1. Ninth-century antiphonal in the Bibliothèque Nationale de France, ed. Léopold Delisle, *Littérature latine & histoire du moyen âge*, Comité des travaux historiques et scientifiques: Section d'histoire et de philologie, Instructions aux correspondants (Paris, 1890), 17; here reproduced after photo of the manuscript in Frank Birkebæk, *Vikingetiden i Danmark* ([Copenhagen?], 2003), 123.
2. *Anglo-Saxon Chronicle*, s.a. 793, ms E, ed. Irvine, 42; trans. Swanton, 55 and 57. An attack from the sea is not very likely in January and the Latin *Annals of Lindisfarne* give the date as 8 June, which a scribe might easily have mistaken for January; see *Annales Lindisfarnenses et Dunelmenses*, s.a. 793, ed. G.H. Pertz, MGH SS 19 (Hanover, 1866), 505.
3. *Alcuini sive Albini epistolae* 20, ed. Dümmler, 56–58; trans. Dutton, *Carolingian Civilization*, 109–110. Alcuin drew on Biblical language, e.g., Isaiah 5:25 and Joel 2:17. See also Zettel, *Bild der Normannen*, 195–196.
4. *Anglo-Saxon Chronicle*, s.a. 796, ms E, ed. Irvine, 42; trans. Swanton, 57.
5. Seán Mac Airt, ed. and trans., *The Annals of Inisfallen MS. Rawlinson B503* (Dublin, 1951), 118–119; Seán Mac Airt and Gearóid Mac Niocaill, eds. and trans., *The Annals of Ulster (to A.D. 1131)* ([Dublin], 1983), 258–259 and 262–263. See also Donnchadh Ó Corráin, "Ireland, Wales, Man, and the Hebrides," in *The Oxford Illustrated History of the Vikings*, ed. Sawyer; Donnchadh Ó Corráin, "The Vikings & Ireland," Corpus of Electronic Texts (CELT), ([c. 1991]), http://www.ucc.ie/celt/General%20Vikings%20in%20Ireland.pdf.

6. Mac Airt and Mac Niocaill, eds. and trans., *Annals of Ulster*, 262–263.

7. Mac Airt and Mac Niocaill, eds. and trans., *Annals of Ulster*, 276–277 and 280–281.

8. Mac Airt and Mac Niocaill, eds. and trans., *Annals of Ulster*, 268–269.

9. *Annales regni Francorum*, s.a. 810, ed. Kurze, 181; trans. Scholz and Rogers, 91–92.

10. *Annales Bertiniani*, s.a. 834–838, ed. G. Waitz, MGH SS rer. Germ. (Hanover, 1883), 9–15; trans. Janet Nelson, *The Annals of St-Bertin*, Ninth-Century Histories 1 (Manchester, 1991), 30–39.

11. *Annales Bertiniani*, s.a. 837, ed. Waitz, 13; trans. Nelson, 37.

12. Mac Airt and Mac Niocaill, eds. and trans., *Annals of Ulster*, 302–305. See also Gwyn Jones, *A History of the Vikings* (London, 1968), 204–206; Alfred P. Smyth, *Scandinavian Kings in the British Isles, 850–880*, Oxford Historical Monographs (Oxford, 1977), 127; and Ó Corráin, "Ireland, Wales, Man, and the Hebrides," 88.

13. B. E. Crawford, *Scandinavian Scotland*, Studies in the Early History of Britain ([Leicester], 1987), 40.

14. *Anglo-Saxon Chronicle*, s.a. 845, ms E, ed. Irvine, 46; trans. Swanton, 64–65.

15. *Annales Bertiniani*, s.a. 844, ed. Waitz, 31; trans. Nelson, 59.

16. *Anglo-Saxon Chronicle*, s.a. 840, ms E, ed. Irvine, 46; trans. Swanton, 64–65.

17. *Annales Xantenses*, s.a. 845, ed. B. de Simson, MGH SS rer. Germ. (Hanover, 1909), 14; trans. Dutton, *Carolingian Civilization*, 391. About Gerward, see Heinz Löwe, "Studien zu den Annales Xantenses," *Deutsche Archiv für Erforschung des Mittelalters* 8 (1951).

18. *Annales Fuldenses*, s.a. 845, ed. Fridericus Kurze, *Annales Fuldenses sive Annales Regni Francorum orientalis*, MGH SS rer. Germ. (Hanover, 1891), 35; trans. Timothy Reuter, *The Annals of Fulda*, Ninth-Century Histories 2 (Manchester, 1992), 23; *Annales Bertiniani*, s.a. 845, ed. Waitz, 32; trans. Nelson, 61; Rimbert, *Vita Anskarii* 16, ed. Waitz 37–38; trans. Robinson, 57–58. See also Hartmut Harthausen, *Die Normanneneinfälle im Elb- und Wesermündungsgebiet mit besonderer Berücksichtigung der Schlacht von 880*, Quellen und Darstellungen zur Geschichte Niedersachsens 68 (Hildesheim, 1966), 10–27; Walther Vogel, *Die Normannen und das fränkische Reich bis zur Gründung der Normandie (799–911)*, Heidelberger Abhandlungen zur mittleren und neueren Geschichte 14 (Heidelberg, 1906), 101–103.

19. *Annales Xantenses*, s.a. 845.

20. *Annales Bertiniani*, s.a. 845, ed. Waitz, 32; trans. Nelson, 60–61; C. Smedt, ed., "Translatio sancti Germani Parisiensis secundum primaevam narrationem," Analecta Bollandiana 2 (1883). See also Vogel, *Normannen und das fränkische Reich*, 104–113; Einar Joranson, *The Danegeld in France* (Rock Island, Ill., 1923), 26–38; Simon Coupland, "The Frankish Tribute Payments to the Vikings and Their Consequences," *Francia* 26 (1999).

21. *Annales Bertiniani*, s.a. 845; *Annales Xantenses*, s.a. 845; trans. Dutton, *Carolingian Civilization*, 391–392.

22. *Annales Bertiniani*, s.a. 844, ed. Waitz, 32; trans. Nelson, 60. See also Vogel, *Normannen und das fränkische Reich*, 116–117.

23. Yves Bonnaz, *Chroniques Asturiennes (fin IXe siècle)* (Paris, 1987), 53–54 and 204–207; Justo Perez de Urbel and Atilano Gonzales Ruiz-Zorrilla, eds., *Historia Silense*, Consejo superior de investigaciones cientificas, Escuela de estudios mediev-

ales: Textos 30 (Madrid, 1959), 143; Juan Gil Fernández, José L. Moralejo, and Juan Ignacio Ruiz de la Peña, *Crónicas asturianas: Crónica de Alfonso III (Rotense y "A Sebastián"): Crónica albeldense (y "profética")*, Publicaciones del Departamento de Historia Medieval / Universidad de Oviedo 11 (Oviedo, 1985), 142, 143, and 262; Jón Stefánsson, "The Vikings in Spain: From Arabic (Moorish) and Spanish Sources," *Saga-Book of the Viking Club* 6 (1908–1909); Roger Collins, *Early Medieval Spain: Unity in Diversity, 400–1000*, 2 ed. (New York, 1995), 193.

24. Rimbert, *Vita Anskarii*, c. 30, ed. Waitz, 60–63; trans. Robinson, 96–100. See also RGA 1.375–376, s.v. "Apoule," by W. Holmqvist; Anders Ekenberg et al., *Boken om Ansgar* (Stockholm, 1986), 106, which dates Ansgar's second visit to Birka to "some point between 849 and 854, and probably after the death of Ebo in 851" (103).

25. DR 334, ed. Erik Moltke and Lis Jacobsen, *Danmarks runeindskrifter* (Copenhagen, 1941–1942), 379–381; "Samnordisk runtextdatabas," (2009), Uppsala universitet, http://www.nordiska.uu.se/forskn/samnord.htm.

26. On the numbers, see Zettel, *Bild der Normannen*, 234–236 and 243–246; Simon Keynes, "The Vikings in England, c. 790–1016," in *The Oxford Illustrated History of the Vikings*, ed. Sawyer, 54.

27. Arnold Angenendt, *Kaiserherrschaft und Königstaufe: Kaiser, Könige und Päpste als geistliche Patrone in der abendländischen Missionsgeschichte*, Arbeiten zur Frühmittelalterforschung 15 (Berlin, 1984), 267–269.

28. Michael Swanton, *Anglo-Saxon Prose*, The Everyman Library (London, 1993), 6–7. *Anglo-Saxon Chronicle*, s.a. 875, 878, and 890, in ed. Janet M. Bately, *MS A*, vol. 3, *The Anglo-Saxon Chronicle: A Collaborative Edition*, ed. David Dumville and Simon Keynes (Cambridge, 1986), 49, 50–51, and 54; ms E, ed. Irvine, 50–51 and 53; trans. Swanton, 76–77 and 82–83.

29. RGA 5.227–236, s.v. "Danelag," by H. Beck and H. R. Loyn; Jones, *A History of the Vikings*, 421–424; Keynes, "The Vikings in England, c. 790–1016," 63–69; S. S. Mastana and R. J. Sokol, "Genetic Variation in the East Midlands," *Annals of Human Biology* 25 (1998). I wish to thank Diana Quinones of Yale University Library and Mary Angelotti of Harvey Cushing/John Hay Whitney Medical Library for helping me get a copy of Mastana and Sokol's article.

30. Christiansen, *Norsemen in the Viking Age*, 3–4.

31. *Anglo-Saxon Chronicle*, s.a. 896, ms A, ed. Bately, 59; trans. Swanton, 89. I translate *feohlease* as "without money or property" (cf. Swanton in note 11) rather than as "without money," as Swanton translates it. Cf. Janet Nelson, "England and the Continent in the Ninth Century: II, The Vikings and Others," *Transactions of the Royal Historical Society, Fifth Series* 13 (2003), who translates it as "moneyless." The point is that those warriors who had not acquired enough wealth to settle down went to France to try their luck.

32. *Annales Vedastini*, s.a. 896–897, ed. B. de Simson, 78. Fulco's letter to Charles is partially quoted in Flodoard of Rheims, *Historia ecclesiae Remensis* 4.5, ed. Flodoard von Rheims, *Die Geschichte der Rheimser Kirche*, ed. Martina Stratmann, MGH SS 36 (Hanover, 1998), 384–385. See also Vogel, *Normannen und das fränkische Reich*, 373–378; Gerhard Schneider, *Erzbischof Fulco von Reims (883–900) und das Frankenreich*, Münchener Beiträge zur Mediävistik und Renaissance-Forschung 14

(München, 1973); Zettel, *Bild der Normannen,* 270–279; Angenendt, *Kaiserherrschaft und Königstaufe,* 262–263.

33. Keynes, "The Vikings in England, c. 790–1016," 73–76.

34. RGA 5.225–227, s.v. "Danegeld," by H. Beck and H. R. Loyn; M. K. Lawson, "The Collection of Danegeld and Heregeld in the Reigns of Aethelred II and Cnut," *English Historical Review* 99 (1984); Keynes, "The Vikings in England, c. 790–1016," 74–76.

35. Peter Sawyer, *Da Danmark blev Danmark: fra ca. år 700 til ca.* 1050, trans. Marie Hvidt, vol. 3, Gyldendal-Politikens Danmarkshistorie (Copenhagen, 1988), 267–277; Carl Löfving, *Gothia som dansk/engelskt skattland: Ett exempel på heterarki omkring år* 1000, new ed., GOTARC, series B: Gothenburg archaeological theses 16 (Göteborg, 2001); Timothy Bolton, *The Empire of Cnut the Great: Conquest and the Consolidation of Power in Northern Europe in the Early Eleventh Century,* The Northern World: North Europe and the Baltic c. 400–1700 A.D: Peoples, Economies and Cultures (Leiden, 2009).

36. *Anglo-Saxon Chronicle,* s.a. 1069, in ed. G. P. Cubbin, *MS D,* vol. 6, *The Anglo-Saxon Chronicle: A Collaborative Edition,* ed. by David Dumville and Simon Keynes (Cambridge, 1991), 84 (s.a. 1068); ms E, ed. Irvine, 88; trans. Swanton, 202–204. See also Ole Fenger, *"Kirker reses alle vegne":* 1050–1250, Gyldendal og Politikens Danmarkshistorie (Copenhagen, 1989), 48.

37. Claes Annerstedt, ed., *Scriptores rerum Suecicarum medii aevi* 3 (Uppsala, 1871–1876), 98.

38. Thomas Lindkvist, "Med Sankt Erik konung mot hedningar och schismatiker: Korståg och korstågsideologi i svensk medeltida östpolitik," in *Väst möter öst: Norden och Ryssland genom tiderna,* ed. Max Engman (Stockholm, 1996).

39. *Annales Bertiniani,* s.a. 838, ed. Waitz, 15; trans. Nelson, 39.

40. *Anglo-Saxon Chronicle,* s.a. 851, ms A, ed. Bately, 44; ms E, ed. Irvine, 46; trans. Swanton, 64–65.

41. *Anglo-Saxon Chronicle,* s.a. 993, ms A, ed. Bately, 79; trans. Swanton, 126.

42. Zettel, *Bild der Normannen,* 250–262; Nelson, "The Frankish Empire," 38–40; Gareth Williams, "Raiding and Warfare," in *The Viking World,* ed. Brink with Price.

43. Zettel, *Bild der Normannen,* 259–260.

44. "The Edict of Pîtres," 25 June 864, c. 25, ed. Alfredus Boretius and Victor Krause, *Capitularia regum Francorum* 2, MGH (Hanover, 1897), 321. See also Ian G. Peirce, *Swords of the Viking Age* (Rochester, N.Y., 2002); A. N. Kirpichnikov, "Connections between Russia and Scandinavia in the 9th and 10th Centuries, as Illustrated by Weapons Finds," in *Varangian Problems,* ed. Knud Hannestad (Copenhagen, 1970); Nelson, "England and the Continent in the Ninth Century: II, The Vikings and Others," 26.

45. *Annales Bertiniani,* s.a. 882, ed. Waitz, 153; trans. Nelson, 224–225.

46. P. H. Sawyer, *Kings and Vikings: Scandinavia and Europe, A.D. 700–1100* (London, 1982).

47. Zettel, *Bild der Normannen,* 128–133 and 213–216.

48. Regino of Prüm, *Chronicle,* s.a. 882, ed. Fridericus Kurze, *Reginonis abbatis Prumensis Chronicon cum continuatione Treverensi,* MGH SS rer. Germ. (Hanover, 1890),

119; trans. Simon MacLean, *History and Politics in Late Carolingian and Ottonian Europe: The Chronicle of Regino of Prüm and Adalbert of Magdeburg*, Manchester Medieval Sources Series (Manchester, 2009).

49. Regino, *Chronicle*, s.a. 884, ed. Kurze, 121.
50. *Annales Bertiniani*, s.a. 865, ed. Waitz, 80; trans. Nelson, 128.
51. *Annales Bertiniani*, s.a. 865, ed. Waitz, 80; trans. Nelson, 129.
52. *Anglo-Saxon Chronicle*, s.a. 1046, ms E, ed. Irvine, 78–79; trans. Swanton, 166–167.
53. Ög 136, ed. Erik Brate, *Östergötlands runinskrifter*, Sveriges runinskrifter 2 (Stockholm, 1911), 231–255. The Rök inscription is difficult to interpret. I have followed Elias Wessén, *Runstenen vid Röks kyrka*, Kungl. Vitterhets-, historie- och antikvitetsakademiens handlingar: Filologisk-filosofiska serien, 5 (Stockholm, 1958). The meaning of the runes here translated as "folktale" is debated. Another interpretation is "to the young men." My translation is inspired by "Samnordisk runtextdatabas." See also Rune Palm, *Vikingarnas språk 750–1100* (Stockholm, 2004), 25–39. Interpretations different from Wessén's are found in Olle Häger and Hans Villius, *Rök: Gåtornas sten* (Stockholm, 1976) and, notably, in Bo Ralph, "Gåtan som lösning—Ett bidrag till förståelsen av Rökstenens runinskrift," *Maal og minne* (2007). However one interprets the inscription, the emphasis on war booty remains clear.
54. Illustrated by Lars Jørgensen, Birger Storgaard, and Lone Gebauer Thomsen, *The Spoils of Victory: The North in the Shadow of the Roman Empire* ([Copenhagen], 2003).
55. Kormákr Ögmundarson, Lausavísa 63, ed. Finnur, *Skjaldedigtning*, B:1, 84–85.
56. *Annales Fuldenses*, s.a. 885, ed. Kurze, 103; trans. Reuter, 98.
57. Flodoard, *Annales*, ed. Ph. Lauer, *Les Annales de Flodoard, publiées d'après les manuscrits*, Collection de textes pour servir à l'étude et à l'enseignement de l'histoire 39 (Paris, 1905), 15–16; trans. Flodoard, *The Annals of Flodoard of Reims, 919–966*, trans. Bernard S. Bachrach and Steven Fanning, Readings in Medieval Civilizations and Cultures 9 (Peterborough, Ont., 2004), 9. See also J. H. Todd, ed., *War of the Gaedhil with the Gaill, or, The Invasions of Ireland by the Danes and Other Norsemen*, Rerum Britannicarum medii aevi scriptores 48 (London, 1867), 114–117, about what King Brian Boru found in a conquered Viking camp on Ireland: "It was in that one place were found the greatest quantities of gold and silver, and bronze, and precious stones, and carbuncle-gems, and buffalo horns, and beautiful goblets . . . Much also of various vestures of all colours was found there likewise."
58. Egon Wamers, "Kristne gjenstander i tidligvikingtidens Danmark," in *Kristendommen i Danmark før 1050*, ed. Niels Lund ([Roskilde], 2004); Egon Wamers and Michael Brandt, *Die Macht des Silbers: Karolingische Schätze im Norden* (Regensburg, 2005).
59. N 540, ed. Terje Spurkland, *I begynnelsen var fuþark: Norske runer og runeinnskrifter*, LNUs skriftserie (Oslo, 2001), 132–133; "Samnordisk runtextdatabas."
60. Barbara H. Rosenwein, *Reading the Middle Ages: Sources from Europe, Byzantium, and the Islamic World* (Peterborough, Ont., 2006), 258.
61. *Annales Bertiniani*, s.a. 860, ed. Waitz, 53; trans. Nelson, 92.
62. Dorothy Whitelock, *English Historical Documents. Vol. 1, C. 500–1042* (London, 1979), no. 98; Somerville and McDonald, *Viking Age*, 235.

63. Alfred was eolderman in Surrey from the 850s to the 880s; see Keynes, "The Vikings in England, c. 790–1016," 60.

64. *Annales Bertiniani*, s.a. 858, ed. Waitz, 49; trans. Nelson, 86.

65. Riché, *The Carolingians*, 136.

66. *Anglo-Saxon Chronicle*, s.a. 914, ms A, ed. Bately, 65; trans. Swanton, 98 and 99.

67. Vg 61, ed. Hugo Jungner and Elisabeth Svärdström, *Västergötlands runinskrifter*, Sveriges runinskrifter 5 (Stockholm, 1958–1970), 90–92; Jansson, *Runes in Sweden*, 76; "Samnordisk runtextdatabas."

68. *Annales Bertiniani*, s.a. 852, ed. Waitz, 41; trans. Nelson, 74.

69. *Annales Bertiniani*, s.a. 868, ed. Waitz, 91; trans. Nelson, 144.

70. David Morgan, *The Mongols* (Oxford, 1990).

71. *Annales Bertiniani*, s.a. 847, ed. Waitz, 35; trans. Nelson, 65.

72. Samuel Hazzard Cross and Olgerd P. Sherbowitz-Wetzor, trans., *The Russian Primary Chronicle: Laurentian Text* (Cambridge, Mass., 1973), 59.

73. Roesdahl, *The Vikings*, 111; Williams, "Raiding and Warfare," 194.

74. *Anglo-Saxon Chronicle*, s.a. 1006, ms E, ed. Irvine, 66; trans. Swanton, 137.

75. U 344, ed. Elias Wessén and Sven B. F. Jansson, *Upplands runinskrifter* 2, Sveriges runinskrifter 7 (Stockholm, 1943), 79–86; Jansson, *Runes in Sweden*, 77–79. About the danegelds, see Keynes, "The Vikings in England, c. 790–1016," 75–77.

76. N 184, ed. Magnus Olsen and Aslak Liestøl, *Norges innskrifter med de yngre runer*, Norges indskrifter indtil reformationen, afd. 2 (Oslo, 1941–), 3.14–33; Spurkland, *I begynnelsen var fuþark*, 109–111; "Samnordisk runtextdatabas."

77. *Annales Fuldenses*, s.a. 882, ed. Kurze, 99; trans. Reuter, 93.

78. For the following, see Timothy Reuter, "Plunder and Tribute in the Carolingian Empire," *Transactions of the Royal Historical Society* 35 (1985).

79. *Annales regni Francorum*, s.a. 796, ed. Kurze, 99–100; trans. Scholz and Rogers, 74. Einhard, *Vita Karoli magni* 13, ed. Waitz, 15–17; trans. Dutton, *Carolingian Civilization*, 31.

80. Einhard, *Vita Karoli magni* 16, ed. Waitz, 20; trans. Dutton, *Carolingian Civilization*, 33.

81. *Annales Fuldenses*, s.a. 882, ed. Kurze, 99; trans. Reuter, 93.

82. *Annales regni Francorum*, s.a. 796, ed. Kurze, 99; trans. Scholz and Rogers, 74.

83. Niels Lund et al., *Two Voyagers at the Court of King Alfred: The Ventures of Ohthere and Wulfstan, together with the Description of Northern Europe from the Old English Orosius* (York, 1984). New translations in Janet Bately and Anton Englert, *Ohthere's Voyages: A Late 9th-century Account of Voyages along the Coasts of Norway and Denmark and Its Cultural Context* (Roskilde, 2007) and in Somerville and McDonald, *Viking Age*, 2–4.

84. Gregory of Tours, *History of the Franks* 3.3, ed. Bruno Krusch and Wilhelmus Levison, *Gregorii episcopi Turonensis Libri Historiarum X*, SS rer. Merov. 1 (Hanover, 1950), 99; trans. Gregory of Tours, *The History of the Franks*, trans. Lewis Thorpe, Penguin Classics (Harmondsworth, 1974), 163–164.

Chapter 3   The Power of Gifts

1. Sighvatr Þórðarson, *Nesjavísur*, ed. Finnur, *Skjaldedigtning*, B:1, 217–220.
2. Marcel Mauss, *The Gift: The Form and Reason for Exchange in Archaic Societies*, trans. by W. D. Halls (London, 1990). Critique in Gadi Algazi, Valentin Groebner, and Bernhard Jussen, *Negotiating the Gift: Pre-Modern Figurations of Exchange*, Veröffentlichungen des Max-Planck-Instituts für Geschichte 188 (Göttingen, 2003).
3. Åke Hyenstrand, *Lejonet, draken och korset: Sverige 500–1000* (Lund, 1996), 92–104. The graves discussed are those of the grave fields in Vendel (14), Valsgärde (15 ship graves plus other graves), Ulltuna (1 grave), and Tuna in Alsike (10 ship graves plus 4 other graves). They come from the period 500–1000. Several of these graves contain most or all of the equipment mentioned.
4. Mette Iversen, ed., *Mammen: Grav, kunst og samfund i vikingetid*, Jysk Arkaeologisk Selskabs skrifter 28 (Højbjerg, 1991).
5. Gabriel Gustafson, Sune Lindqvist, and Fredrik Nordin, *Gotlands Bildsteine* (Stockholm, 1941), 1.74–76; Erik Nylén and Jan Peder Lamm, *Bildstenar*, 3d ed. (Stockholm, 2003).
6. Gustafson, Lindqvist, and Nordin, *Gotlands Bildsteine*, 1, plates 135–136, and 2.113–115, plates 303–304.
7. Roberta Frank, *Old Norse Court Poetry: The Dróttkvætt Stanza*, Islandica 42 (Ithaca, N.Y., 1978), 142–153.
8. Finnur, ed., *Skjaldedigtning*, B:1, 177; Öl 1, ed. Sven Söderberg and Erik Brate, *Ölands runinskrifter*, Sveriges runinskrifter 1 (Stockholm, 1900), 14–37; Sven B. F. Jansson, *Runinskrifter i Sverige*, 3d ed. (Stockholm, 1984), 139–141; Jesse L. Byock, *Feud in the Icelandic Saga* (Berkeley, 1982).
9. Thorleif Sjøvold, *Vikingeskipene i Oslo* (Oslo, 1985); *Levd liv: En utstilling om skjelettene fra Oseberg og Gokstad*, ([Oslo], 2008), 6–7.
10. *Annales regni Francorum*, s.a. 814, ed. Kurze, 141; trans. Scholz and Rogers, 97–99.
11. Jones, *A History of the Vikings*, 51; K. L. Maund, "'A Turmoil of Warring Princes': Political Leadership in Ninth-century Denmark," *The Haskins Society Journal: Studies in Medieval History* 6 (1994); Wickham, *Framing the Early Middle Ages*, 371–372, n. 161; cf. Zettel, *Bild der Normannen*, 69–84.
12. Anders Götherström, *Acquired or Inherited Prestige? Molecular Studies of Family Structures and Local Horses in Central Svealand during the Early Medieval Period*, Theses and Papers in Scientific Archaeology 4 (Stockholm, 2001).
13. Einar, *Vellekla* 37, ed. Finnur, *Skjaldedigtning*, B:1, 124.
14. Sighvatr, *Erfidrápa Óláfs helga* 2, ed. Finnur, *Skjaldedigtning*, B:1, 239. See also Christiansen, *Norsemen in the Viking Age*, 150.
15. Sighvatr, *Austrfararvísur* 16, ed. Finnur, *Skjaldedigtning*, B:1, 224.
16. Ernst Leisi, "Gold und Manneswert im Beowulf," *Anglia*, n.s., 59 = 71 (1953); Pierre Bourdieu, *The Logic of Practice*, trans. Richard Nice (Stanford, Calif., 1990), 122; Jón Viðar Sigurðsson, *Det norrøne samfunnet: Vikingen, kongen, erkebiskopen og bonden* (Oslo, 2008), 78–90; RGA 11.466–477, s.v. "Geschenke."
17. Egill Skallagrímsson, *Arinbjarnarkviða* 22, ed. Finnur, *Skjaldedigtning*, B:1, 41.

18. Diana Whaley, *The Poetry of Arnórr Jarlaskáld: An Edition and Study*, Westfield Publications in Medieval Studies 8 (Turnhout, 1998), 134.

19. Leisi, "Gold und Manneswert im Beowulf"; Jos Bazelmans, "Beyond Power: Ceremonial Exchanges in Beowulf," in *Rituals of Power: From Late Antiquity to the Early Middle Ages*, ed. Frans Theuws and Janet Nelson, The Transformation of the Roman World (Leiden, 2000).

20. *Beowulf*, lines 1020–1057, ed. Fulk, Bjork, and Niles, 36–37; trans. Liuzza, 84–85.

21. *Beowulf*, lines 2633–2638, ed. Fulk, Bjork, and Niles, 90; trans. Liuzza, 134.

22. Sö 174, ed. Erik Brate and Elias Wessén, *Södermanlands runinskrifter*, Sveriges runinskrifter 3 (Stockholm, 1924), 135–136; "Samnordisk runtextdatabas."

23. Hákon inn góði Haraldsson, Lausavísa, ed. Finnur, *Skjaldedigtning*, B:1, 54. The stanza is probably not Håkon's and was written later; however, the sentiment expressed is representative of the gift-exchange system.

24. Þórbjorn hornklofi, *Haraldskvæði* (Hrafnsmál), 16, ed. Finnur, *Skjaldedigtning*, B:1, 24. Some words in the stanza are difficult to interpret exactly. *Málmr* ("ore") is often used in kennings for either gold or, when iron ore is imagined, weapons. The poet might well have wanted to conjure both images. Finnur Jónsson understands the Hunnish ore here to be spears. *Hunn* can refer to the knob at the top of a mast, or a bear cub, but the derived meaning of "game piece, dice" is more likely. See Sveinbjörn Egilsson and Finnur Jónsson, *Lexicon poeticum antiquæ linguæ Septentrionalis: Ordbog over det norsk-islandske skjaldesprog*, 2d ed. (Copenhagen, 1931).

25. Sveinbjörn and Finnur, *Lexicon poeticum*, 36–37 and 280–282; Richard Cleasby, Guðbrandur Vigfússon, and William A. Craigie, *An Icelandic-English Dictionary*, 2d ed., (Oxford, 1957), 285; RGA 25.5, s.v. "Ring und Ringschmuck," by Ch. Zimmermann and T. Capelle.

26. Jonas Ström, "Världens största vikingatida silverskatt," Historiska museet (2002), http://www.historiska.se/historia/manadensforemal/2002/mfjuni2002/. For the Hägvalds hoard, see Birgitta Radhe, ed., *Klenoder i Gotlands Fornsal*, Gotländskt arkiv 75 (Visby, 2003).

27. Iversen, ed., *Mammen*; RGA 19.197–205, s.v. "Mammen und Mammenstil," by E. Nyman and I. Skibsted Klæsø.

28. Signe Horn Fuglesang, "The Axehead from Mammen and the Mammen Style," in *Mammen*, ed. Iversen.

29. Bjarne Lønborg, *Vikingetidens metalbearbejdning*, Fynske studier 17 (Odense, 1998), 106, n. 143.

30. *Beowulf*, line 1038, ed. Fulk, Bjork, and Niles, 37; trans. Liuzza, 85.

31. Arnórr jarlaskáld, Þorfinnsdrápa, 2, ed. and trans. Whaley, *The Poetry of Arnórr Jarlaskáld*, 123; Kari Ellen Gade, ed. *Poetry from the Kings' Sagas, 2: From c. 1035 to c. 1300*, Skaldic Poetry of the Scandinavian Middle Ages (Turnhout, 2009), 2:232.

32. Herschend, *Livet i hallen*, 61–89. About hospitality, see also Christiansen, *Norsemen in the Viking Age*, 143–146.

33. RGA, 13.414–425, s.v. "Halle," by F. Herschend. See also Rosemary Cramp, "The Hall in Beowulf and in Archeology," in *Heroic Poetry in the Anglo-Saxon Period: Studies in Honor of Jess B. Bessinger, Jr.*, ed. Helen Damico and John Leyerly (Kalamazoo, Mich., 1993); Leslie Webster, "Archaeology and Beowulf," in *Beowulf:*

An Edition with Relevant Shorter Texts, ed. Bruce Mitchell and Fred C. Robinson (Oxford, 1998); Herschend, *Livet i hallen*; Birkebæk, *Vikingetiden i Danmark*, 51–53; John D. Niles, "Beowulf's Great Hall," *History Today* 56 (2006); Niles, Christensen, and Osborn, eds., *Beowulf and Lejre*.

34. Thietmar of Merseburg, *Chronicon* 1.17, ed. Robert Holtzmann, *Die Chronik des Bischofs Thietmar von Merseburg und ihre Korveier Überarbeitung*, MGH SS rer. Germ. NS 9 (Berlin, 1935), 23; trans. David Warner, *Ottonian Germany: The Chronicon of Thietmar of Merseburg*, Manchester Medieval Sources Series (Manchester, 2001), 80.

35. Sm 44, ed. Ragnar Kinander, *Smålands runinskrifter*, Sveriges runinskrifter 4 (Stockholm, 1935), 1.136–140; "Samnordisk runtextdatabas." Many similar inscriptions exist, e.g.: "Holmbjörn had the stone raised in memory of himself. He was generous with food and eloquent" (U 739, ed. Elias Wessén and Sven B. F. Jansson, *Upplands runinskrifter*, vol. 3, Sveriges runinskrifter 8 [Stockholm, 1949], 280–283). "He was the best of estate-holders (bomanna) and the most generous with food" (DR 291, ed. Moltke and Jacobsen, *Danmarks runeindskrifter*, 343–344). See also Jansson, *Runes in Sweden*, 126–129 and "Samnordisk runtextdatabas."

36. Helmer Gustavson, Thorgunn Snædal, and Marit Åhlén, "Runfynd 1989 och 1990," *Fornvännen* 87 (1992): 166; "Samnordisk runtextdatabas." It is difficult to interpret such a short line of text without much context, as its editors point out. It could be an example of irony, a literary quotation, or a put-down. However it was meant, it is hard to argue that it was not normal, or desired, that a participant at a feast should be impressed by the host.

37. Sighvatr, *Bersöglisvísur* 17, ed. Finnur, *Skjaldedigtning*, B:1, 238; ed. Gade, *Poetry from the Kings' Sagas*, 2:29.

38. See the Introduction.

Chapter 4 Carving Out Power

1. *Íslendingabók* 6, ed. Jakob Benediktsson, *Íslendingabók: Landnámabók*, Íslenzk fornrit 1 (Reykjavik, 1968), 13–14; trans. Siân Grønlie, *Íslendingabók = The Book of the Icelanders: Kristni Saga = The Story of the Conversion*, Viking Society for Northern Research: Text Series 18 (London, 2006), 7; Keneva Kunz, *The Vinland Sagas: The Icelandic Sagas about the First Documented Voyages across the North Atlantic*, Penguin Classics (London, 2008), 26–28.

2. Agnar Helgason et al., "Estimating Scandinavian and Gaelic Ancestry in the Male Settlers of Iceland," *American Journal of Human Genetics* 67 (2000); Agnar Helgason et al., "mtDNA and the Islands of the North Atlantic: Estimating the Proportions of Norse and Gaelic Ancestry," *American Journal of Human Genetics* 68 (2001).

3. RGA 13.637–638, s.v. "Haraldr," by A. Krause; Dansk biografisk lexicon 6 (Copenhagen, 1980), 1, s.v. "Harald Klak," by Aksel E. Christensen. Ian Wood, "Christians and Pagans in Ninth-Century Scandinavia," in *The Christianization of Scandinavia: Report of a Symposium Held at Kungälv, Sweden 4–9 August 1985*, ed. Birgit Sawyer, Peter Sawyer, and Ian Wood (Alingsås, Sweden, 1987).

4. Jesse L. Byock, *Viking Age Iceland* (London, 2001).

5. Jones, *A History of the Vikings*, 295–306; Birgitta L. Wallace, *Westward Vikings: The Saga of L'Anse aux Meadows* (St. John's, NF, 2006). While there is no doubt that Scandinavians reached North America during the Viking Age, the so-called Vinland map (Yale University, Beinecke Rare Book and Manuscript Library MS 350A), showing the northeastern corner of North America, is clearly a modern forgery, see, e.g., Kirsten A. Seaver, *Maps, Myths, and Men: The Story of the Vinland Map* (Stanford, Calif., 2004).

6. S. Goodacre et al., "Genetic Evidence for a Family-based Scandinavian Settlement of Shetland and Orkney during the Viking Periods," *Heredity* 95 (2005).

7. Crawford, *Scandinavian Scotland*; A. D. M. Forte, Richard D. Oram, and Frederik Pedersen, *Viking Empires* (Cambridge, 2005) .

8. Crawford, *Scandinavian Scotland*, 40.

9. Mac Airt and Mac Niocaill, eds. and trans., *Annals of Ulster*, 298–299; Ó Corráin, "Ireland, Wales, Man, and the Hebrides," 88.

10. Alfred P. Smyth, *Scandinavian York and Dublin: The History and Archaeology of Two Related Viking Kingdoms* (Dublin, 1987); Benjamin T. Hudson, *Viking Pirates and Christian Princes: Dynasty, Religion, and Empire in the North Atlantic* (Oxford, 2005).

11. Brian McEvoy et al., "The Scale and Nature of Viking Settlement in Ireland from Y-chromosome Admixture Analysis," *European Journal of Human Genetics* 14 (2006).

12. *Anglo-Saxon Chronicle*, s.a. 851, ms E, ed. Irvine, 46; trans. Swanton, 65.

13. *Anglo-Saxon Chronicle*, s.a. 880, ms A, ed. Bately, 50–51; ms E, ed. Irvine, 50–51; trans. Swanton, 74–77.

14. Peter Heather, *Empires and Barbarians: The Fall of Rome and the Birth of Europe* (New York, 2010), 484–487.

15. Mastana and Sokol, "Genetic Variation in the East Midlands"; Georgina R. Bowden et al., "Excavating Past Population Structures by Surname-Based Sampling: The Genetic Legacy of the Vikings in Northwest England," *Molecular Biology and Evolution* 25 (2008).

16. Levin L. Schücking, "Wann entstand der Beowulf? Glossen, Zweifel, und Fragen," *Beiträge zur Geschichte der deutschen Sprache und Literatur* 42 (1917), presents a plausible argument for placing the origin of *Beowulf* in the Danelaw.

17. Gillian Fellows-Jenssen, *The Vikings and Their Victims: The Evidence of the Names* (London, 1995), 13; Ó Corráin, "Ireland, Wales, Man, and the Hebrides"; Keynes, "The Vikings in England, c. 790–1016."

18. Ó Corráin, "Ireland, Wales, Man, and the Hebrides," 89–90.

19. Keynes, "The Vikings in England, c. 790–1016," 69.

20. Simon Coupland, "From Poachers to Game-Keepers: Scandinavian Warlords and Carolingian Kings," *Early Medieval Europe* 7 (1998): 105.

21. Simon Franklin and Jonathan Shepard, *The Emergence of Rus: 750–1200*, Longman History of Russia (London, 1996), 33, 39, and 66–68.

22. Cross and Sherbowitz-Wetzor, *Russian Primary Chronicle*, 59.

Chapter 5   Weland, Ulfberht, and Other Artisans

1. RGA 31.393–404, s.v. "Ulfberht-Schwerter," by M. Müller-Wille and A. Stalsberg.
2. KLNM 20.350–351, s.v. "Völundr," by Eyvind Fjeld Halvorsen; RGA 33.604–622, s.v. "Wieland," by A. Pesch, R. Nedoma, and J. Insley.
3. Gustafson, Lindqvist, and Nordin, *Gotlands Bildsteine*, 2.22–24 and fig. 311; Nylén and Lamm, *Bildstenar*, 71 and 181; Jessica Eriksson, "Bilden av Bödvild: Ett genusperspektiv på berättelserna om Völund," in *Spaden och pennan: Ny humanistisk forskning i andan av Erik B Lundberg och Bengt G Söderberg*, ed. Thorsten Svensson (Stockholm, 2009); RGA 1.398–399, s.v. "Ardre," by W. Holmqvist, with plate 32.
4. RGA 1.514–523, s.v. "Auzon, das Bilder- und Runenkästchen," by K. Hauck, W. Krause, and H. Beck, with plates 41–45; Leslie Webster and Michelle P. Brown, *The Transformation of the Roman World AD 400–900* (London, 1997), 239 and plate 235; Richard Abels, "What Has Weland to Do with Christ? The Franks Casket and the Acculturation of Christianity in Early Anglo-Saxon England," *Speculum* 84 (2009).
5. *Völundarkviða* 6 and 21, ed. and trans. Ursula Dronke, *The Poetic Edda* (Oxford, 1969–), 1.245 and 249.
6. *Beowulf*, line 406, ed. Fulk, Bjork, and Niles, 16; trans. Liuzza, 65. I use the felicitous translation in Burton Raffel, *Beowulf* (New York, 2008), 20.
7. *Beowulf*, lines 452–455, ed. Fulk, Bjork, and Niles, 17; trans. Liuzza, 67.
8. *Þiðreks saga af Bern* 130, ed. Henrik Bertelsen, Samfund til udgivelse af gammel nordisk litteratur, Skrifter 34 (Copenhagen, 1905–11), 125–126; RGA 30.466–471, s.v. "Þiðreks saga af Bern," by S. Kramarz-Bein.
9. Lønborg, *Vikingetidens metalbearbejdning*.
10. *Beowulf*, line 1038, ed. Fulk, Bjork, and Niles, 37; trans. Liuzza, 85.
11. *Beowulf*, lines 2192–2193, ed. Fulk, Bjork, and Niles, 74; trans. Liuzza, 120. Most translations are inexact about the sword. I thank Professor Fred C. Robinson for advice on the meaning of these lines.
12. Þorbjörn hornklofi, *Haraldskvæði (Hrafnsmál)*19, ed. Finnur, *Skjaldedigtning*, B:1, 24–25.
13. Sighvatr, *Erfidrápa Óláfs helga* 27, ed. Finnur, *Skjaldedigtning*, B:1, 245.
14. KLNM 17.511–542, s.v. "Sverd," by Aslak Liestøl, Signe Horn Nordhagen, Rikke Agnete Olsen, Olle Cederlöf, and Lena Thålin; RGA 27.593–597, s.v. "Schwert, § 7. Karolinger- und Wikingerzeit," by A. Pedersen; RGA 31.393–404, s.v. "Ulfberht-Schwerter."
15. RGA 29.164, s.v. "Snartemo," by F.-A. Stylegar; Cato Guhnfeldt, "Nazijakt på et skjult sverd," *Aftenposten*, 12 April 2003.
16. Märta Strömberg, *Untersuchungen zur jüngeren Eisenzeit in Schonen: Völkerwanderungszeit, Wikingerzeit* (Bonn, 1961), 1.138, 2.166–167, and plate 165; Fedir Androschchuk, "The Hvoshcheva Sword: An Example of Contacts between Britain and Scandinavia in the Late Viking Period," *Fornvännen* 98 (2003).
17. KLNM 16.290 and 297, s.v. "Smykker: Sverige: Vikingatid," by Mårten Stenberger, and s.v. "Smykker: Danmark: Vikingatid," by Elisabeth Munksgaard.

18. Statens historiska museum, Stockholm, Huvudkatalog, inv. no. 33759, http://catview. historiska.se/catview/index.jsp; RGA, 29.366–367, s.v. "Spillings," by M. Östergren; Ström, "Världens största vikingatida silverskatt."

19. Statens historiska museum, Stockholm, inv. no. SHM 5671, catalogue entry and photographs accessible at http://mis.historiska.se.

20. Roesdahl, The Vikings, 169.

21. The following overview is based on KLNM 3.406–411, s.v. "Dyreornamentikk," by Ole Henrik Moe; Ole Klindt-Jensen and David M. Wilson, Viking art, 2d ed., Nordic Series 6 (Minneapolis, 1980); James Graham-Campbell, Viking Artefacts: Select Catalogue (London, 1980); LMA 9.106–110, s.v. "Wikingerkunst," by D. M. Wilson; David M. Wilson, Vikingatidens konst, trans. Henrika Ringbom, Signums svenska konsthistoria (Lund, 1995); Roesdahl, The Vikings, 168–177; and Birkebæk, Vikingetiden i Danmark, 182–186; RGA 34.64–72, s.v. "Wikinger, § 3. Kunst," by D. M. Wilson.

22. A. W. Brøgger et al., Osebergfundet (Kristiania, 1917); KLNM 13.38–42, s.v. "Osebergstil," by Thorleif Sjøvold.

23. KLNM 2.170–172, s.v. "Borrestilen," by Wenche Slomann.

24. KLNM 7.570–571, s.v. "Jellingstilen," by Thorkild Ramskou.

25. RGA 19.197–205, s.v. "Mammen und Mammenstil," by E. Nyman and I. Skibsted Klæsø.

26. Roesdahl, The Vikings, 175.

27. KLNM 14.327–329, s.v. "Ringerikstil," by Signe Horn Nordhagen.

28. KLNM 19.358–360, s.v. "Urnesstillen," by David Wilson.

29. See the map of Frankish silver and gold objects found in Scandinavia in Wamers and Brandt, Macht des Silbers, 114.

30. Wamers and Brandt, Macht des Silbers, 142.

31. Greta Arwidsson and Gösta Berg, The Mästermyr Find: A Viking Age Tool Chest from Gotland (Stockholm, 1983); Birkebæk, Vikingetiden i Danmark, 168–169; RGA 19. 118–119, s.v. "Mästermyr," by L. Thunmark-Nylén.

32. Franklin and Shepard, Emergence of Rus, 13.

33. Wilhelm Holmqvist, Excavations at Helgö, 13 vols. (Stockholm, 1961–1997); Agneta Lundström, ed., Thirteen studies on Helgö (Stockholm, 1988); RGA 14.286–291, s.v. "Helgö," by K. Lamm.

34. Åke Hyenstrand, Järn och bebyggelse: Studier i Dalarnas äldre kolonisationshistoria, Dalarnas hembygdsbok, 1974 (Falun, 1974).

35. Stig Jensen, "Det ældste Ribe—og vikingetidens begyndelse," in Femte tværfaglige vikingesymposium Aarhus Universitet 1986, ed. Torben Kisbye and Else Roesdahl (Højbjerg, Denmark, 1986); Claus Feveile, "The Latest News from Viking Age Ribe: Archaeological Excavations 1993," in Developments, ed. Björn Ambrosiani and Helen Clarke (Stockholm, 1993); Claus Feveile, Ribe studier, Jysk Arkæologisk Selskabs skrifter, 51 (Højbjerg, 2006); RGA 24.549–556, s.v. "Ribe," by Claus Feveile, Eva Nyman, and Marie Stoklund.

Chapter 6 The Lure of the Exotic

1. Sjøvold, "Vikingeskipene i Oslo," 53. KLNM 13.612–616, s.v. "Påfågel," by John Bernström; LMA 6.2026–2027, s.v. "Pfau," by Ch. Hünemörder and J. Engemann. See also ch. 3.

2. Wamers and Brandt, *Macht des Silbers*.

3. Grierson, "Commerce in the Dark Ages," is the classic statement.

4. Sighvatr, Lausavísa 10, ed. Finnur, *Skjaldedigtning*, B.1, 248. Translation adapted from Russell Poole, "Claiming Kin Skaldic Style," in *Verbal Encounters: Anglo-Saxon and Old Norse Studies for Roberta Frank*, ed. Russell Poole and Antonina Harbus, Toronto Old English Series 13 (Toronto, 2005), 273. About the meter, see Frank, *Old Norse Court Poetry*. About Sighvatr, see KLNM 15.231–238, s.v. "Sighvatr Þórðarson," by Hallvard Lie; Pulsiano and Wolf, eds., *Medieval Scandinavia*, 580–581, s.v. "Sighvatr Þórðarson," by Russell Poole.

5. Sighvatr, *Bersöglisvisur* 17, ed. Finnur, *Skjaldedigtning*, B:1, 238; ed. Gade, *Poetry from the Kings' Sagas*, 2.29.

6. Karl Bertsch and Franz Bertsch, *Geschichte unserer Kulturpflanzen*, 2d ed. (Stuttgart, 1949), 119–122; KLNM 4.664, s.v. "Frugt," by Johan Lange; Jonathan D. Sauer, *Historical Geography of Crop Plants: A Select Roster* (Boca Raton, Fla., 1993), 90–92; RGA 33.150–155, s.v. "Walnuß," by W. Heizemann and J. Wiethold.

7. James E. McKeithen, "The Risalah of Ibn Fadlan: An Annotated Translation with Introduction" (PhD diss., Indiana University, 1979), 64 and 69; Richard N. Frye, *Ibn Fadlan's Journey to Russia: A Tenth-Century Traveler from Baghad to the Volga River* (Princeton, 2005), 37 and 40.

8. Jens Holmboe, "Nytteplanter og ugræs i Osebergfundet," in *Osebergfundet*, ed. A. W. Brøgger and Haakon Shetelig (Oslo, 1927), 5.16–17.

9. Hakon Hjelmqvist, "Frön och frukter från det äldsta Lund," in *Thulegrävningen 1961*, ed. Ragnar Blomqvist and Anders W. Mårtensson, Archaeologica Lundensia: Investigationes de antiqvitatibus urbis Lundae 2 (Lund, 1963), 249–251.

10. Karl-Ernst Behre and Hans Reichstein, *Untersuchungen des botanischen Materials der frühmittelalterlichen Siedlung Haithabu. (Ausgrabung 1963–1964)*, Berichte über die Ausgrabungen in Haithabu, Bericht 2 (Neumünster, 1969), 31.

11. Agnes Geijer, *Die Textilfunde aus den Gräbern*, Birka: Untersuchungen und Studien 3 (Stockholm, 1938); KLNM 15.174–180, s.v. "Siden," by Agnes Geijer; Inga Hägg, "Birkas orientaliska praktplagg," *Fornvännen* 78 (1983); Annika Larsson, "Vikingar begravda i kinesiskt siden," *Valör* (2008).

12. Inga Hägg, Gertrud Grenander Nyberg, and Helmut Schweppe, *Die Textilfunde aus dem Hafen von Haithabu*, Berichte über die Ausgrabungen in Haithabu 20 (Neumünster, 1984); Inga Hägg, *Die Textilfunde aus der Siedlung und aus den Gräbern von Haithabu: Beschreibung und Gliederung*, Berichte über die Ausgrabungen in Haithabu 29 (Neumünster, 1991); Else Østergård, "Textilfragmenterne fra Mammengraven," in *Mammen: Grav, kunst og samfund i vikingetid*, Jysk Arkæologisk Selskabs skrifter 28 (Viborg, 1991); Pirko-Liisa Lehtosalo-Hilander, "Le Viking finnois," *Finskt museum* (1990): 57.

13. Einarr Helgason skálaglamm, *Vellekla* 13, ed. Finnur, *Skjaldedigtning*, B:1, 119.
14. KLNM 9.288–289, s.v. "Kristall," by Holger Arbman.
15. Graham-Campbell, *Viking Artefacts*, 46 and 226, n. 157.
16. KLNM 9.288–289.
17. *Rígsþula* 32, ed. and trans. Dronke, *The Poetic Edda*, 2.169. Cf. Somerville and McDonald, *Viking Age*, 24. The date of Rígsþula is much debated.
18. Rimbert, *Vita Anskari* 20, ed. Waitz, 44; trans. Robinson, 71.
19. KLNM 20.120–123, s.v. "Vinhandel: Sverige," by Hugo Yrwing.
20. Heiko Steuer, "Der Handel der Wikingerzeit zwischen Nord- und Westeuropa aufgrund archäologischer Zeugnisse," in *Der Handel der Karolinger- und Wikingerzeit: Bericht über die Kolloquien der Kommission für die Altertums-kunde Mittel-und Nordeuropas in den Jahren 1980 bis 1983*, ed. Klaus Düwel, Untersuchungen zu Handel und Verkehr der vor- und frühgeschichtlichen Zeit in Mittel-und Nordeuropa 4 = Abhandlungen der Akademie der Wissenschaften in Göttingen: Philologisch-historische Klasse, 3. Folge, 156 (Göttingen, 1987), 131–134.
21. Göran Burenhult, *Arkeologi i Norden* (Stockholm, 1999), 2.178–181.
22. *Annales Bertiniani*, s.a. 864, 866, and 869, ed. Waitz, 67, 81, and 107; trans. Nelson, 112, 130, and 164.
23. Coupland, "From Poachers to Game-Keepers," 111; Angenendt, *Kaiserherrschaft und Königstaufe*, 260–262.
24. *Anglo-Saxon Chronicle*, s.a. 1012, ms E, ed. Irvine, 69; trans. Swanton, 142.
25. C. J. Lamm, *Oriental Glass of Mediaeval Date Found in Sweden and the Early History of Lustre-Painting* (Stockholm, 1941); KLNM 5.342–349, s.v. "Glas," by Holger Arbman and Nils Cleve.
26. KLNM 8.382, s.v. "Keramik," by Carl-Olof Cederlund; RGA 30.296–300, s.v. "Tatinger Keramik," by Ch. Ruhmann.
27. *Beowulf*, lines 612–615 and 1160–1163, ed. Fulk, Bjork, and Niles, 23–24 and 44; trans. Liuzza, 72 and 89.

Chapter 7 Networks of Trade

1. Heiko Steuer, "Eine dreieckige Bronzeschale aus Haithabu bei Schleswig," *Archäologisches Korrespondenzblatt* 3 (1975). Steuer quotes the interpretation of Professor János Harmatta of the Hungarian Academy of Sciences: "Erwäge [einen] Rat: Trinke—heiß liebe! Befolge!"
2. P. H. Sawyer, "Kings and Merchants," in *Early Medieval Kingship*, ed. P. H. Sawyer and I. N. Wood (Leeds, 1977); Ross Samson, "Fighting with Silver: Rethinking Trading, Raiding, and Hoarding," in *Social Approaches to Viking Studies*, ed. Ross Samson (Glasgow, 1991).
3. Sture Bolin, "Muhammed, Karl den store, och Rurik," *Scandia* 12 (1939); Sture Bolin, "Mohammed, Charlemagne and Rurik," *Scandinavian Economic History Review* 1 (1953); Richard Hodges and David Whitehouse, *Mohammed, Charlemagne, and the Origins of Europe: Archaeology and the Pirenne Thesis* (London, 1983); Michael McCormick, *Origins of the European Economy: Communications and Commerce*

A.D. 300–900 (Cambridge, 2001), coined the felicitous phrase "The northern arc of commerce."

4. Thomas S. Noonan, "The Vikings in the East: Coins and Commerce," in *Developments Around the Baltic and the North Sea in the Viking Age*, ed. Björn Ambrosiani and Helen Clarke, Birka Studies 3 (Stockholm, 1994).

5. Roman K. Kovalev and Alexis C. Kaelin, "Circulation of Arab Silver in Medieval Afro-Eurasia: Preliminary Observations," *History Compass* 5, no. 2 (2007), http://www.blackwell-synergy.com/doi/abs/10.1111/j.1478–0542.2006.00376.x.

6. See, e.g., the maps in RGA 13.497–593, s.v. "Handel," by Heinrich Beck, Brigitte Bulitta, Klaus Düwel, Heiko Steuer, and David M. Wilson; and in Helen Clarke and Björn Ambrosiani, *Towns in the Viking Age* (Leicester, 1991).

7. Lund et al., *Two Voyagers*, 309.

8. Charlotte Blindheim and Roar L. Tollnes, *Kaupang, vikingenes handelsplass* (Oslo, 1972); KLNM 6.133–138, s.v. "Handelsplasser, Norge," by Charlotte Blindheim. RGA 16.338–344, s.v. "Kaupang," by Th. Andersson and D. Skre.

9. Dietrich Hoffmann, *Hollingstedt: Untersuchungen zum Nordseehafen von Haithabu/Schleswig*, Berichte über die Ausgrabungen in Haithabu 25 (Neumünster, 1987), reports on the failure to find any traces of a Viking Age harbor at Hollingstedt, on the Treene River, which flows into the North Sea. Earlier generations had guessed that this was the site of Hedeby's harbor on the North Sea.

10. German translation in Georg Jacob, *Arabische Berichte von Gesandten an germanische Fürstenhöfe aus dem 9. und 10. Jahrhundert ins Deutsche übertragen und mit Fussnoten versehen* (Berlin, 1927), 29; French translation in André Miquel, "L'Europe occidentale dans la relation arabe d'Ibrâhîm b. Ya'qûb (Xᵉ s.)," *Annales Économies, Sociétés, Civilisations* 21 (1966): 1062; Norwegian translation in Harris Birkeland, *Nordens historie i middelalderen etter arabiske kilder*, vol. 1954:2, Skrifter utgitt av Det Norske Videnskaps-Akademi i Oslo, II. Hist.-Filos. Klasse (Oslo, 1954), 103–104. About al-Tartushi, see *The Encyclopaedia of Islam*, new ed. (Leiden, 1954–2002), 3:991, s.v. "Ibrāhīm b. Ya'ḳūb," by A. Miquel; and *Lexikon des Mittelalters* 5 (Zürich, 1991), 321–322.

11. The last dendrochronologically secured date from Hedeby is 1020, and a coin from 1042 was found in a grave.

12. Behre and Reichstein, *Untersuchungen des botanischen Materials*, 31. Fragments of six walnut shells were discovered during excavations in 1963–64, but at least two other fragments had been previously found.

13. Accounts for the excavations in Hedeby are found in the series Berichte über die Ausgrabungen in Haithabu (Neumünster, 1969–). They are summarized, e.g., in Herbert Jankuhn, *Haithabu: Ein Handelsplatz der Wikingerzeit*, 3d ed. (Neumünster, 1956), and in RGA 13.361–387, s.v. "Haiðabu," by Wolfgang Laur, Christian Radtke, Marie Stoklund, and Ralf Weichmann.

14. The existence of the trade route is vouched for by Rimbert, *Vita Anskari*, 10, ed. Waitz, 31–32; trans. Robinson, 47.

15. Adam of Bremen calls Mälaren a bay; see Adam, *Gesta* 1.60, ed. Schmeidler, 58; trans. Tschan, 51. During the last one thousand years, the land in eastern Sweden has risen about five meters.

16. Adam, *Gesta*, scholion 142, ed. Schmeidler, 262; trans. Tschan, 210.

17. Björn Ambrosiani, "What Is Birka?" in *Investigations in the Black Earth*, ed. Björn Ambrosiani and Helen Clarke, Birka Studies: Birka Project (1992).

18. Ola Kyhlberg, "Vågar och viktlod: Diskussion kring frågor om precision och nog-grannhet," *Fornvännen* 70 (1975); Ola Kyhlberg, *Vikt och värde: Arkeologiska studier i värdemätning, betalningsmedel och metrologi under yngre järnålder: 1. Helgö, 2. Birka*, Stockholm Studies in Archaeology 1 (Stockholm, 1980); Steuer, "Handel der Wikingerzeit"; Ingrid Gustin, "Means of Payment and the Use of Coins in the Viking Age Town of Birka in Sweden: Preliminary Results," *Current Swedish Archaeology* 6 (1998).

19. Peter Johanek, "Der fränkische Handel der Karolingerzeit im Spiegel der Schrift-quellen," in *Handel der Karolinger- und Wikingerzeit*, ed. Düwel, 310.

20. *Annales Bertiniani*, s.a. 873, ed. Waitz, 124; trans. Nelson, 185.

21. Michael McCormick, "New Light on the 'Dark Ages': How the Slave Trade Fuelled the Carolingian Economy," *Past and Present* (2002).

22. About trade between the Frankish Empire and England, see Johanek, "Der frän-kische Handel der Karolingerzeit"; Simon Coupland, "Trading Places: Quentovic and Dorestad Reassessed," *Early Medieval Europe* 11 (2002).

23. Steuer, "Handel der Wikingerzeit," 119, 122, and 142–146; Volkmar Schön, *Die Mühlsteine von Haithabu und Schleswig: Ein Beitrag zur Entwicklungsgeschichte des mittelalterlichen Mühlenwesens in Nordwesteuropa*, Berichte über die Ausgrabungen in Haithabu 31 (Neumünster, 1995).

24. Steuer, "Handel der Wikingerzeit."

25. Rimbert, *Vita Anskarii* 20, ed. Waitz, 44–46.

26. Kovalev and Kaelin, "Circulation of Arab Silver." See, in general on trade in eastern Europe, Ingmar Jansson, "Communications between Scandinavia and Eastern Europe in the Viking Age," in *Handel der Karolinger- und Wikingerzeit*, ed. Düwel.

27. "Sembi": the inhabitants of Samland, which is an area in Prussia, northwest of modern Kaliningrad.

28. Lund et al., *Two Voyagers*.

29. Marek F. Jagodziński and Maria Kasprzycka, "The Early Medieval Craft and Com-mercial Center at Janów Pomorski near Elblag on the South Baltic Coast," *Antiquity* 65 (1991); Marek F. Jagodziński, "Truso—Siedlung und Hafen im slawisch-estnischen Grenzgebiet," in *Europas Mitte um 1000: Handbuch zur Ausstellung*, ed. Alfred Wieczorek and Hans-Martin Hinz (Stuttgart, 2000).

30. Rune Edberg, "Vikingar mot strömmen: Några synpunkter på möjliga och omöjliga skepp vid färder i hemmavatten och i österled," *Fornvännen* 91 (1996).

31. Cross and Sherbowitz-Wetzor, *Russian Primary Chronicle*, 53.

32. KLNM 12.310–318, s.v. "Niveauforandring," by Niels Kingo Jacobsen, Lars Erik Åse, Aslak Liestøl, and Jón Jónsson.

33. RGA 1.220–225, s.v. "Alt-Ladoga," by H. Arbman, W. Krause, H. Kuhn, and K. Zernack; Thomas S. Noonan, "Why the Vikings First Came to Russia," *Jahrbücher für Geschichte Osteuropas* 34 (1986): 330–340, repr. in Thomas S. Noonan, *The Islamic World, Russia and the Vikings, 750–900: The Numismatic Evidence* (Aldershot, U.K., 1998), no. I; Eduard Mühle, "Review of Srednevekovaia Ladoga," *Jahrbücher für Ge-*

schichte Osteuropas 35 (1987); Anatol N. Kirpičnikov, "Staraja Ladoga/Alt-Ladoga und seine überregionalen Beziehungen im 8.–10. Jahrhundert: Anmerkungen zur Verbreitung von Dirhems im eurasischen Handel," *Bericht der römisch-germanischen Kommission* 69 (1988), 307–337; Eduard Mühle, *Die städtischen Handelszentren der nordwestlichen Rus: Anfänge und frühe Entwicklung altrussischer Städte (bis gegen Ende des 12. Jahrhunderts)*, Quellen und Studien zur Geschichte des östlichen Europa 32 (Stuttgart, 1991), 19–73; Clarke and Ambrosiani, *Towns in the Viking Age*, 119–121; Franklin and Shepard, *Emergence of Rus*, 12–21; RGA 29.519–522, s.v. "Staraja Ladoga," by S. Brather and K. Düwel.

34. Eyvindr dáðaskald, *Bandadrápa* 7, ed. Finnur, *Skjaldedigtning*, B:1, 191–192.
35. Vladimir L. Janin, "Das frühe Novgorod," Bericht der römisch-germanischen Kommission 69 (1988), 338–343; Clarke and Ambrosiani, *Towns in the Viking Age*, 121–122; and Franklin and Shepard, *Emergence of Rus*, 33–36.
36. Cross and Sherbowitz-Wetzor, *Russian Primary Chronicle*, 53.
37. Erik Nylén, *Vikingaskepp mot Miklagård: Krampmacken i Österled* (Stockholm, 1987).
38. Ole Crumlin-Pedersen, "Vikingernes 'søvej' til Byzans—om betingelser for sejlads ad flodvejene fra Østersø till Sortehav," in *Beretning fra Ottonde tværfaglige vikingesymposium*, ed. Torben Kisbye and Else Roesdahl (Højbjerg, 1989); Edberg, "Vikingar mot strömmen"; Rune Edberg, "Med Aifur till Aifur: Slutrapport från en experimentell österledsfärd," *Fornvännen* 94 (1999).
39. Robert J. Kerner, *The Urge to the Sea: The Course of Russian History: The Role of Rivers, Portages, Ostrogs, Monasteries, and Furs* (Berkeley, 1942), esp. pp. 15 and 107–151; Hildegard Adam, *Das Zollwesen im fränkischen Reich und das spätkarolingische Wirtschaftsleben: Ein Überblick über Zoll, Handel und Verkehr im 9. Jahrhundert*, Vierteljahrschrift für Sozial- und Wirtschaftsgeschichte, Beihefte 126 (Stuttgart, 1996), 92; Detlev Ellmers, "Die Archäologie der Binnenschiffahrt in Europa nördlich der Alpen," in *Der Verkehr, Verkehrswege, Verkehrsmittel, Organisation*, ed. Else Ebel, Herbert Jankuhn, and Wolfgang Kimmig, Untersuchungen zur Handel und Verkehr der vor- und frühgeschichtlichen Zeit in Mittel- und Nordeuropa 5 = Abhandlungen der Akademie der Wissenschaften in Göttingen: Philologisch-historische Klasse, 3d series, 180 (Göttingen, 1989), 324. Place names often reflect the presence of portages, cf., e.g., Jürgen Udolph, " 'Handel' und 'Verkehr' in slavischen Ortsnamen," in *Handel der Karolinger- und Wikingerzeit*, ed. Düwel, esp. 599–606, where the author charts place names deriving from "volok," the Slavic word for portage. Such place names are concentrated at the water divides between the various Russian river systems (cf. the maps on pp. 602 and 604). See also Christiansen, *Norsemen in the Viking Age*, 178.
40. The timber seems now to be lost, but local inhabitants remembered that the herring-bone-pattern revetment of a portage trench was still visible in the 1920s; see Björn Ambrosiani, "Birka: Its Waterways and Hinterland," in *Aspects of Maritime Scandinavia AD 200–1200: Proceedings of the Nordic Seminar on Maritime Aspects of Archaeology, Roskilde, 13th–15th March, 1989*, ed. Ole Crumlin-Pedersen (Roskilde, 1991), 102.
41. Constantine Porphyrogenitus, *De administrando imperio*, ed. Gy. Moravcsik and trans. R. J. H. Jenkins (Budapest, 1949), 50–51.

42. Franklin and Shepard, *Emergence of Rus*, 101.

43. Franklin and Shepard, *Emergence of Rus*, 127.

44. Adam, *Gesta* 2.22, ed. Schmeidler, 80; trans. Tschan, 67.

45. Constantine, *De administrando imperio*, 50–51.

46. RGA, s.v. "Dnjepr," by Heinrich Beck, Carsten Goehrke, Helmut Jäger, Renate Rolle, and Wolfgang P. Schmid.

47. G 280; "Samnordisk runtextdatabas"; Helmer Gustavson, *Gamla och nya runor: Artiklar 1982–2001*, Runica et mediaevalia: Opuscula, 9 (Stockholm, 2003): 9–36.

48. T. J. Arne, "Den svenska runstenen från ön Berezanj utanför Dnjeprmynningen: Referat efter prof. F. Brauns redogörelse i Ryska arkeol. kommissionens meddelanden 1907," *Fornvännen* 9 (1914); Jansson, *Runinskrifter i Sverige*, 65.

49. Cross and Sherbowitz-Wetzor, *Russian Primary Chronicle*, 53.

50. About Bulghar: Janet Martin, *Treasure of the Land of Darkness: The Fur Trade and Its Significance for Medieval Russia* (Cambridge, 1986), 5–14; Peter B. Golden, "The Peoples of the Russian Forest Belt," in *The Cambridge History of Early Inner Asia*, ed. Denis Sinor (Cambridge, 1990), 238–239; V. L. Ianin, *Otechestvennaia istoriia: istoriia Roccii c drevneyshikh vremen do 1917 goda* (Moscow, 1994), 306, s.v. "Bulgar," by M. D. Poluboiarinova; Franklin and Shepard, *Emergence of Rus*, 61–65; Thomas S. Noonan, "European Russia, c. 500–c. 1050," in *The New Cambridge Medieval History*, vol. 3, *c. 900–c. 1024*, ed. Timothy Reuter (Cambridge, 1999); *Encyclopaedia of Islam* 1. 1304–1308, s.v. "Bulghar," by I. Hrbek.

51. Ahmed Zeki Velidi Togan, *Ibn Fadlan's Reisebericht*, Abhandlungen für die Kunde des Morgenlandes, 24.3 (Leipzig, 1939), reprinted as Ahmed Zeki Velidi Togan, *Ibn Fadlan's Reisebericht*, Islamic Geography 168 (Frankfurt am Main, 1994); trans. McKeithen, "The Risalah of Ibn Fadlan"; Frye, *Ibn Fadlan's Journey to Russia*. The section on the Rus has been translated separately many times, e.g., in James E. Montgomery, "Ibn Fadlan and the Russiyah," *Journal of Arabic and Islamic Studies* 3 (2000).

52. Martin, *Treasure of the Land of Darkness*.

53. Franklin and Shepard, *Emergence of Rus*, 28–29.

54. For example: Sö 131, Sö 279, Sö 281, ed. Brate and Wessén, *Södermanlands runinskrifter*, 98–99, 243–244, and 246–247; U 785, ed. Wessén and Jansson, *Upplands runinskrifter* 3.368–369. See also "Samnordisk runtextdatabas"; Sven B. F. Jansson, "Några okända uppländska runinskrifter," *Fornvännen* 41 (1946), and Jansson, *Runinskrifter i Sverige*, 68–69.

55. Vs 1, ed. Sven B. F. Jansson, *Västmanlands runinskrifter*, Sveriges runinskrifter 13 (Stockholm, 1964), 6–9; "Samnordisk runtextdatabas"; Helmer Gustavson, "Runmonumentet i Rytterne," in *Nya anteckningar om Rytterns socken: Medeltidsstudier tillägnade Göran Dahlbäck*, ed. Olle Ferm, Agneta Paulsson, and Krister Ström, Västmanlands läns museum: Västmanlands fornminnesförening, Årsbok 78 (2002).

56. Sö 179, ed. Brate and Wessén, *Södermanlands runinskrifter*, 153–156; Jansson, *Runinskrifter i Sverige*, 69–71.

57. Kovalev and Kaelin, "Circulation of Arab Silver."

58. Thomas S. Noonan, "The Impact of the Silver Crisis in Islam upon Novgorod's Trade with the Baltic," *Bericht der römisch-germanischen Kommission* 69 (1988): 423–424; Noonan, "Vikings in the East," 233.

59. Noonan, "Why the Vikings First Came to Russia."

60. McCormick, *Origins of the European Economy*, 610 and 762; RGA 29.14–16, s.v. "Sklave," by G. Horsmann.

61. *Annales regni Francorum*, s.a. 808, ed. Kurze, 195; trans. Scholz and Rogers, 88.

62. Else Roesdahl, "Dendrochronology in Denmark, with a Note on the Beginning of the Viking Age," in *Developments around the Baltic and the North Sea in the Viking Age*, ed. Björn Ambrosiani and Helen Clarke (Stockholm, 1994), 107.

63. Feveile, *Ribe studier*, 25–28.

64. Władysław Filipowiak, "Handel und Handelsplätze an der Ostseeküste Westpommerns," *Bericht der römisch-germanischen Kommission* 69 (1988): 694–699; Clarke and Ambrosiani, *Towns in the Viking Age*, 112–115; Władysław Filipowiak, "Wollin—ein frühmittelalterliche Zentrum an der Ostsee," in *Europas Mitte um 1000*, ed. Alfried Wieczorek and Hans-Martin Hinz (Stuttgart, 2000).

Chapter 8 The Story of Conversion

1. Arne Odd Johnsen, *Studier vedrørende kardinal Nicolaus Brekespears legasjon til Norden* (Oslo, 1945).

2. Ekenberg et al., *Boken om Ansgar*; Bertil Nilsson, *Missionstid och tidig medeltid*, Sveriges kyrkohistoria 1 (Stockholm, 1998); Eric Knibbs, "The Origins of the Archdiocese of Hamburg-Bremen" (PhD diss., Yale University, 2009).

3. Rimbert, *Vita Anskari* 17 and 33, ed. Waitz, 38 and 64; trans. Robinson, 59 and 104. The names of the martyrs were Nithard and Ragenbert.

4. Much scholarship has in recent years been devoted to conversion in Scandinavia, e.g., Birgit Sawyer and Peter Sawyer, eds., *The Christianization of Scandinavia: Report of a Symposium Held at Kungälv, Sweden 4–9 August 1985* (Alingsås, Sweden, 1987); Bertil Nilsson, ed., *Kristnandet i Sverige: Gamla källor och nya perspektiv*, Publikationer Projektet Sveriges kristnande, 5 (Uppsala, 1996); R. A. Fletcher, *The Conversion of Europe: From Paganism to Christianity 371–1386 AD* (London, 1997); Nilsson, *Missionstid och tidig medeltid*; Dagfinn Skree, "Missionary Activity in Early Medieval Norway: Strategy, Organization, and the Course of Events," *Scandinavian History Review* 23 (1998); Thomas A. DuBois, *Nordic Religions in the Viking Age* (Philadelphia, 1999); Orri Vésteinsson, *The Christianization of Iceland: Priests, Power, and Social Change, 1000–1300* (Oxford, 2000); Guyda Armstrong and I. N. Wood, *Christianizing Peoples and Converting Individuals*, International Medieval Research (Turnhout, 2000); Jón Viðar Sigurðsson, *Kristninga i Norden 750–1200*, Utsyn & innsikt (Oslo, 2003); Alexandra Sanmark, *Power and Conversion: A Comparative Study of Christianization in Scandinavia*, Occasional Papers in Archaeology 34 (Uppsala, 2004); Niels Lund, *Kristendommen i Danmark før 1050: Et symposium i Roskilde den 5.–7. februar 2003* ([Roskilde], 2004); Lutz von Padberg, *Christianisierung im Mittelalter* (Stuttgart, 2006); Nora Berend, *Christianization and the Rise of Christian Monarchy: Scandinavia, Central Europe and Rus' c. 900–1200* (Cambridge, 2007). In addition, almost every general book on Vikings and on Scandinavian history of the early Middle Ages contains sections devoted to conversion.

5. Emile Durkheim, *The Elementary Forms of the Religious Life*, trans. Karen E. Fields (New York, 1995), 44.

6. Tore Nyberg, *Die Kirche in Skandinavien: Mitteleuropäischer und englischer Einfluss im 11. und 12. Jahrhundert: Anfänge der Domkapitel Børglum und Odense in Dänemark*, Beiträge zur Geschichte und Quellenkunde des Mittelalters 10 (Sigmaringen, 1986), 11–78.

7. Thomas Lindkvist, "Ny tro i nya riken: Kristnandet som en del av den politiska historien," in *Kyrka—samhälle—stat: Från kristnande till etablerad kyrka*, ed. Göran Dahlbäck, Historiallinen Arkisto 110:3 (Helsinki, 1997), 55–56; Sverre Bagge, "Ideologies and Mentalities," in *Cambridge History of Scandinavia*, ed. Knut Helle (Cambridge, 2003).

8. The honor of being the first missionary in Scandinavia is usually given to Willibrord of Utrecht, but we have seen above in chapter 1 that there is no reason to take as factual what his relative and biographer Alcuin claimed in this respect many decades later.

9. JE 2553, ed. MGH Epp. 5.68, n. 11.

10. *Annales Xantenses*, s.a. 823, ed. Simson, 6. *Annales regni Francorum*, s.a. 823, ed. Kurze, 163; trans. Scholz and Rogers, 114; Rimbert, *Vita Anskari* 13, ed. Waitz, 35; trans. Robinson, 54; MGH Epp. 6, 163. Ermoldus Nigellus, *In honorem Hludowici christianissimi caesaris augusti*, lines 1882–1993 and 2028–2061, ed. and trans. Edmond Faral, in *Poème sur Louis le Pieux et Épîtres au roi Pépin*, Les classiques de l'histoire de France au moyen âge 14 (Paris, 1932), 144–153 and 154–157; see also Wamers, "Kristne gjenstander i tidligvikingtidens Danmark."

11. Flodoard, *Historia ecclesiae Remensis* 2.20, ed. Stratmann, 184.

12. About Ansgar, see Odilo Engels and Stefan Weinfurter, *Series episcoporum Ecclesiae Catholicae occidentalis ab initio ad annum MCXCVIII* 5.2: *Archiepiscopatus Hammaburgensis sive Bremensis* (Stuttgart, 1984), 12–16; Georg Dehio, *Geschichte der Erzbistums Hamburg-Bremen bis zum Ausgang des Mission* (Berlin, 1877), 1:42–92; Lauritz Weibull, "Ansgarius," *Scandia* 14 (1942), reprinted in Weibull, *Nordisk historia*, 1.175–189; Ekenberg et al., *Boken om Ansgar*; Nilsson, *Missionstid och tidig medeltid*, 42–51. Knibbs, "The Origins of the Archdiocese of Hamburg-Bremen," overturns much of the standard biography of Ansgar. See also Eric Knibbs, *Ansgar, Rimbert and the Forged Foundations of Hamburg-Bremen*, Church, Faith and Culture in the Medieval West (Farnham, U.K., 2011).

13. Rimbert's *Vita Anskari* was edited for the MGH SS rer. Germ. by Georg Waitz in 1884. The English translation by Charles H. Robinson (1921) is outdated. Valuable for interpreting the *Vita Anskari* are the commentaries and accompanying essays in Ekenberg et al., *Boken om Ansgar*. Rimbert's authorship of the *Life* is vouched for only by the anonymous *Vita Rimberti*. See also Ian Wood, *The Missionary Life: Saints and the Evangelisation of Europe, 400–1050* (Harlow, U.K., 2001).

14. *Annales regni Francorum*, s.a. 814 and 819, ed. Kurze, 141 and 152; trans. Scholz and Rogers, 99 and 106.

15. Böhmer, Mühlbacher, and Lechner, *Die Regesten des Kaiserreichs unter den Karolingern, 751–918*, 326; Angenendt, *Kaiserherrschaft und Königstaufe*, 215–223; Wood, "Christians and Pagans in Ninth-Century Scandinavia."

16. Rimbert, *Vita Anskari* 11, ed. Waitz, 32; trans. Robinson, 49.

17. Gauzbert probably was made a bishop earlier than Ansgar; see Knibbs, "The Origins of the Archdiocese of Hamburg-Bremen," 182. Rimbert, *Vita Anskari* 14, ed. Waitz, 26; trans. Robinson, 55–56. Rimbert says Gauzbert was a relative (*propinquus*) of Ebo, while Adam claims more exactly that he was the archbishop's nephew; see Adam, *Gesta* 1.18, ed. Schmeidler, 24; trans. Tschan, 24. About Gauzbert, see Odilo Engels and Stefan Weinfurter, *Series episcoporum Ecclesiae Catholicae occidentalis ab initio ad annum MCXCVIII* 5.1: *Archiepiscopatus Coloniensis* (Stuttgart, 1982), 141–142.

18. Rimbert, *Vita Anskari* 17, ed. Waitz, 38; trans. Robinson, 59.

19. Rimbert, *Vita Anskari* 16, ed. Waitz, 37; trans. Robinson, 57.

20. Rimbert, *Vita Anskari* 24, ed. Waitz, 52–53; trans. Robinson, 84.

21. Rimbert, *Vita Anskari* 28, ed. Waitz, 59; trans. Robinson, 95.

22. Rimbert, *Vita Anskari* 33, ed. Waitz, 64; trans. Robinson, 104.

23. Birkebæk, *Vikingetiden i Danmark*, 155.

24. Rimbert, *Vita Anskari* 32, ed. Waitz, 64; trans. Robinson, 103.

25. Adam, *Gesta* 1.58 and 60, ed. Schmeidler, 57 and 58; trans. Tschan, 50 and 51.

26. Adam, *Gesta* 4.43, ed. Schmeidler, 279–280; trans. Tschan, 222.

27. Edited in Rimbert, *Vita Anskari auctore Rimberto: Accedit Vita Rimberti*, ed. Waitz, 80–100.

28. *Vita Rimberti* 12, ed. Waitz, 91.

29. *Vita Rimberti* 16, ed. Waitz, 94–95.

30. *Vita Rimberti* 11, ed. Waitz, 90.

31. Adam, *Gesta* 1.40 and 46, ed. Schmeidler, 44 and 47; trans. Tschan 40 and 43.

32. Karl Heinz Brandt and Margareta Nockert, *Ausgrabungen im Bremer St.-Petri-Dom 1974–76: Ein Vorbericht*, Bremer archäologische Blätter (Bremen, 1976), 41, and see also fig. 21 on p. 38.

33. Adam, *Gesta* 1.58–62, ed. Schmeidler, 57–60; trans. Tschan, 50–53.

34. Adam, *Gesta* 1.61, ed. Schmeidler, 59; trans. Tschan, 52–53.

35. Peter Sawyer, "The Process of Scandinavian Christianization in the Tenth and Eleventh Centuries," in *The Christianization of Scandinavia*, ed. Sawyer, Sawyer, and Wood, 75; Jan Arvid Hellström, *Vägar till Sveriges kristnande* (Stockholm, 1996), 161–175.

36. Adam, *Gesta* 1.52, ed. Schmeidler, 53; trans. Tschan 47.

37. MGH Concilia 6,1.140 and 158; see also p. 137. Adam, *Gesta*, 2.4, ed. Schmeidler, 64; trans. Tschan, 57. See also Helmuth Kluger et al., *Series episcoporum Ecclesiae Catholicae occidentalis ab initio ad annum MCXCVIII* 6.2: *Archiepiscopatus Lundensis* (Stuttgart, 1992), 40–41, 67, and 100–101.

38. Leaving aside the Danish king Chnuba or Wurm, who after his defeat in 934 by King Henry I of Germany supposedly underwent baptism; see Widukind of Corvey, *Res gestae Saxonicae* 1.40, ed. Hirsch and Lohmann, 59, and *Annales Corbeienses*, s.a. 934, ed. G. H. Pertz, MGH SS 3 (Hanover, 1839), 4. It is possible that Harald was baptized at that time.

39. Knud J. Krogh, *Gåden om Kong Gorms grav: Historien om Nordhøjen i Jelling*, Vikingekongernes monumenter i Jelling 1 (Copenhagen, 1993).

40. Adam, *Gesta*, 2.3, ed. Schmeidler, 63–64; trans. Tschan, 55–57; Lauritz Weibull, *Kritiska undersökningar i Nordens historia omkring år 1000* (Lund, 1911), reprinted in Weibull, *Nordisk historia*, 1.269–274; Sawyer, *Da Danmark blev Danmark*, 237.

41. Widukind, *Res gesta Saxonicae*, 3.65, ed. Hirsch and Lohmann, 140–141; Robert Bartlett, *Trial by Fire and Water: The Medieval Judicial Ordeal* (Oxford, 1986); Angenendt, *Kaiserherrschaft und Königstaufe*, 276–282.

42. DR 42, ed. Moltke and Jacobsen, *Danmarks runeindskrifter*, 1.65–81; "Samnordisk runtextdatabas"; Jansson, *Runinskrifter i Sverige*, 102; Birgit Sawyer, *The Viking-Age Rune-Stones: Custom and Commemoration in Early Medieval Scandinavia* (Oxford, 2000), 159; Anders Winroth, "Christianity Comes to Denmark," in Barbara Rosenwein, *Reading the Middle Ages*, (Peterborough, Ont., 2006); Somerville and McDonald, *Viking Age*, 440.

43. Krogh, *Gåden om Kong Gorms grav.*

44. The following sketch of the Norwegian conversion is mostly based on Erik Gunnes, *Rikssamling og kristning: 800–1177*, Norges historie 2 (Oslo, 1976); Jón Viðar Sigurðsson, *Norsk historie 800–1300*, Samlagets Norsk historie 800–2000 (Oslo, 1999); Claus Krag, *Norges historie fram til 1319* (Oslo, 2000); Knut Helle, ed., *The Cambridge History of Scandinavia* (Cambridge, 2003); and Jón Viðar, *Kristninga i Norden.*

45. Snorri Sturluson, *Heimskringla*, ed. Bjarni Aðalbjarnarson, Íslenzk fornrit, 26–28 (Reykjavik, 1941); Snorri Sturluson, *Heimskringla: History of the Kings of Norway*, trans. Lee M. Hollander (Austin, 1964). Diana Whaley, *Heimskringla: An Introduction*, Viking Society for Northern Research: Text Series 8 (London, 1991). I accept the argument that there is no reason to believe that Snorri was the author of the *Heimskringla*: Tommy Danielsson, *Sagorna om Norges kungar: Från Magnús góði till Magnús Erlingsson* ([Hedemora], 2002), 350–363.

46. Lesley Abrams, "The Anglo-Saxons and the Christianization of Scandinavia," *Anglo-Saxon England* 24 (1995): 217–219.

47. Jón Viðar, *Norsk historie 800–1300*; Krag, *Norges historie fram til 1319*, 59–66; Jón Viðar, *Kristninga i Norden*; Sverre Bagge and Sæbjørg Walaker Nordeide, "The Kingdom of Norway," in *Christianization and the Rise of Christian Monarchy*, ed. Berend; Jón Viðar, *Det norrøne samfunnet.*

48. N 449, ed. Olsen and Liestøl, *Norges innskrifter med de yngre runer*, 4.280–286; Spurkland, *I begynnelsen var fuþark*, 120–124; RGA 17.412–414, s.v. "Kuli," by J. E. Knirk.

49. Torgeir Landro, "Kristenrett og kyrkjerett: Borgartingskristenretten i eit komparativt perspektiv" (PhD diss., University of Bergen (Norway), 2010).

50. Adam, *Gesta* 2.38, ed. Schmeidler, 98–99; trans. Tschan, 80–81.

51. Adam, *Gesta* 2.58, ed. Schmeidler, 118; trans. Tschan, 95.

52. Adam, *Gesta* 3.15, ed. Schmeidler, 156; trans. Tschan, 125–126. Osmund retired to Ely monastery in England, where he was much appreciated for being able to perform episcopal functions for the monastery, which was constantly in conflict with its diocesan bishop in Lincoln; see *Liber Eliensis* 2.99 and 3.50, ed. E. O. Blake, *Liber Eliensis*, Camden Third Series 92 (London, 1962), 168–169 and 293. See also Abrams, "The Anglo-Saxons and the Christianization of Scandinavia," 235–236;

Hellström, *Vägar till Sveriges kristnande*, 149–152; Nilsson, *Missionstid och tidig medeltid*, 58–59.

53. E.g., Gabriel Turville-Petre and Christopher Tolkien, eds., *Hervarar saga ok Heiðreks*, Viking Society for Northern Research: Text Series (London, 1976), 70–71. See also Olof Sundqvist, "Cult Leaders, Rulers and Religion," in *The Viking World*, ed. Brink with Price, 225.

54. Johnsen, *Studier vedrørende kardinal Nicolaus Brekespears legasjon*; *Svenskt biografiskt lexikon* 33 (Stockholm, 2009), 372–376, s.v. "Stephanus," by Anders Winroth.

55. Adam, *Gesta*, 2.27–28, ed. Schmeidler 87–89; trans. Tschan 72–73; Lauritz Weibull, *Historisk-kritisk metod och nordisk medeltidsforskning* (Lund, 1913), reprinted in Weibull, *Nordisk historia*, 1.274–287; Sawyer, *Da Danmark blev Danmark*, 244–245.

56. Wolfgang Seegrün, *Das Papsttum und Skandinavien bis zur Vollendung der nordischen Kirchenorganisation*, Quellen und Forschungen zur Geschichte Schleswig-Holsteins 51 (Neumünster, 1967), 28; Britt Hedberg, *Uppsala stifts herdaminne: Från missionstid till år 1366*, Uppsala stifts herdaminne 4:1 (Uppsala, 2007), 23 and 45.

57. See above, n. 52.

58. Adam, *Gesta* 2.26, ed. Schmeidler, 85; trans. Tschan, 71.

59. See above, n. 37.

60. Sawyer, *Da Danmark blev Danmark*, 241; Forte, Oram, and Pedersen, *Viking Empires*, 358.

61. Adam, *Gesta*, scholion 147, ed. Schmeidler, 268; trans. Tschan, 214

62. Sawyer, *Da Danmark blev Danmark*, 206–297; Kluger et al., *Series episcoporum* 6.2.

63. Lauritz Weibull, "Den skånska kyrkans älsta historia," in *Nordisk historia*, 2.27–33; Seegrün, *Das Papsttum und Skandinavien*; Fenger, *"Kirker reses alle vegne,"* 100–102.

Chapter 9 Writing Conversion

1. Wood, *Missionary Life*, discusses how the authors of early medieval saints' lives inspired each other. About the *Life of Ansgar*, see also Wood, "Christians and Pagans in Ninth-Century Scandinavia."

2. A careful survey of the sources is in Abrams, "The Anglo-Saxons and the Christianization of Scandinavia," 220–223.

3. See Introduction.

4. Cleasby, Vigfússon, and Craigie, *An Icelandic-English Dictionary*, 311: "the horg was an altar of stone . . . erected on a high place, or a sacrificial cairn . . . built in open air . . .: hence such phrases as, to 'break' the horg but to 'burn' the temples." See also Olaf Olsen, *Hørg, hov og kirke: Historiske og arkæologiske vikingetidsstudier* (Copenhagen, 1966).

5. Adam, *Gesta* 2.40, ed. Schmeidler, 100–101; trans. Tschan, 82.

6. Adam, *Gesta* 2.37, ed. Schmeidler, 98; trans. Tschan 80. See also Abrams, "The Anglo-Saxons and the Christianization of Scandinavia," 229.

7. For the same reason, Adam condemns Bishop Osmund (consecrated in Poland, active in Sweden); see above, ch. 8, n. 52.

8. Konrad von Maurer, *Die Bekehrung des norwegischen Stammes zum Christenthume in ihrem geschichtlichen Verlaufe quellenmässig geschildert*, 2 vols. (Munich, 1855–56; reprint, Osnabrück, 1965).

9. Theodore M. Andersson, "The Conversion of Norway according to Oddr Snorrason and Snorri Sturluson," *Mediaeval Scandinavia* 10 (1976); Whaley, *Heimskringla: An Introduction*, 112–143.

10. Oddr, *The Saga of Olaf Tryggvason*. Oddr wrote the text in Latin, but it survives only in an Old Norse translation.

11. Theodoricus is edited in Gustav Storm, *Monumenta historica Norvegiae: Latinske kildeskrifter til Norges historie i middelalderen*, Skrifter utg. for Kjeldeskriftfondet (Kristiania, 1880; reprint, Oslo, 1973), 1–68, translation in Theodoricus, *Historia de antiquitate regum Norwagiensium: An Account of the Ancient History of the Norwegian Kings*, trans. David McDougall and Ian McDougall, Viking Society for Northern Research: Text Series 11 (London, 1998). The *Historia Norwegie* is edited and translated in Inger Ekrem, Peter Fischer, and Lars Boje Mortensen, *Historia Norwegie* (Copenhagen, 2003). *Ágrip* is edited in Bjarni Einarsson, *Ágrip af Nóreg-skonunga sǫgum: Fagrskinna = Nóregs konunga tal*, Íslenzk fornrit 29 (Reykjavik, 1984), and translated in Matthew James Driscoll, *Ágrip af Nóregskonungasǫgum: A Twelfth-Century Synoptic History of the Kings of Norway* (London, 1995). The sections in these works that treat Olav Tryggvason are helpfully translated in the appendix of Oddr, *The Saga of Olaf Tryggvason*, 151–165.

12. See, most recently, Danielsson, *Sagorna om Norges kungar*, and Theodore M. Andersson, *The Growth of the Medieval Icelandic Sagas (1180–1280)* (Ithaca, N.Y., 2006).

13. Jakob, ed., *Íslendingabók*; translation in Grønlie, *Íslendingabók*.

14. Mortensen in Ekrem, Fischer, and Mortensen, eds. and trans., *Historia Norwegie*, 207.

15. Lars Lönnroth, "Studier i Olaf Tryggvasons saga," *Samlaren* 84 (1963); Ekrem, Fischer, and Mortensen, eds. and trans., *Historia Norwegie*, 207.

16. Oddr, *Óláfs saga Tryggvasonar* 44/54, ed. Ólafur, 271–272; trans. Andersson, 102. Theodoricus, *Historia* 13, ed. Storm, 22; trans. McDougall, 17.

17. William of Jumièges, *Gesta Normannorum ducum*, 5.12, ed. and trans. Elisabeth M. C. Van Houts, *The "Gesta Normannorum ducum" of William of Jumièges, Orderic Vitalis, and Robert of Torigni*, Oxford Medieval Texts (Oxford, 1992–1995), 2.26. See also 1.li. Scandinavian writers knew about his baptism in Rouen; see Theodoricus, *Historia* 13, ed. Storm, 22; trans. McDougall, 17; Passio S. Olavi, ed. Storm, *Monumenta historica Norvegiae*, 128; trans. Carl Phelpstead and Devra Levingson Kunin, *A History of Norway, and the Passion and Miracles of Blessed Óláfr* (London, 2001), 27.

18. Oddr, *Óláfs saga Tryggvasonar* 37, ed. Ólafur, 231–232; trans. Andersson, 84.

19. Ekrem, Fischer, and Mortensen, eds. and trans., *Historia Norwegie*, 94–95.

20. Theodoricus, *Historia* 11, ed. Storm, 18; trans. McDougall, 14; I quote the translation of Andersson in Oddr, *Saga of Óláf Tryggvason*, 155.

21. Oddr, *Óláfs saga Tryggvasonar* 46/56, ed. Ólafur, 279–280; trans. Andersson, 105.

22. See, e.g., Adam's account of an English missionary in Sweden chopping up a statue of Tor: Adam, *Gesta* 2.62, ed. Schmeidler, 122; trans. Tschan, 97–98. The account by Saxo Grammaticus about a Danish army chopping up a statue of Svantevit after they had conquered Ancona might report actual events; see Saxo, *Gesta Danorum*

14.39.31–33, ed. Jørgen Olrik and Hans Raeder, eds., *Saxonis Gesta Danorum* (Copenhagen, 1931), 472.

23. Chapter 4, "Kristningskongene ca. 995–1035," in the excellent Krag, *Norges historie fram til 1319*, 56–66, contains four sections: two that are devoted to the Olavs, a section on church organization, and one on the fall of Olav Haraldsson.

24. Rimbert, *Vita Anskari* 24, ed. Waitz, 53; trans. Robinson, 85.

25. Oddr, *Ólafs saga Tryggvasonar* 35, ed. Ólafur, 232; trans. Andersson, 84.

26. Eloquent critique in Brit Solli, "Narratives of Encountering Religions: On the Christianization of the Norse around AD 900–1000," *Norwegian Archaeological Review* 29 (1996).

27. James C. Russell, *The Germanization of Early Medieval Christianity: A Sociohistorical Approach to Religious Transformation* (New York, 1994).

28. See, for example, Ulf Näsman, "Sea Trade during the Scandinavian Iron Age: Its Character, Commodities and Routes," in *Aspects of Maritime Scandinavia AD 200–1200: Proceedings of the Nordic Seminar on Maritime Aspects of Archaeology, Roskilde, 13th–15th March, 1989*, ed. Ole Crumlin-Pedersen (Roskilde, 1991); Skree, "Missionary Activity in Early Medieval Norway: Strategy, Organization, and the Course of Events," 2.

29. Jordanes, *Getica* 3.21, ed. Mommsen, 59; trans. Mierow, 7.

30. B. Weber, "Norwegian Reindeer Antler Export to Orkney: An Analysis of Combs from Pictish/Early Norse Sites," *Universitetets Oldsaksamlings Årbok 1991–1992* (1993); J. Hines, "På tvers av Nordsjøen: Britiske perspektiver på Skandinaviens senare jernalder," *Universitetets Oldsaksamlings Årbok 1991–1992* (1993).

31. Ulla Lund Hansen, *Römischer Import im Norden: Warenaustausch zwischen dem Römischen Reich und dem freien Germanien während der Kaiserzeit unter besonderer Berücksichtigung Nordeuropas*, Nordiske fortidsminder. Serie B—in quarto 10 (Copenhagen, 1987); Lennart Lind, *Roman Denarii Found in Sweden*, Stockholm Studies in Classical Archaeology 11 (Stockholm, 1981); Joan Marie Fagerlie, *Late Roman and Byzantine Solidi Found in Sweden and Denmark*, Numismatic notes and monographs 157 (New York, 1967); Kent Andersson and Frands Herschend, *Germanerna och Rom: The Germans and Rome*, Occasional Papers in Archaeology 13 (Uppsala, 1997).

32. Gad Rausing, "Barbarian Mercenaries or Roman citizens?" *Fornvännen* 82 (1987); Andersson and Herschend, *Germanerna och Rom: The Germans and Rome* , ch. 4, at n. 50.

33. Ulf Erik Hagberg et al., *The Archaeology of Skedemosse* (Stockholm, 1967), conveniently summarized in Ulf Erik Hagberg, "Offren i Skedemosse på Öland och handeln med romarriket," in *Arkeologi i Norden*, by Göran Burenhult (Stockholm, 1999).

34. Forte, Oram, and Pedersen, *Viking Empires*, 24–27.

35. Anne-Sofie Gräslund, "Charonsmynt i vikingatida gravar?" *Tor: Tidskrift för nordisk fornkunskap* 11 (1967); Kent Andersson, "Intellektuell import eller romersk dona?" *Tor: Tidskrift för nordisk fornkunskap* 20 (1985); Kent Andersson, *Romartida guldsmide i Norden*, Occasional Papers in Archaeology 6 (Uppsala, 1993); Andersson and Herschend, *Germanerna och Rom: The Germans and Rome*, note 45.

36. *Capitulare de partibus Saxoniae* 7, ed. Alfred Boretius, *Capitularia regum Francorum* 1, MGH (Hanover, 1883), 69. About cremation versus inhumation, usefully,

Anne-Sofie Gräslund, "Den tidiga missionen i arkeologisk belysning—problem och synpunkter," *Tor: Tidskrift för nordisk fornkunskap* 20 (1985): 297–298, and Caroline Walker Bynum, *The Resurrection of the Body in Western Christianity, 200–1336*, Lectures on the History of Religions New Series 15 (New York, 1995), 1–52.

37. Anne-Sofie Gräslund, "Arkeologin och kristnandet," in *Kristnandet i Sverige*, ed. Nilsson, 28–29; Nilsson, *Missionstid och tidig medeltid*, 35; Inga Lundström, Claes Theliander, and Pirjo Lahtiperä, *Såntorp: Ett gravfält i Västergötland från förromersk järnålder till tidig medeltid: anläggningsbeskrivningar, dokumentation och analyser*, GOTARC, series C: Arkeologiska skrifter, 49 (Göteborg, 2004); Claes Theliander, *Västergötlands kristnande: Religionsskifte och gravskickets förändring 700–1200*, new ed., GOTARC, series B: Gothenburg Archaeological Theses 41 (Göteborg, 2005).

38. Ann Sandwall and Björn Ambrosiani, *Vendeltid*, Historia i fickformat (Stockholm, 1980).

39. Gräslund, "Arkeologin och kristnandet," 28–29; Nilsson, *Missionstid och tidig medeltid*, 35; Lundström, Theliander, and Lahtiperä, *Såntorp*; Theliander, *Västergötlands kristnande*.

40. Brøgger et al., *Osebergfundet*; Sandwall and Ambrosiani, *Vendeltid*; Krogh, *Gåden om Kong Gorms grav*.

41. Gräslund, "Den tidiga missionen."

42. Bodil Leth-Larsen, "Mammenlyset," in *Mammen*, ed. Iversen; Anne-Sofie Gräslund, "Var Mammen-mannen kristen?" in *Mammen*, ed. Iversen; Krogh, *Gåden om Kong Gorms grav*.

43. Anne-Sofie Gräslund, *The Burial Customs: A Study of the Graves on Björkö*, Birka: Untersuchungen und Studien 4 (Stockholm, 1980), 83; Theliander, *Västergötlands kristnande*.

44. Gräslund, "Var Mammen-mannen kristen?"

45. The either-or question often appears in the scholarly literature; see, e.g., Birgit Sawyer and Peter Sawyer, "Scandinavia enters Christian Europe," in *Cambridge History of Scandinavia*, ed. Helle, 154; Stefan Brink, *Sockenbildning och sockennamn: Studier i äldre territoriell indelning i Norden* (Uppsala, 1990), 374; Skree, "Missionary Activity in Early Medieval Norway: Strategy, Organization, and the Course of Events," 8–9.

46. DuBois, *Nordic Religions in the Viking Age*, 139–172.

47. KLNM 18.502–506, s.v. "Torshamrar," by Olav Bø and Krister Ström; Anne-Sofie Gräslund, "Kreuzanhänger, Kruzifix und Reliquiar-Anhänger," in *Birka*, ed. Greta Arwidsson (Stockholm, 1984); John Lindow, "Thor's 'hamarr,'" *Journal of Germanic and English Philology* 93 (1994); DuBois, *Nordic Religions in the Viking Age*, 159.

48. Gräslund, "Kreuzanhänger, Kruzifix und Reliquiar-Anhänger"; Gräslund, "Arkeologin och kristnandet," 37–40; DuBois, *Nordic Religions in the Viking Age*, 139–172.

49. Birkebæk, *Vikingetiden i Danmark*, 119.

50. Michael Müller-Wille, *Das wikingerzeitliche Gräberfeld von Thumby-Bienebek (Kr. Rendsburg-Eckernförde)*, Offa-Bücher 36 (Neumünster, 1976), 54–55.

51. Anne-Sofie Gräslund, "Tor eller Vite Krist? Några reflektioner med anledning av Lugnås-hammaren," *Västergötlands fornminnesförenings tidskrift* 1983–1984 (1983).

52. Graham-Campbell, *Viking Artefacts*.

53. Gräslund, "Kreuzanhänger, Kruzifix und Reliquiar-Anhänger," 118; DuBois, *Nordic Religions in the Viking Age*, 153, Franklin and Shepard, *Emergence of Rus*, 174; Christiansen, *Norsemen in the Viking Age*, 266.

54. Krogh, *Gåden om Kong Gorms grav*. Cf. Jörn Staecker, "Jelling—Mythen und Realität," in *Der Ostseeraum und Kontinentaleuropa 1100–1600: Einflußnahme—Rezeption—Wandel* (Schwerin, 2004).

55. Sö 101, ed. Brate and Wessén, *Södermanlands runinskrifter.*

56. Widukind, *Res gestae Saxonicae* 3.65, ed. Hirsch and Lohmann, 140.

Chapter 10 The Gift of Christianity

1. Durkheim, *The Elementary Forms of the Religious Life*, 44.

2. Heinz Löwe, *Die karolingische Reichsgründung und der Südosten: Studien zum Werden des Deutschtums und seiner Auseinandersetzung mit Rom*, Forschungen zur Kirchen- und Geistesgeschichte 13 (Stuttgart, 1937), 116–124. Löwe edits the *Ordo de cathecizandis rudibus*, containing advice for missionaries and ascribed to Alcuin, on pp. 171–177. See also Russell, *Germanization of Early Medieval Christianity*, 198; Richard E. Sullivan, *Christian Missionary Activity in the Early Middle Ages*, Variorum Reprints: Collected Studies Series 431 (Aldershot, U.K., 1994); Gunhild Kværness, *Blote kan ein gjere om det berre skjer i løynd: Kristenrettane i Gulatings-lova og Grágás og forholdet mellom dei*, KULTs skriftserie 5 (Oslo, 1996).

3. See ch. 11.

4. Krogh, *Gåden om Kong Gorms grav.*

5. Cross and Sherbowitz-Wetzor, *Russian Primary Chronicle*, 93.

6. Ursula Perkow, "Wasserweihe, Taufe und Patenschaft bei den Nordgermanen" (PhD diss., Hamburg University, 1972); Angenendt, *Kaiserherrschaft und Königstaufe*; Joseph H. Lynch, *Godparents and Kinship in Early Medieval Europe* (Princeton, N.J., 1986); Joseph H. Lynch, *Christianizing Kinship: Ritual Sponsorship in Anglo-Saxon England* (Ithaca, N.Y., 1998).

7. See ch. 9.

8. N 210, ed. Olsen and Liestøl, *Norges innskrifter med de yngre runer*, 3.73–100; Spurkland, *I begynnelsen var fuþark*, 124–128. There is some question about how the word translated as "holy" should be rendered. The inscription reads "hala" (gen. sing.), which also could be interpreted as "slippery, crooked," rather than "halga" ("holy "). See also James E. Knirk, "Arbeidet ved Runearkivet, Oslo," *Nytt om runer* 2 (1987): 9.

9. Sighvatr, Lausavísa 11, ed. Finnur, *Skjaldedigtning*, B:1, 248. Olav was the half brother of King Harald Sigurdsson, hence the circumlocution "Harald's brother" refers to Olav.

10. Sighvatr, *Bersöglisvisur* 18, ed. Finnur, *Skjaldedigtning*, B:1, 238–239: meðal okkar alt's háligt ("the relationship between us two is truly sacred"). The *Heimskringla* interprets this as referring to Sigvat's being Magnus's godfather, but this is not the only possible interpretation. Morkinskinna does not suggest this interpretation, and cf. Gade's too unspecific translation of the line: "between us two all is well"; Theodore M. Andersson and Kari Ellen Gade, *Morkinskinna: The Earliest Icelandic Chronicle of the Norwegian Kings (1030–1157)*, Islandica 51 (Ithaca, N.Y., 2000), 108.

11. *Anglo-Saxon Chronicle*, s.a. 994, ms E, ed. Irvine, 62; ed. Katherine O'Brien O'Keeffe, *MS C*, vol. 5, *The Anglo-Saxon Chronicle: A Collaborative Edition*, ed. David Dumville and Simon Keynes (Cambridge, 2000), 87; trans. Swanton, 128–129. Cf. Dorothy Whitelock, *The Anglo-Saxon Chronicle: A Revised Translation* (New Brunswick, N.J., 1962), 83. Whitelock claims that Olav was confirmed, not baptized. See also Angenendt, *Kaiserherrschaft und Königstaufe*, 272–273.

12. Einarr, *Vellekla* 13, 17, and 37, ed. Finnur, *Skjaldedigtning*, B:1, 119–124.

13. Einarr, *Vellekla* 15–16, ed. Finnur, *Skjaldedigtning*, B:1, 119.

14. Hallfredr, *Óláfsdrápa* 4, Lausavísa 4, 11, and 25, ed. Finnur, *Skjaldedigtning*, B:1, 149, 158, 159, and 162–163.

15. Sighvatr, *Erfidrápa Óláfs Tryggvasonar* 26, 28, ed. Finnur, *Skjaldedigtning*, B:1, 156. There is no reason to doubt the authenticity of the Erfidrápa; see Strömbäck, *Conversion of Iceland*.

16. Hallfredr, *Óláfsdrápa* 4 and Lausavísa 6, ed. Finnur, *Skjaldedigtning*, B:1, 149 and 158. See also ch. 9.

Chapter 11 Kings of God's Grace

1. A recent summary: Robert Bartlett, "From Paganism to Christianity in Medieval Europe," in *Christianization and the Rise of Christian Monarchy*, ed. Berend.

2. Olsen, *Hørg, hov og kirke*; Berta Stjernquist, "Offerplatsen och samhällsstrukturen," in *Uppåkra: Centrum och sammanhang*, ed. Birgitta Hårdh, Acta archaeologica Lundensia, series in 80 34 (Lund, 2001); Anders Hultgård, "The Religion of the Vikings," in *The Viking World*, ed. Brink with Price, 215–216; RGA 23.424–435, s.v. "Priester und Priesterinnen," by O. Sundqvist.

3. Olsen, *Hørg, hov og kirke*, 19–54; Klaus Düwel, *Das Opferfest von Lade: Quellenkritische Untersuchungen zur germanischen Religionsgeschichte*, Wiener Arbeiten zur germanischen Altertumskunde und Philologie 27 (Vienna, 1985).

4. Thietmar, *Chronicon* 1.17, ed. Holtzmann, 23–24; trans. Warner, 80.

5. Marijane Osborn, "Legends of Lejre, Home of Kings," in *Beowulf and Lejre*, ed. Niles, Christensen, and Osborn, 123–124.

6. Adam, *Gesta* 4.27, ed. Schmeidler, 259–260; trans. Tschan, 208. See also Olsen, *Hørg, hov og kirke*, 116–166.

7. J. Asmussen, *De fontibus Adami Bremensis commentarius* (Kiel, 1834), and J. M. Lappenberg, "Von den Quellen, Handschriften und Bearbeitungen des Adam von Bremen," *Archiv der Gesellschaft für ältere deutsche Geschichtskunde* 6 (1838), do not mention Thietmar as a possible source of Adam, and neither does Schmeidler's introduction to his edition, lvii–lxiv.

8. Anne-Sofie Gräslund, "New Perspectives on an Old Problem: Uppsala and the Christianization of Sweden," in *Christianizing Peoples and Converting Individuals*, ed. Gyuda Armstrong and Ian N. Wood, International Medieval Research (Turnhout, 2000).

9. Henrik Janson, *Templum nobilissimum: Adam av Bremen, Uppsalatemplet och konfliktlinjerna i Europa kring år 1075*, Avhandlingar från Historiska institutionen i Göteborg 21 (Göteborg, 1998), 22–23.

10. Janson, *Templum nobilissimum*. About Olav, see ch. 8.

11. Ibn Fadlan's report of the rituals surrounding the burial of a Rus chieftain in the neighborhood of Bulghar is often used as a source for Scandinavian pre-Christian religious practices, but it remains highly uncertain to what degree these rituals reflect Scandinavian practice.

12. Sighvatr, *Austrfararvísur* 4–5, ed. Finnur, *Skjaldedigtning*, B:1, 221; trans. R. I. Page, *Chronicles of the Vikings: Records, Memorials, and Myths* (Toronto, 1995), 50. A very free translation is in Snorri Sturluson, *Heimskringla*, trans. Lee M. Hollander (Austin, 1964), 336–337. Much has been written about this stanza; see, e.g., Finnur Jónsson, *Austrfararvísur* (Oslo, 1932), and Olsen, *Hørg, hov og kirke*, 86–91.

13. Catharina Raudvere, "Popular Religion in the Viking Age," in *The Viking World*, ed. Brink with Price, 237.

14. Gräslund, "Arkeologin och kristnandet," 22–24; Elisabeth Iregren, "Under Frösö kyrka—ben från en vikingatida offerlund?" in *Arkeologi och religion: Rapport från arkeologidagarna 16–18 januari 1989*, ed. Lars Larsson and Bożena Wyszomirska, Institute of Archaeology Report Series 34 (Lund, 1989); Neil S. Price, *The Viking Way: Religion and War in Late Iron Age Scandinavia* (Uppsala, 2002), 61–62; Anne-Sofie Gräslund, "The Material Culture of Old Norse Religion," in *The Viking World*, ed. Brink with Price, 253.

15. Lars Larsson and Birgitta Hårdh, "Kulthuset i Uppåkra," in *Odens öga—mellan människor och makter i det förkristna Norden*, ed. Anders Andrén and Peter Carelli, Stadshistoriska avdelningen, Dunkers kulturhus, Skrifter 6 (Helsingborg, 2006); Birgitta Hårdh and Lars Larsson, *Uppåkra—Lund före Lund*, Föreningen Gamla Lund: Årsbok (Lund, 2007), 39–58; Birgitta Hårdh, "Viking Age Uppåkra and Lund," in *The Viking World*, ed. Brink with Price.

16. Olsen, *Hørg, hov og kirke*, 112–114; Thorsten Andersson, "Orts- und Personennamen als Aussagequelle für die altgermanische Religion," in *Germanische Religionsgeschichte: Quellen und Quellenprobleme*, ed. Heinrich Beck, Detlev Ellmers, and Kurt Schier, Ergänzungsbände zum Reallexikon der Germanischen Altertumskunde (Berlin, 1992).

17. Olsen, *Hørg, hov og kirke*, 92–93. The English definition of *hof* from p. 280.

18. Jón Viðar, *Det norrøne samfunnet*, 69–70; Lindkvist, "Ny tro i nya riken," 43.

19. Medieval laws from Scandinavia typically contain such prohibitions; see, e.g., Kværness, *Blote kan ein gjere*, 148–149.

20. Widukind, *Res gestae Saxonicae* 3.65, ed. Hirsch and Lohmann, 141.

21. Hallfredr, *Óláfsdrápa* 3–4, ed. Finnur, *Skjaldedigtning*, B:1, 149.

22. Ari, *Íslendingabók* 7, ed. Jakob, 17; trans. Grønlie, 9. See also Jenny Jochens, "Late and Peaceful: Iceland's Conversion through Arbitration in 1000," *Speculum* 74 (1999).

23. About horseflesh, compare the prohibition in the Icelandic lawbook known as Grágás; see Andrew Dennis, Peter Godfrey Foote, and Richard Perkins, trans., *Laws of Early Iceland: The Codex Regius of Grágás with Material from Other Manuscripts*, University of Manitoba Icelandic Studies 3 (Winnipeg, Man., 1980), 49, and see KLNM 7.280–281, s.v. "Hästkött," by Brita Egardt; Kværness, *Blote kan ein gjere*, 79–81, and Landro, "Kristenrett og kyrkjerett," 131–146.

24. Vésteinsson, *The Christianization of Iceland*, 37, e.g., argues persuasively that priests were rare in Iceland during the first century after the conversion. Similarly,

for Denmark, Michael H. Gelting, "The Kingdom of Denmark," in *Christianization and the Rise of Christian Monarchy*, ed. Berend, 96.

25. Nora Berend, "Introduction," in *Christianization and the Rise of Christian Monarchy*, ed. Berend, 36.

26. Winroth, "Christianity Comes to Denmark."

27. Henrik Williams, "Runjämtskan på Frösöstenen och Östmans bro," in *Jämtlands kristnande*, Projektet Sveriges kristnande: Publikationer 4 (Uppsala, 1996); Henrik Williams, "Vad säger runstenarna om Sveriges kristnande?" in *Kristnandet i Sverige: Gamla källor och nya perspektiv*, Projektet Sveriges kristnande: Publikationer 5 (Uppsala, 1996); Sawyer, *The Viking-Age Rune-Stones*, 133; "Samnordisk runtextdatabas."

28. Sawyer, *Kings and Vikings*, 147.

29. Vésteinsson, *The Christianization of Iceland*, 26–37 and 182–194.

30. See ch. 8.

31. Adam, *Gesta*, 2.55, ed. Schmeidler, 116; trans. Tschan 93.

32. Byock, *Feud in the Icelandic Saga*.

33. Ari, *Íslendingabók* 8, ed. Jakob, 18–19; trans. Grønlie, 10. About these bishops see also Grønlie's commentary, p. 26–27; Vésteinsson, *The Christianization of Iceland*, 20–21; and Byock, *Viking Age Iceland*, 303.

34. It has also been suggested that the adjective *ermskr* ("Armenian") should be read to suggest that they did not come from Armenia but from Ermland, which is a district on the southeastern coast of the Baltic Sea; see Grønlie, trans., *Íslendingabók*, 27, with references. That steadfastly pagan region, however, had no bishops in the eleventh century. Ermskr certainly means "Armenian." See also Cleasby, Vigfússon, and Craigie, *An Icelandic-English Dictionary*, 133. The oldest Icelandic law code, Grágás, clearly counts on the possibility that bishops without knowledge of Latin were active in Iceland; see Dennis, Foote, and Perkins, *Laws of Early Iceland*, 38. See also Margaret Cormack, "Irish and Armenian Ecclesiastics in Medieval Iceland," in *West over Sea: Studies in Scandinavian Seaborne Expansion and Settlement: A Festschrift in Honour of Dr. Barbara E. Crawford*, ed. Beverley Ballin Smith, Simon Taylor, and Gareth Williams (Leiden, 2007).

35. Kluger et al., *Series episcoporum* 6.2, 13–14.

36. Vésteinsson, *The Christianization of Iceland*.

37. About Isleif, see Ari, *Íslendingabók* 9, ed. Jakob, 20–21; trans. Grønlie, 10–11, and commentary, 27–28; Adam, *Gesta* 3.77 and 4.36, ed. Schmeidler, 224 and 273; trans. Tschan, 183 and 218. See also Vésteinsson, *The Christianization of Iceland*, 19–24; Byock, *Viking Age Iceland*, 306.

38. Eljas Orrman, "Church and Society," in *The Cambridge History of Scandinavia*, ed. Helle, 443–448; Carl Göran Andræ, *Kyrka och frälse i Sverige under äldre medeltid* (Stockholm, 1960); Carsten Breengaard, *Muren om Israels hus: Regnum og sacerdotium i Danmark 1050–1170*, Kirkehistoriske studier (Copenhagen, 1982); Knut Helle, "The Organisation of the Twelfth-Century Norwegian Church," in *St. Magnus Cathedral and Orkney's Twelfth-Century Renaissance*, ed. B. Crawford (Aberdeen, 1988).

39. Kluger et al., *Series episcoporum* 6.2, 80.

40. Adam, *Gesta* 4.8, ed. Schmeidler, 235–236; trans. Tschan, 191–192.

41. Paul Hinschius, *System des katholischen Kirchenrechts mit besonderen Rücksicht auf Deutschland* (Berlin, 1869–1897), 2.400.

42. Eskil of Lund stayed in France from 1161–1167 (but he also visited the Holy Land and Italy during this period); see, e.g., Lauritz Weibull, "Skånes kyrka från älsta tid till Jacob Erlandsens död 1274," in *Lunds domkyrkas historia*, ed. Ernst Newman (1946), 237–241, repr. in Weibull, *Nordisk historia*, 2.507–509. Øystein of Nidaros was in England from c. 1180 to 1183; see Erik Gunnes, *Erkebiskop Øystein: Statsmann og kirkebygger* (Oslo, 1996). Stephanus of Uppsala was in Italy and Denmark in 1169 and 1170; see Svenskt biografiskt lexikon 33.373–374.

43. *Annales regni Francorum*, s.a. 814, ed. Kurze, 141; trans. Scholz and Rogers, 99.

44. Gelting, "Kingdom of Denmark," 76.

45. Sawyer, *Da Danmark blev Danmark*; Gelting, "Kingdom of Denmark," 82.

46. Roesdahl, *The Vikings*, 136–139; Birkebæk, *Vikingetiden i Danmark*, 201–205. Cf. Sawyer, *Da Danmark blev Danmark*, 305–306; Gelting, "Kingdom of Denmark," 82. The trelleborg in Trelleborg, Scania, is slightly different from the other four.

47. Sawyer, *Da Danmark blev Danmark*, 91–92; Birkebæk, *Vikingetiden i Danmark*, 207; Gelting, "Kingdom of Denmark," 82.

48. Lars Ersgård, "Two Magnate's Farms and Their Landscape—a Postscript," in *Slöinge och Borg: Stormansgårdar i öst och väst*, ed. Lars Lundqvist, Anders Andersson, and Richard Hedvall, Arkeologiska undersökningar (Stockholm, 1996); Johan Callmer and Erik Rosengren, *"Gick Grendel att söka det höga huset": Arkeologiska källor till aristokratiska miljöer i Skandinavien under yngre järnålder: Rapport från ett seminarium i Falkenberg 16–17 november 1995*, Slöinge projektet 1 (Halmstad, 1997); Johan Callmer, "Extinguished Solar Systems and Black Holes: Traces of Estates in the Scandinavian Late Iron Age," in *Uppåkra: Centrum och sammanhang*, ed. Birgitta Hårdh, Acta archaeologica Lundensia, series in 8o 34 (Lund, 2001); Lars Lundqvist, *Slöinge 1992–1996: Undersökningar av en boplats från yngre järnålder*, GOTARC, series C: Arkeologiska skrifter (Göteborg, 2003).

49. Niles, Christensen, and Osborn, *Beowulf and Lejre*; Gelting, "Kingdom of Denmark," 83; Tom Christensen, "Lejre and Roskilde," in *The Viking World*, ed. Brink with Price.

50. Hårdh, "Viking Age Uppåkra and Lund."

51. *Beowulf*, lines 1151–1152, ed. Fulk, Bjork, and Niles, 40–41; trans. Liuzza, 88.

52. Bolton, *The Empire of Cnut the Great*, 202–240.

53. Axel Christophersen, "Ports and Trade in Norway during the Transition to Historical Time," in *Aspects of Maritime Scandinavia AD 200–1200: Proceedings of the Nordic Seminar on Maritime Aspects of Archaeology, Roskilde, 13th–15th March, 1989*, ed. Ole Crumlin-Pedersen (Roskilde, 1991), 168.

54. Bolton, *The Empire of Cnut the Great*.

55. Gelting, "Kingdom of Denmark," 93.

Chapter 12 Scandinavia in European History

1. The classic statement of this view is Robert Bartlett, *The Making of Europe: Conquest, Colonization, and Cultural Change, 950–1350* (Princeton, 1993).

2. Stephen Neill, *A History of Christian Missions*, 2d ed., The Pelican History of the Church (Harmondsworth, 1986), is perhaps a relatively recent representative of this understanding.

3. Berend, "Introduction," esp. 30–37.

4. Rimbert, *Vita Anskari* 24 and 32, ed. Waitz, 52 and 64; trans. Robinson, 83–84 and 103.

5. Stefan Brink, "Tidig kyrklig organisation i Norden—aktörerna i sockenbildningen," in *Kristnandet i Sverige*, ed. Nilsson.

6. The bibliography is enormous. For a recent engagement with this debate, see Dominique Barthélemy, *The Serf, the Knight and the Historian*, trans. Graham Robert Edwards (Ithaca, N.Y., 2009).

7. See, e.g., McCormick, *Origins of the European Economy* and McCormick, "New Light on the 'Dark Ages.'"

8. Nelson, "The Frankish Empire."

9. *Annales Bertiniani*, s.a. 866, ed. Waitz, 81; trans. Nelson, 130. A mansus was a Frankish tax unit.

10. Lawson, "Collection of Danegeld and Heregeld."

11. *Annales Bertiniani*, s.a. 858, ed. Waitz, 49; trans. Nelson, 86. Cf. above, ch. 2.

12. Lawson, "Collection of Danegeld and Heregeld," 728.

13. Georges Duby, *The Early Growth of the European Economy: Warriors and Peasants from the Seventh to the Twelfth Century*, World Economic History (Ithaca, N.Y., 1974).

14. Bolin, "Mohammed, Charlemagne and Rurik"; Hodges and Whitehouse, *Mohammed, Charlemagne, and the Origins of Europe.*

15. McCormick, "New Light on the 'Dark Ages.'"

16. Steuer, "Handel der Wikingerzeit."

17. Classical statements are Henri Pirenne, *Medieval Cities: Their Origins and the Revival of Trade*, trans. Frank D. Halsey (Princeton, 1925); Robert S. Lopez, *The Commercial Revolution of the Middle Ages, 950–1350* (Cambridge, 1976).

18. Thomas Lindkvist, *Plundring, skatter och den feodala statens framväxt: Organisatoriska tendenser i Sverige under övergången från vikingatid till tidig medeltid*, 3d ed., Opuscula historica Upsaliensia 1 (Uppsala, 1993); Carl F. Hallencreutz, *När Sverige blev europeiskt: Till frågan om Sveriges kristnande*, Vitterhetsakademiens skriftserie om Europa (Stockholm, 1993); Thomas Lindkvist, "Early Political Organization: a) Introductory Survey," in *Cambridge History of Scandinavia*, ed. Helle; Berend, *Christianization and the Rise of Christian Monarchy*; Eric Christiansen, *The Northern Crusades: The Baltic and the Catholic Frontier, 1100–1525* (Minneapolis, 1980); Lars Ivar Hansen and Bjørnar Olsen, *Samenes historie fram til 1750* (Oslo, 2004), 151–155.

19. Useful surveys of the early administration of the Scandinavian kingdoms are in Berend, ed., *Christianization and the Rise of Christian Monarchy*.

Bibliography

Abels, Richard. "What Has Weland to Do with Christ? The Franks Casket and the Acculturation of Christianity in Early Anglo-Saxon England." *Speculum* 84 (2009): 549–581.

Abrams, Lesley. "The Anglo-Saxons and the Christianization of Scandinavia." *Anglo-Saxon England* 24 (1995): 213–250.

Acta sanctorum, Novembris 3. Edited by Carolus de Smedt, Franciscus van Ortroy, Hippolytus Delahaye, Albertus Poncelet, and Paulus Peeters. Brussels, 1910.

Adam, Hildegard. *Das Zollwesen im fränkischen Reich und das spätkarolingische Wirtschaftsleben: Ein Überblick über Zoll, Handel und Verkehr im 9. Jahrhundert*, Vierteljahrschrift für Sozial- und Wirtschaftsgeschichte, Beihefte 126. Stuttgart, 1996.

Adam of Bremen. *Hamburgische Kirchengeschichte*. Edited by Bernhard Schmeidler, MGH SS rer. Germ. Hanover, 1917.

——. *History of the Archbishops of Hamburg-Bremen*. Translated with an introduction and notes by Francis J. Tschan, with a new introduction and selected bibliography by Timothy Reuter. Records of Western Civilization. New York, 2002.

Algazi, Gadi, Valentin Groebner, and Bernhard Jussen. *Negotiating the Gift: Pre-Modern Figurations of Exchange*, Veröffentlichungen des Max-Planck-Instituts für Geschichte 188. Göttingen, 2003.

Ambrosiani, Björn. "Birka: Its Waterways and Hinterland." In *Aspects of Maritime Scandinavia AD 200–1200: Proceedings of the Nordic Seminar on Maritime Aspects of Archaeology, Roskilde, 13th-15th March, 1989*, edited by Ole Crumlin-Pedersen, 99–104. Roskilde, Denmark, 1991.

——. "What Is Birka?" In *Investigations in the Black Earth*, vol. 1, *Early Investigations and Future Plans*, edited by Björn Ambrosiani and Helen Clarke, 10–22. Stockholm, 1992.

Andersson, Kent. "Intellektuell import eller romersk dona?" *Tor: Tidskrift för nordisk fornkunskap* 20 (1985).

——. *Romartida guldsmide i Norden*, Occasional Papers in Archaeology 6. Uppsala, 1993.

Andersson, Kent, and Frands Herschend. *Germanerna och Rom: The Germans and Rome*, Occasional Papers in Archaeology 13. Uppsala, 1997.

Andersson, Theodore M. "The Conversion of Norway according to Oddr Snorrason and Snorri Sturluson." *Mediaeval Scandinavia* 10 (1976): 83–95.

——. *The Growth of the Medieval Icelandic Sagas (1180–1280)*. Ithaca, 2006.

Andersson, Theodore M., and Kari Ellen Gade. *Morkinskinna: The Earliest Icelandic Chronicle of the Norwegian Kings (1030–1157)*, Islandica 51. Ithaca, N.Y., 2000.

Andersson, Thorsten. "Orts- und Personennamen als Aussagequelle für die altgermanische Religion." In *Germanische Religionsgeschichte: Quellen und Quellenprobleme*, edited by Heinrich Beck, Detlev Ellmers, and Kurt Schier, 508–540. Berlin, 1992.

Andræ, Carl Göran. *Kyrka och frälse i Sverige under äldre medeltid*. Stockholm, 1960.

Androschchuk, Fedir. "The Hvoshcheva Sword: An Example of Contacts between Britain and Scandinavia in the Late Viking Period." *Fornvännen* 98 (2003): 35–43.

Angenendt, Arnold. *Kaiserherrschaft und Königstaufe: Kaiser, Könige und Päpste als geistliche Patrone in der abendländischen Missionsgeschichte*, Arbeiten zur Frühmittelalterforschung 15. Berlin, 1984.

Annales Bertiniani. Edited by G. Waitz, MGH SS rer. Germ. Hanover, 1883.

Annales Fuldenses sive Annales Regni Francorum orientalis. Edited by Fridericus Kurze, MGH SS rer. Germ. Hanover, 1891.

Annales regni Francorum inde ab a. 741 usque ad a. 829, qui dicuntur Annales Laurissenses maiores et Einhardi. Edited by Fridericus Kurze, MGH SS rer. Germ. Hanover, 1895.

Annales Xantenses et Annales Vedastini. Edited by B. de Simson, MGH SS rer. Germ. Hanover, 1909.

Annerstedt, Claes, ed. *Scriptores rerum Suecicarum medii aevi* 3. Uppsala, 1871–1876.

Armstrong, Guyda, and Ian N. Wood. *Christianizing Peoples and Converting Individuals*, International Medieval Research 7. Turnhout, 2000.

Arne, T. J. "Den svenska runstenen från ön Berezanj utanför Dnjeprmynningen: Referat efter prof. F. Brauns redogörelse i Ryska arkeol. kommissionens meddelanden 1907." *Fornvännen* 9 (1914): 44–48.

Arwidsson, Greta, and Gösta Berg. *The Mästermyr Find: A Viking Age Tool Chest from Gotland*. Stockholm, 1983.

Asmussen, J. *De fontibus Adami Bremensis commentarius*. Kiel, 1834.

Bachrach, Bernard S., and Steven Fanning. *The Annals of Flodoard of Reims, 919–966*. Readings in Medieval Civilizations and Cultures 9. Peterborough, Ont., 2004.

Bagge, Sverre. "Ideologies and Mentalities." In *The Cambridge History of Scandinavia*, edited by Knut Helle, 1: 465–486. Cambridge, 2003.

Bagge, Sverre, and Sæbjørg Walaker Nordeide. "The Kingdom of Norway." In *Christianization and the Rise of Christian Monarchy: Scandinavia, Central Europe and Rus' c. 900–1200*, edited by Nora Berend, 121–166. Cambridge, 2007.

Barthélemy, Dominique. *The Serf, the Knight and the Historian.* Translated by Graham Robert Edwards. Ithaca, N.Y., 2009.

Bartlett, Robert. "From Paganism to Christianity in Medieval Europe." In *Christianization and the Rise of Christian Monarchy: Scandinavia, Central Europe and Rus' c. 900–1200,* edited by Nora Berend, 47–72. Cambridge, 2007.

———. *The Making of Europe: Conquest, Colonization, and Cultural Change, 950–1350.* Princeton, N.J., 1993.

———. *Trial by Fire and Water: The Medieval Judicial Ordeal.* Oxford, 1986.

Bately, Janet M., ed. *MS A.* Vol. 3 of *The Anglo-Saxon Chronicle: A Collaborative Edition,* edited by David Dumville and Simon Keynes. Cambridge, 1986.

Bately, Janet, and Anton Englert. *Ohthere's Voyages: A Late 9th-century Account of Voyages along the Coasts of Norway and Denmark and Its Cultural Context.* Roskilde, 2007.

Bazelmans, Jos. "Beyond Power: Ceremonial Exchanges in *Beowulf.*" In *Rituals of Power: From Late Antiquity to the Early Middle Ages,* edited by Frans Theuws and Janet Nelson, 311–375. Leiden, 2000.

Behre, Karl-Ernst, and Hans Reichstein. *Untersuchungen des botanischen Materials der frühmittelalterlichen Siedlung Haithabu. (Ausgrabung 1963–1964.),* Berichte über die Ausgrabungen in Haithabu, Bericht 2. Neumünster, 1969.

Benediktsson, Jakob. See Jakob Benediktsson.

Berend, Nora, ed. *Christianization and the Rise of Christian Monarchy: Scandinavia, Central Europe and Rus' c. 900–1200.* Cambridge, 2007.

———. "Introduction." In *Christianization and the Rise of Christian Monarchy: Scandinavia, Central Europe and Rus' c. 900–1200,* edited by Nora Berend, 1–46. Cambridge, 2007.

Berichte über die Ausgrabungen in Haithabu. Neumünster, 1969–.

Bertelsen, Henrik, ed. *Þiðreks saga af Bern,* Samfund til udgivelse af gammel nordisk litteratur, Skrifter 34. Copenhagen, 1905–1911.

Bertsch, Karl, and Franz Bertsch. *Geschichte unserer Kulturpflanzen.* 2d ed. Stuttgart, 1949.

Birkebæk, Frank. *Vikingetiden i Danmark.* [Copenhagen], 2003.

Birkeland, Harris. *Nordens historie i middelalderen etter arabiske kilder.* Vol. 1954: 2, Skrifter utgitt av Det Norske Videnskaps-Akademi i Oslo, II. Hist.-Filos. Klasse. Oslo, 1954.

Bjarni Einarsson. *Ágrip af Nóregskonunga sǫgum: Fagrskinna = Nóregs konunga tal,* Íslenzk fornrit 29. Reykjavik, 1984.

Blake, E. O., ed. *Liber Eliensis,* Camden Third Series 92. London, 1962.

Blindheim, Charlotte, and Roar L. Tollnes. *Kaupang, vikingenes handelsplass.* Oslo, 1972.

Böhmer, Johann Friedrich, Engelbert Mühlbacher, and Johann Lechner. *Die Regesten des Kaiserreichs unter den Karolingern, 751–918.* 2d ed, Regesta imperii. Innsbruck, 1908.

Bolin, Sture. "Mohammed, Charlemagne and Rurik." *Scandinavian Economic History Review* 1 (1953): 5–39.

———. "Muhammed, Karl den store, och Rurik." *Scandia* 12 (1939): 181–222.

Bolton, Timothy. *The Empire of Cnut the Great: Conquest and the Consolidation of Power in Northern Europe in the Early Eleventh Century,* The Northern World:

North Europe and the Baltic c. 400–1700 A.D.: Peoples, Economies and Cultures. Leiden, 2009.

Bonnaz, Yves. *Chroniques Asturiennes (fin IXe siècle)*. Paris, 1987.

Bourdieu, Pierre. *The Logic of Practice*. Translated by Richard Nice. Stanford, Calif., 1990.

Bowden, Georgina R., Patricia Balaresque, Turi E. King, Ziff Hansen, Andrew C. Lee, Giles Pergl-Wilson, Emma Hurley, Stephen J. Roberts, Patrick Waite, Judith Jesch, Abigail L. Jones, Mark G. Thomas, Stephen E. Harding, and Mark A. Jobling. "Excavating Past Population Structures by Surname-Based Sampling: The Genetic Legacy of the Vikings in Northwest England." *Molecular Biology and Evolution* 25 (2008): 301–309.

Brandt, Karl Heinz, and Margareta Nockert. *Ausgrabungen im Bremer St.-Petri-Dom 1974–76: Ein Vorbericht*, Bremer archäologische Blätter. Bremen, 1976.

Brate, Erik. *Östergötlands runinskrifter*, Sveriges runinskrifter 2. Stockholm, 1911.

Brate, Erik, and Elias Wessén. *Södermanlands runinskrifter*, Sveriges runinskrifter 3. Stockholm, 1924.

Breengaard, Carsten. *Muren om Israels hus: Regnum og sacerdotium i Danmark 1050–1170*, Kirkehistoriske studier. Copenhagen, 1982.

Brink, Stefan. *Sockenbildning och sockennamn: Studier i äldre territoriell indelning i Norden*. Uppsala, 1990.

——. "Tidig kyrklig organisation i Norden—aktörerna i sockenbildningen." In *Kristnandet i Sverige: Gamla källor och nya perspektiv*, edited by Bertil Nilsson, 269–290. Uppsala, 1996.

Brink, Stefan, ed. *The Viking World*. In collaboration with Neil Price. Routledge Worlds. London, 2008.

Brøgger, A. W., Hjalmar Falk, G. Gustafson, and Haakon Shetelig. *Osebergfundet*. Kristiania [Oslo], 1917.

Burenhult, Göran. *Arkeologi i Norden*. Stockholm, 1999.

Burström, Mats. *Arkeologisk samhällsavgränsning: En studie av vikingatida samhällsterritorier i Smålands inland*, Stockholm Studies in Archaeology 9. Stockholm, 1991.

Bynum, Caroline Walker. *The Resurrection of the Body in Western Christianity, 200–1336*, Lectures on the History of Religions, new series 15. New York, 1995.

Byock, Jesse L. *Feud in the Icelandic Saga*. Berkeley, 1982.

——. *Viking Age Iceland*. London, 2001.

Callmer, Johan. "Extinguished Solar Systems and Black Holes: Traces of Estates in the Scandinavian Late Iron Age." In *Uppåkra: Centrum och sammanhang*, edited by Birgitta Hårdh, 109–137. Lund, 2001.

Callmer, Johan, and Erik Rosengren. *"Gick Grendel att söka det höga huset": Arkeologiska källor till aristokratiska miljöer i Skandinavien under yngre järnålder: Rapport från ett seminarium i Falkenberg 16–17 november 1995*, Slöinge projektet 1. Halmstad, 1997.

Christensen, Tom. "Lejre and Roskilde." In *The Viking World*, edited by Stefan Brink, in collaboration with Neil Price, 121–125. London, 2008.

Christiansen, Eric. *The Norsemen in the Viking Age*, Peoples of Europe. Oxford, 2002.

——. *The Northern Crusades: The Baltic and the Catholic Frontier, 1100–1525.* Minneapolis, 1980.

Christophersen, Axel. "Ports and Trade in Norway during the Transition to Historical Time." In *Aspects of Maritime Scandinavia AD 200–1200: Proceedings of the Nordic Seminar on Maritime Aspects of Archaeology, Roskilde, 13th-15th March, 1989,* edited by Ole Crumlin-Pedersen, 159–170. Roskilde, 1991.

Clarke, Helen, and Björn Ambrosiani. *Towns in the Viking Age.* Leicester, 1991.

Cleasby, Richard, Guðbrandur Vigfússon, and William A. Craigie. *An Icelandic-English Dictionary.* 2d ed. Oxford, 1957.

Collins, Roger. *Early Medieval Spain: Unity in Diversity, 400–1000.* 2d ed. New York, 1995.

Cormack, Margaret. "Irish and Armenian Ecclesiastics in Medieval Iceland." In *West over Sea: Studies in Scandinavian Seaborne Expansion and Settlement: A Festschrift in Honour of Dr. Barbara E. Crawford,* edited by Beverley Ballin Smith, Simon Taylor, and Gareth Williams, 227–234. Leiden, 2007.

Coupland, Simon. "The Frankish Tribute Payments to the Vikings and Their Consequences." *Francia* 26 (1999): 57–75.

——. "From Poachers to Game-Keepers: Scandinavian Warlords and Carolingian Kings." *Early Medieval Europe* 7 (1998): 85–114.

——. "Trading Places: Quentovic and Dorestad Reassessed." *Early Medieval Europe* 11 (2002): 209–232.

Cramp, Rosemary. "The Hall in *Beowulf* and in Archeology." In *Heroic Poetry in the Anglo-Saxon Period: Studies in Honor of Jess B. Bessinger, Jr.,* edited by Helen Damico and John Leyerly, 331–346. Kalamazoo, Mich., 1993.

Crawford, B. E. *Scandinavian Scotland,* Studies in the Early History of Britain. [Leicester], 1987.

Cross, Samuel Hazzard, and Olgerd P. Sherbowitz-Wetzor, trans. *The Russian Primary Chronicle: Laurentian Text.* Cambridge, Mass., 1973.

Crumlin-Pedersen, Ole. "Vikingernes 'søvej' til Byzans—om betingelser for sejlads ad flodvejene fra Østersø till Sortehav." In *Beretning fra Ottonde tværfaglige vikingesymposium,* edited by Torben Kisbye and Else Roesdahl, 33–51. Højbjerg, 1989.

Cubbin, G. P., ed. *MS D.* Vol. 6 of *The Anglo-Saxon Chronicle: A Collaborative Edition,* edited by David Dumville and Simon Keynes. Cambridge, 1991.

Danielsson, Tommy. *Sagorna om Norges kungar: Från Magnús góði till Magnús Erlingsson.* [Hedemora], 2002.

Dehio, Georg. *Geschichte der Erzbistums Hamburg-Bremen bis zum Ausgang des Mission.* 2 vols. Berlin, 1877.

Delisle, Léopold. *Littérature latine et histoire du moyen âge,* Comité des travaux historiques et scientifiques: Section d'histoire et de philologie, Instructions aux correspondants. Paris, 1890.

Dennis, Andrew, Peter Godfrey Foote, and Richard Perkins, trans. *Laws of Early Iceland: The Codex Regius of Grágás with Material from Other Manuscripts,* University of Manitoba Icelandic Studies 3. Winnipeg, Man., 1980.

Diekamp, Wilhelm. *Die Vitae sancti Liudgeri,* Die Geschichtsquellen des Bisthums Münster 4. Münster, 1881.

Driscoll, Matthew James, trans. *Ágrip af Nóregskonungasǫgum: A Twelfth-Century Synoptic History of the Kings of Norway*. London, 1995.

Dronke, Ursula, ed. *The Poetic Edda*. Oxford, 1969–.

DuBois, Thomas A. *Nordic Religions in the Viking Age*. Philadelphia, 1999.

Duby, Georges. *The Early Growth of the European Economy: Warriors and Peasants from the Seventh to the Twelfth Century*, World Economic History. Ithaca, N.Y., 1974.

Durkheim, Emile. *The Elementary Forms of the Religious Life*. Translated by Karen E. Fields. New York, 1995.

Dutton, Paul Edward. *Carolingian Civilization: A Reader*. Peterborough, Ont., 1993.

Düwel, Klaus. *Das Opferfest von Lade: Quellenkritische Untersuchungen zur germanischen Religionsgeschichte*, Wiener Arbeiten zur germanischen Altertumskunde und Philologie 27. Vienna, 1985.

Edberg, Rune. "Med Aifur till Aifur: Slutrapport från en experimentell österledsfärd." *Fornvännen* 94 (1999): 1–12.

———. "Vikingar mot strömmen: Några synpunkter på möjliga och omöjliga skepp vid färder i hemmavatten och i österled." *Fornvännen* 91 (1996): 37–42.

Egilsson, Sveinbjörn. See Sveinbjörn Egilsson.

Einarsson, Bjarni. See Bjarni Einarsson.

Einhard. *Einhardi Vita Karoli magni*. Edited by G. Waitz. 6th ed., MGH SS rer. Germ. Hanover, 1911.

Ekenberg, Anders, Eva Odelman, Carl Fredrik Hallencreutz, and Tore Hållander. *Boken om Ansgar*. Stockholm, 1986.

Ekrem, Inger, Peter Fischer, and Lars Boje Mortensen, eds. and trans. *Historia Norwegie*. Copenhagen, 2003.

Ellmers, Detlev. "Die Archäologie der Binnenschiffahrt in Europa nördlich der Alpen." In *Der Verkehr, Verkehrswege, Verkehrsmittel, Organisation*, edited by Else Ebel, Herbert Jankuhn, and Wolfgang Kimmig, 291–350. Untersuchungen zu Handel und Verkehr der vor- und frühgeschichtlichen Zeit in Mittel- und Nordeuropa 5 = Abhandlungen der Akademie der Wissenschaften in Göttingen: Philologisch-historische Klasse, 3. Folge, 180. Göttingen, 1989.

The Encyclopaedia of Islam. New ed. Leiden, 1954–2002.

Engels, Odilo, and Stefan Weinfurter. *Series episcoporum Ecclesiae Catholicae occidentalis ab initio ad annum MCXCVIII 5.1: Archiepiscopatus Coloniensis*. Stuttgart, 1982.

———. *Series episcoporum Ecclesiae Catholicae occidentalis ab initio ad annum MCXCVIII 5.2: Archiepiscopatus Hammaburgensis sive Bremensis*. Stuttgart, 1984.

Enoksen, Lars Magnar. *Runor: Historia, tydning, tolkning*. Lund, 1998.

Enright, Michael J. *Lady with a Mead Cup: Ritual, Prophecy, and Lordship in the European Warband from La Tène to the Viking Age*. Blackrock, Ireland, 1996.

Eriksson, Jessica. "Bilden av Bödvild: Ett genusperspektiv på berättelserna om Völund." In *Spaden och pennan: Ny humanistisk forskning i andan av Erik B Lundberg och Bengt G Söderberg*, edited by Thorsten Svensson, 157–166. Stockholm, 2009.

Ermoldus Nigellus. "In honorem Hludowici." In *Poème sur Louis le Pieux et Épîtres au roi Pépin*, edited and translated by Edmond Faral, Les classiques de l'histoire de France au moyen âge 14. Paris, 1932.

Ersgård, Lars. "Two Magnate's Farms and Their Landscape—a Postscript." In *Slöinge och Borg: Stormansgårdar i öst och väst*, edited by Lars Lundqvist, Anders Andersson, and Richard Hedvall, 116–122. Stockholm, 1996.

Fagerlie, Joan Marie. *Late Roman and Byzantine Solidi Found in Sweden and Denmark*, Numismatic Notes and Monographs 157. New York, 1967.

Fellows-Jenssen, Gillian. *The Vikings and Their Victims: The Evidence of the Names*. London, 1995.

Fenger, Ole. *"Kirker reses alle vegne": 1050–1250*, Gyldendal og Politikens Danmarkshistorie. Copenhagen, 1989.

Feveile, Claus. "The Latest News from Viking Age Ribe: Archaological Excavations 1993." In *Developments*, edited by Björn Ambrosiani and Helen Clarke, 91–99. Stockholm, 1993.

——. *Ribe studier*, Jysk Arkaeologisk Selskabs skrifter 51. Højbjerg, 2006.

Filipowiak, Władysław. "Handel und Handelsplätze an der Ostseeküste Westpommerns." *Bericht der römisch-germanischen Kommission* 69 (1988): 690–719.

——. "Wollin—ein frühmittelalterliche Zentrum an der Ostsee." In *Europas Mitte um 1000*, edited by Alfried Wieczorek and Hans-Martin Hinz, 152–155. Stuttgart, 2000.

Finnur Jónsson. *Austrfararvísur*. Oslo, 1932.

——. *Den norsk-islandske skjaldedigtning*. Copenhagen, 1912.

Fletcher, R. A. *The Conversion of Europe: From Paganism to Christianity 371–1386 AD*. London, 1997.

Flodoard of Rheims. *Les Annales de Flodoard, publièes d'après les manuscrits*. Edited and translated by Ph. Lauer. Collection de textes pour servir à l'étude et à l'enseignement de l'histoire 39. Paris, 1905.

——. *Die Geschichte der Rheimser Kirche*. Edited by Martina Stratmann, MGH SS 36. Hanover, 1998.

Forte, A. D. M., Richard D. Oram, and Frederik Pedersen. *Viking Empires*. Cambridge, 2005.

Frank, Roberta. *Old Norse Court Poetry: The Dróttkvætt Stanza*, Islandica 42. Ithaca, N.Y., 1978.

——. "A Scandal in Toronto: *The Dating of 'Beowulf'* a Quarter Century On." *Speculum* 82 (2007): 843–864.

Franklin, Simon, and Jonathan Shepard. *The Emergence of Rus: 750–1200*, Longman History of Russia. London, 1996.

Frye, Richard N. *Ibn Fadlan's Journey to Russia: A Tenth-Century Traveler from Baghdad to the Volga River*. Princeton, N.J., 2005.

Fulk, R. D., Robert E. Bjork, and John D. Niles. *Klaeber's Beowulf and the Fight at Finnsburg*. Toronto, 2008.

Gade, Kari Ellen, ed. *Poetry from the Kings' Sagas, 2: From c. 1035 to c. 1300*. Skaldic Poetry of the Scandinavian Middle Ages 2. Turnhout, 2009.

Geijer, Agnes. *Die Textilfunde aus den Gräbern*, Birka: Untersuchungen und Studien 3. Stockholm, 1938.

Gelting, Michael H. "The Kingdom of Denmark." In *Christianization and the Rise of Christian Monarchy: Scandinavia, Central Europe and Rus' c. 900–1200*, edited by Nora Berend, 73–120. Cambridge, 2007.

Gil Fernández, Juan, José L. Moralejo, and Juan Ignacio Ruiz de la Peña. *Crónicas asturianas: Crónica de Alfonso III (Rotense y "A Sebastián"): Crónica albeldense (y "profética")*, Publicaciones del Departamento de Historia Medieval / Universidad de Oviedo 11. Oviedo, 1985.

Godman, Peter, ed. *Poetry of the Carolingian Renaissance*. Norman, Okla., 1985.

——. *Poets and Emperors: Frankish Politics and Carolingian Poetry*. Oxford, 1987.

Goffart, Walter. *The Narrators of Barbarian History (A.D. 550–800): Jordanes, Gregory of Tours, Bede, and Paul the Deacon*. 2d ed., Publications in Medieval Studies. Notre Dame, Ind., 2005.

Golden, Peter B. "The Peoples of the Russian Forest Belt." In *The Cambridge History of Early Inner Asia*, edited by Denis Sinor, 229–255. Cambridge, 1990.

Goodacre, S., A. Helgason, J. Nicholson, L. Southam, L. Ferguson, E. Hickey, E. Vega, K. Stefánsson, R. Ward, and B. Sykes. "Genetic Evidence for a Family-based Scandinavian Settlement of Shetland and Orkney during the Viking Periods." *Heredity* 95 (2005): 129–135.

Götherström, Anders. *Acquired or Inherited Prestige? Molecular Studies of Family Structures and Local Horses in Central Svealand during the Early Medieval Period*, Theses and Papers in Scientific Archaeology 4. Stockholm, 2001.

Graham-Campbell, James. *Viking Artefacts: Select Catalogue*. London, 1980.

Gräslund, Anne-Sofie. "Arkeologin och kristnandet." In *Kristnandet i Sverige: Gamla källor och nya perspektiv*, edited by Bertil Nilsson, 19–44. Uppsala, 1996.

——. *The Burial Customs: A Study of the Graves on Björkö*, Birka: Untersuchungen und Studien 4. Stockholm, 1980.

——. "Charonsmynt i vikingatida gravar?" *Tor: Tidskrift för nordisk fornkunskap* 11 (1967).

——. "Den tidiga missionen i arkeologisk belysning—problem och synpunkter." *Tor: Tidskrift för nordisk fornkunskap* 20 (1985): 291–313.

——. "Kreuzanhänger, Kruzifix und Reliquiar-Anhänger." In *Birka*, edited by Greta Arwidsson, 111–118. Stockholm, 1984.

——. "The Material Culture of Old Norse Religion." In *The Viking World*, edited by Stefan Brink, in collaboration with Neil Price. London, 2008.

——. "New Perspectives on an Old Problem: Uppsala and the Christianization of Sweden." In *Christianizing Peoples and Converting Individuals*, edited by Gyuda Armstrong and Ian N. Wood. Turnhout, 2000.

——. "Tor eller Vite Krist? Några reflektioner med anledning av Lugnås-hammaren." *Västergötlands fornminnesförenings tidskrift 1983–1984* (1983): 229–235.

——. "Var Mammen-mannen kristen?" In *Mammen: Grav, kunst og samfund i vikingetid*, edited by Mette Iversen, 205–210. Viborg, 1991.

Gregory of Tours. *Gregorii episcopi Turonensis Libri Historiarum X*. Edited by Bruno Krusch and Wilhelmus Levison, SS rer. Merov. 1. Hanover, 1950.

——. *The History of the Franks*. Translated by Lewis Thorpe, Penguin Classics. Harmondsworth, 1974.

Grierson, Philip. "Commerce in the Dark Ages: A Critique of the Evidence." *Transactions of the Royal Historical Society, Fifth Series* 9 (1959): 123–140.

Grønlie, Siân, trans. *Íslendingabók = The Book of the Icelanders: Kristni Saga = The Story of the Conversion*, Viking Society for Northern Research: Text Series 18. London, 2006.

Guhnfeldt, Cato. "Nazijakt på et skjult sverd." *Aftenposten*, 12 (April 2003).

Gunnes, Erik. *Erkebiskop Øystein: Statsmann og kirkebygger*. Oslo, 1996.

———. *Rikssamling og kristning: 800–1177*. Vol. 2 of *Norges historie*. Oslo, 1976.

Gustafson, Gabriel, Sune Lindqvist, and Fredrik Nordin. *Gotlands Bildsteine*. Stockholm, 1941.

Gustavson, Helmer. *Gamla och nya runor: Artiklar 1982–2001*, Runica et mediaevalia: Opuscula 9. Stockholm, 2003.

———. "Runmonumentet i Rytterne." In *Nya anteckningar om Rytterns socken: Medeltidsstudier tillägnade Göran Dahlbäck*, edited by Olle Ferm, Agneta Paulsson, and Krister Ström, 145–153. Västerås, 2002.

Gustavson, Helmer, Thorgunn Snædal, and Marit Åhlén. "Runfynd 1989 och 1990." *Fornvännen* 87 (1992).

Gustin, Ingrid. "Means of Payment and the Use of Coins in the Viking Age Town of Birka in Sweden: Preliminary Results." *Current Swedish Archaeology* 6 (1998): 73–83.

Hagberg, Ulf Erik. "Offren i Skedemosse på Öland och handeln med romarriket." In *Arkeologi i Norden*, by Göran Burenhult, 274–277. Stockholm, 1999.

Hagberg, Ulf Erik, Margareta Beskow-Sjöberg, Joachim Boessneck, Nils Gustaf Gejvall, and Angela von den Driesch Karpf. *The Archaeology of Skedemosse*. Stockholm, 1967.

Häger, Olle, and Hans Villius. *Rök: Gåtornas sten*. Stockholm, 1976.

Hägg, Inga. "Birkas orientaliska praktplagg." *Fornvännen* 78 (1983): 204–223.

———. *Die Textilfunde aus der Siedlung und aus den Gräbern von Haithabu: Beschreibung und Gliederung*, Berichte über die Ausgrabungen in Haithabu 29. Neumünster, 1991.

Hägg, Inga, Gertrud Grenander Nyberg, and Helmut Schweppe. *Die Textilfunde aus dem Hafen von Haithabu*, Berichte über die Ausgrabungen in Haithabu 20. Neumünster, 1984.

Halldórsson, Ólafur. See Ólafur Halldórsson.

Hallencreutz, Carl F. *När Sverige blev europeiskt: Till frågan om Sveriges kristnande*, Vitterhetsakademiens skriftserie om Europa. Stockholm, 1993.

Hansen, Lars Ivar, and Bjørnar Olsen. *Samenes historie fram til 1750*. Oslo, 2004.

Hårdh, Birgitta. "Viking Age Uppåkra and Lund." In *The Viking World*, edited by Stefan Brink, in collaboration with Neil Price, 145–149. London, 2008.

Hårdh, Birgitta, and Lars Larsson. *Uppåkra—Lund före Lund*, Föreningen Gamla Lund: Årsbok. Lund, 2007.

Harthausen, Hartmut. *Die Normanneneinfälle im Elb- und Wesermündungsgebiet mit besonderer Berücksichtigung der Schlacht von 880*, Quellen und Darstellungen zur Geschichte Niedersachsens 68. Hildesheim, 1966.

Heather, Peter. *Empires and Barbarians: The Fall of Rome and the Birth of Europe*. New York, 2010.

Hedberg, Britt. *Uppsala stifts herdaminne: Från missionstid till år 1366*, Uppsala stifts herdaminne 4:1. Uppsala, 2007.

Helgason, Agnar, Eileen Hickey, Sara Goodacre, Vidar Bosnes, Kári Stefánsson, Ryk Ward, and Bryan Sykes. "mtDNA and the Islands of the North Atlantic: Estimating the Proportions of Norse and Gaelic Ancestry." *American Journal of Human Genetics* 68 (2001): 723–737.

Helgason, Agnar, Sigrún Sigurðardóttir, Jayne Nicholson, Bryan Sykes, Emmeline W. Hill, Daniel G. Bradley, Vidar Bosnes, Jeffery R. Gulcher, Ryk Ward, and Kári Stefánsson. "Estimating Scandinavian and Gaelic Ancestry in the Male Settlers of Iceland." *American Journal of Human Genetics* 67 (2000): 697–717.

Helle, Knut, ed. *The Cambridge History of Scandinavia.* Cambridge, 2003.

——. "The Organisation of the Twelfth-Century Norwegian Church." In *St. Magnus Cathedral and Orkney's Twelfth-Century Renaissance,* edited by B. Crawford. Aberdeen, 1988.

Hellström, Jan Arvid. *Vägar till Sveriges kristnande.* Stockholm, 1996.

Herschend, Frands. "Hus på Helgö." *Fornvännen* 90 (1995): 221–228.

——. *Livet i hallen: Tre fallstudier i den yngre järnålderns aristokrati,* Occasional Papers in Archaeology 14. Uppsala, 1997.

Hines, J. "På tvers av Nordsjøen: Britiske perspektiver på Skandinaviens senare jernalder." *Universitetets Oldsaksamlings Årbok 1991–1992,* 1993, 103–124.

Hinschius, Paul. *System des katholischen Kirchenrechts mit besonderen Rücksicht auf Deutschland.* Berlin, 1869–1897.

Hjelmqvist, Hakon. "Frön och frukter från det äldsta Lund." In *Thulegrävningen 1961,* edited by Ragnar Blomqvist and Anders W. Mårtensson, 233–267. Lund, 1963.

Hodges, Richard, and David Whitehouse. *Mohammed, Charlemagne, and the Origins of Europe: Archaeology and the Pirenne Thesis.* London, 1983.

Hoffmann, Dietrich. *Hollingstedt: Untersuchungen zum Nordseehafen von Haithabu/Schleswig,* Berichte über die Ausgrabungen in Haithabu 25. Neumünster, 1987.

Holmboe, Jens. "Nytteplanter og ugræs i Osebergfundet." In *Osebergfundet,* edited by A. W. Brøgger and Haakon Shetelig, 5.1–78. Oslo, 1927.

Holmqvist, Wilhelm. *Excavations at Helgö.* Stockholm, 1961–1997.

Horn Fuglesang, Signe. "The Axehead from Mammen and the Mammen Style." In *Mammen: Grav, kunst og samfund i vikingetid,* edited by Mette Iversen, 83–108. Højbjerg, 1991.

Hudson, Benjamin T. *Viking Pirates and Christian Princes: Dynasty, Religion, and Empire in the North Atlantic.* Oxford, 2005.

Hultgård, Anders. "The Religion of the Vikings." In *The Viking World,* edited by Stefan Brink, in collaboration with Neil Price, 212–218. London, 2008.

Hyenstrand, Åke. *Järn och bebyggelse: Studier i Dalarnas äldre kolonisationshistoria,* Dalarnas hembygdsbok 1974. Falun, 1974.

——. *Lejonet, draken och korset: Sverige 500–1000.* Lund, 1996.

Ianin, V. L. *Otechestvennaia istoriia: istoriia Roccii c drevneyshikh vremen do 1917 goda.* Moscow, 1994.

Iregren, Elisabeth. "Under Frösö kyrka—ben från en vikingatida offerlund?" In *Arkeologi och religion: Rapport från arkeologidagarna 16–18 januari 1989,* edited by Lars Larsson and Bożena Wyszomirska, 119–133. Lund, 1989.

Iversen, Mette, ed. *Mammen: Grav, kunst og samfund i vikingetid,* Jysk Arkaeologisk Selskabs skrifter 28. Højbjerg, 1991.

Jacob, Georg. *Arabische Berichte von Gesandten an germanische Fürstenhöfe aus dem 9. und 10. Jahrhundert ins Deutsche übertragen und mit Fussnoten versehen.* Berlin, 1927.

Jaffé, Philipp. *Regesta pontificum Romanorum.* 2d ed. Leipzig, 1885–1888.

Jagodziński, Marek F. "Truso—Siedlung und Hafen im slawisch-estnischen Grenzgebiet." In *Europas Mitte um 1000: Handbuch zur Ausstellung,* edited by Alfried Wieczorek and Hans-Martin Hinz, 170–174. Stuttgart, 2000.

Jagodziński, Marek F., and Maria Kasprzycka. "The Early Medieval Craft and Commercial Center at Janów Pomorski near Elblag on the South Baltic Coast." *Antiquity* 65 (1991): 696–715.

Jakob Benediktsson, ed. *Íslendingabók: Landnámabók,* Íslenzk fornrit 1. Reykjavik, 1968.

Janin, Vladimir L. "Das frühe Novgorod." *Bericht der römisch-germanischen Kommission* 69 (1988): 338–343.

Jankuhn, Herbert. *Haithabu: Ein Handelsplatz der Wikingerzeit.* 3d ed. Neumünster, 1956.

Janson, Henrik. *Templum nobilissimum: Adam av Bremen, Uppsalatemplet och konfliktlinjerna i Europa kring år 1075,* Avhandlingar från Historiska institutionen i Göteborg 21. Göteborg, 1998.

Jansson, Ingmar. "Communications between Scandinavia and Eastern Europe in the Viking Age." In *Der Handel der Karolinger- und Wikingerzeit: Bericht über die Kolloquien der Kommission für die Altertumskunde Mittel- und Nordeuropas in den Jahren 1980 bis 1983,* edited by Klaus Düwel, 773–807. Untersuchungen zu Handel und Verkehr der vor- und frühgeschichtlichen Zeit in Mittel- und Nordeuropa 4 = Abhandlungen der Akademie der Wissenschaften in Göttingen: Philologisch-historische Klasse, 3. Folge, 156. Göttingen, 1987.

Jansson, Sven B. F. "Några okända uppländska runinskrifter." *Fornvännen* 41 (1946): 257–280.

——. *Runes in Sweden.* [Stockholm], 1987.

——. *Runinskrifter i Sverige.* 3d ed. Stockholm, 1984.

——. *Västmanlands runinskrifter,* Sveriges runinskrifter 13. Stockholm, 1964.

Jensen, Jørgen. *The Prehistory of Denmark.* London, 1982.

Jensen, Stig. "Det ældste Ribe—og vikingetidens begyndelse." In *Femte tværfaglige vikingesymposium Aarhus Universitet 1986,* edited by Torben Kisbye and Else Roesdahl, 7–22. Højbjerg, 1986.

Jochens, Jenny. "Late and Peaceful: Iceland's Conversion through Arbitration in 1000." *Speculum* 74 (1999): 621–655.

Johanek, Peter. "Der fränkische Handel der Karolingerzeit im Spiegel der Schriftquellen." In *Der Handel der Karolinger- und Wikingerzeit: Bericht über die Kolloquien der Kommission für die Altertumskunde Mittel- und Nordeuropas in den Jahren 1980 bis 1983,* edited by Klaus Düwel, 7–68. Untersuchungen zu Handel und Verkehr der vor- und frühgeschichtlichen Zeit in Mittel- und Nordeuropa 4 = Abhandlungen der Akademie der Wissenschaften in Göttingen: Philologisch-historische Klasse, 3. Folge, 156. Göttingen, 1987.

Johnsen, Arne Odd. *Studier vedrørende kardinal Nicolaus Brekespears legasjon til Norden.* Oslo, 1945.

Jón Viðar Sigurðsson. *Det norrøne samfunnet: Vikingen, kongen, erkebiskopen og bonden.* Oslo, 2008.

———. *Kristninga i Norden 750–1200,* Utsyn & innsikt. Oslo, 2003.

———. *Norsk historie 800–1300,* Samlagets Norsk historie 800–2000. Oslo, 1999.

Jones, Gwyn. *A History of the Vikings.* London, 1968.

Jónsson, Finnur. See Finnur Jónsson.

Joranson, Einar. *The Danegeld in France.* Rock Island, Ill., 1923.

Jordanes. *Jordanis Romana et Getica.* Edited by Theodor Mommsen, MGH Auctores antiquissimi 5. Berlin, 1882.

Jørgensen, Lars, Birger Storgaard, and Lone Gebauer Thomsen. *The Spoils of Victory: The North in the Shadow of the Roman Empire.* [Copenhagen], 2003.

Jungner, Hugo, and Elisabeth Svärdström. *Västergötlands runinskrifter,* Sveriges runin-skrifter 5. Stockholm, 1958–1970.

Kerner, Robert J. *The Urge to the Sea: The Course of Russian History: The Role of Rivers, Portages, Ostrogs, Monasteries, and Furs.* Berkeley, 1942.

Keynes, Simon. "The Vikings in England, c. 790–1016." In *The Oxford Illustrated History of the Vikings,* edited by Peter Sawyer, 48–82. Oxford, 1997.

Kinander, Ragnar. *Smålands runinskrifter,* Sveriges runinskrifter 4. Stockholm, 1935.

Kirpichnikov, A. N. "Connections between Russia and Scandinavia in the 9th and 10th Centuries, as Illustrated by Weapons Finds." In *Varangian Problems,* edited by Knud Hannestad, 57–61. Copenhagen, 1970.

Kirpičnikov, Anatol N. "Staraja Ladoga/Alt-Ladoga und seine überregionalen Beziehungen im 8.–10. Jahrhundert: Anmerkungen zur Verbreitung von Dirhems im eurasischen Handel." *Bericht der römisch-germanischen Kommission* 69 (1988): 307–337, 1988.

Klindt-Jensen, Ole, and David M. Wilson. *Viking Art.* 2d ed., Nordic series 6. Min-neapolis, 1980.

Kluger, Helmuth, Odilo Engels, Tore Nyberg, and Stefan Weinfurter. *Series episcoporum Ecclesiae Catholicae occidentalis ab initio ad annum MCXCVIII 6.2: Archiepiscopatus Lundensis.* Stuttgart, 1992.

Knibbs, Eric. "The Origins of the Archdiocese of Hamburg-Bremen." PhD diss., Yale University, 2009.

———. *Ansgar, Rimbert and the Forged Foundations of Hamburg-Bremen,* Church, Faith and Culture in the Medieval West. Farnham, U.K., 2011.

Knirk, James E. "Arbeidet ved Runearkivet, Oslo." *Nytt om runer* 2 (1987).

Kovalev, Roman K., and Alexis C. Kaelin. "Circulation of Arab Silver in Medieval Afro-Eurasia: Preliminary Observations." *History Compass,* no. 2 (2007). http://www.blackwell-synergy.com/doi/abs/10.1111/j.1478-0542.2006.00376.x.

Krag, Claus. *Norges historie fram til 1319.* Oslo, 2000.

Krogh, Knud J. *Gåden om Kong Gorms grav: Historien om Nordhøjen i Jelling,* Vikingekongernes monumenter i Jelling 1. Copenhagen, 1993.

Kulturhistoriskt lexikon för nordisk medeltid från vikingatid till reformationstid. 22 vols. Malmö, 1956–1982.

Kunz, Keneva. *The Vinland Sagas: The Icelandic Sagas about the First Documented Voyages across the North Atlantic,* Penguin Classics. London, 2008.

Kværness, Gunhild. *Blote kan ein gjere om det berre skjer i løynd: Kristenrettane i Gulatingslova og Grágás og forholdet mellom dei*, KULTs skriftserie 65. Oslo, 1996.

Kyhlberg, Ola. "Vågar och viktlod: Diskussion kring frågor om precision och noggrannhet." *Fornvännen* 70 (1975): 156–165.

——. *Vikt och värde: Arkeologiska studier i värdemätning, betalningsmedel och metrologi under yngre järnålder: 1. Helgö, 2. Birka*, Stockholm Studies in Archaeology 1. Stockholm, 1980.

Lamm, C. J. *Oriental Glass of Mediaeval Date Found in Sweden and the Early History of Lustre-Painting*. Stockholm, 1941.

Landro, Torgeir. "Kristenrett og kyrkjerett: Borgartingskristenretten i eit komparativt perspektiv." PhD diss., University of Bergen (Norway), 2010.

Lappenberg, J. M. "Von den Quellen, Handschriften und Bearbeitungen des Adam von Bremen." *Archiv der Gesellschaft für ältere deutsche Geschichtskunde* 6 (1838): 766–892.

Larsen, Nicolai Garhøj. "Virtual Reconstruction: The Viking Hall at Lejre." In *Beowulf and Lejre*, edited by John D. Niles, Tom Christensen, and Marijane Osborn, 159–166. Tempe, Ariz., 2007.

Larsson, Annika. "Vikingar begravda i kinesiskt siden." *Valör* (2008): 33–43.

Larsson, Lars, and Birgitta Hårdh. "Kulthuset i Uppåkra." In *Odens öga—mellan människor och makter i det förkristna Norden*, edited by Anders Andrén and Peter Carelli, 176–183, 309–311. Helsingborg, 2006.

Lawson, M. K. "The Collection of Danegeld and Heregeld in the Reigns of Aethelred II and Cnut." *English Historical Review* 99 (1984): 721–738.

Lehtosalo-Hilander, Pirko-Liisa. "Le Viking finnois." *Finskt museum* (1990): 55–72.

Leisi, Ernst. "Gold und Manneswert im Beowulf." *Anglia* n.s. 59 = 71 (1953): 259–273.

Leth-Larsen, Bodil. "Mammenlyset." In *Mammen: Grav, kunst og samfund i vikingetid*, edited by Mette Iversen, 109–121. Viborg, 1991.

Levd liv: En utstilling om skjelettene fra Oseberg og Gokstad. [Oslo], 2008.

Lexikon des Mittelalters 5. Zürich, 1991.

Lind, Lennart. *Roman Denarii Found in Sweden*, Stockholm Studies in Classical Archaeology 11. Stockholm, 1981.

Lindkvist, Thomas. "Early Political Organization: a) Introductory Survey." In *The Cambridge History of Scandinavia*, edited by Knut Helle, 160–167. Cambridge, 2003.

——. "Med Sankt Erik konung mot hedningar och schismatiker. Korståg och korstågsideologi i svensk medeltida östpolitik." In *Väst möter öst. Norden och Ryssland genom tiderna*, edited by Max Engman, 13–33. Stockholm, 1996.

——. "Ny tro i nya riken: Kristnandet som en del av den politiska historien." In *Kyrka—samhälle—stat: Från kristnande till etablerad kyrka*, edited by Göran Dahlbäck, 37–58. Helsinki, 1997.

——. *Plundring, skatter och den feodala statens framväxt: Organisatoriska tendenser i Sverige under övergången från vikingatid till tidig medeltid*. 3d ed, Opuscula historica Upsaliensia 1. Uppsala, 1993.

Lindow, John. "Thor's 'hamarr.' " *Journal of Germanic and English Philology* 93 (1994): 485–503.

Liuzza, R. M. *Beowulf: A New Verse Translation*, Broadview Literary Texts. Peterborough, Ont., 2000.

Löfving, Carl. *Gothia som dansk/engelskt skattland: Ett exempel på heterarki omkring år 1000*. New ed., GOTARC, series B: Gothenburg Archaeological Theses 16. Göteborg, 2001.

Lønborg, Bjarne. *Vikingetidens metalbearbejdning*, Fynske studier 17. Odense, 1998.

Lönnroth, Lars. "Hövdingahallen i fornnordisk myt och saga: Ett mentalitetshistoriskt bidrag till förståelsen av Slöingefyndet." In *"Gick Grendel att söka det höga huset"*, edited by Callmer and Rosengren, 31–37.

———. "Studier i Olaf Tryggvasons saga." *Samlaren* 84 (1963): 54–94.

Lopez, Robert S. *The Commercial Revolution of the Middle Ages, 950–1350*. Cambridge, 1976.

Löwe, Heinz. *Die karolingische Reichsgründung und der Südosten: Studien zum Werden des Deutschtums und seiner Auseinandersetzung mit Rom*, Forschungen zur Kirchen- und Geistesgeschichte 13. Stuttgart, 1937.

———. "Studien zu den Annales Xantenses." *Deutsche Archiv für Erforschung des Mittelalters* 8 (1951): 59–99.

Lund, Niels. *Kristendommen i Danmark før 1050: Et symposium i Roskilde den 5.-7. februar 2003*. [Roskilde], 2004.

Lund, Niels, Ole Crumlin-Pedersen, P. H. Sawyer, and Christine E. Fell. *Two Voyagers at the Court of King Alfred: The Ventures of Ohthere and Wulfstan, together with the Description of Northern Europe from the Old English Orosius*. York, U.K., 1984.

Lund Hansen, Ulla. *Römischer Import im Norden: Warenaustausch zwischen dem Römischen Reich und dem freien Germanien während der Kaiserzeit unter besonderer Berücksichtigung Nordeuropas*, Nordiske fortidsminder. Serie B—in quarto 10. Copenhagen, 1987.

Lundqvist, Lars. *Slöinge 1992–1996: Undersökningar av en boplats från yngre järnålder*, GOTARC, series C: Arkeologiska skrifter. Göteborg, 2003.

Lundström, Agneta, ed. *Thirteen Studies on Helgö*. Stockholm, 1988.

Lundström, Inga, Claes Theliander, and Pirjo Lahtiperä. *Såntorp: Ett gravfält i Västergötland från förromersk järnålder till tidig medeltid: anläggningsbeskrivningar, dokumentation och analyser*, GOTARC, series C: Arkeologiska skrifter 49. Göteborg, 2004.

Lynch, Joseph H. *Christianizing Kinship: Ritual Sponsorship in Anglo-Saxon England*. Ithaca, N.Y., 1998.

———. *Godparents and Kinship in Early Medieval Europe*. Princeton, N.J., 1986.

Mac Airt, Seán, ed. and trans. *The Annals of Inisfallen MS. Rawlinson B503*. Dublin, 1951.

Mac Airt, Seán, and Gearóid Mac Niocaill, eds. and trans. *The Annals of Ulster (to A.D. 1131)*. [Dublin], 1983.

MacLean, Simon. *History and Politics in Late Carolingian and Ottonian Europe: The Chronicle of Regino of Prüm and Adalbert of Magdeburg*, Manchester Medieval Sources Series. Manchester, 2009.

Martin, Janet. *Treasure of the Land of Darkness: The Fur Trade and Its Significance for Medieval Russia*. Cambridge, 1986.

Mastana, S. S., and R. J. Sokol. "Genetic Variation in the East Midlands." *Annals of Human Biology* 25 (1998): 43–68.

Maund, K. L. "'A Turmoil of Warring Princes': Political Leadership in Ninth-century Denmark." *Haskins Society Journal: Studies in Medieval History* 6 (1994): 29–47.

Maurer, Konrad von. *Die Bekehrung des norwegischen Stammes zum Christenthume in ihrem geschichtlichen Verlaufe quellenmässig geschildert.* Munich, 1855–56. Reprint, Osnabrück, 1965.

Mauss, Marcel. *The Gift: The Form and Reason for Exchange in Archaic Societies.* Translated by W. D. Halls. London, 1990.

McCormick, Michael. "New Light on the 'Dark Ages': How the Slave Trade Fuelled the Carolingian Economy." *Past and Present* (2002): 17–54.

——. *Origins of the European Economy: Communications and Commerce A.D. 300–900.* Cambridge, 2001.

McEvoy, Brian, Claire Brady, Laoise T. Moore, and Daniel G. Bradley. "The Scale and Nature of Viking Settlement in Ireland from Y-chromosome Admixture Analysis." *European Journal of Human Genetics* 14 (2006): 1288–1294.

McKeithen, James E. "The Risalah of Ibn Fadlan: An Annotated Translation with Introduction." PhD diss., Indiana University, 1979.

Mierow, Charles C., trans. *Jordanes, The Origin and Deeds of the Goths, in English Version.* Princeton, N.J., 1908.

Miquel, André. "L'Europe occidentale dans la relation arabe d'Ibrâhîm b. Ya'qûb (Xᵉ s.)." *Annales Économies, Sociétés, Civilisations* 21 (1966): 1048–1064.

Moltke, Erik, and Lis Jacobsen. *Danmarks runeindskrifter.* Copenhagen, 1941–1942.

Montgomery, James E. "Ibn Fadlan and the Russiyah." *Journal of Arabic and Islamic Studies* 3 (2000): 1–25.

Monumenta Germaniae Historica: Capitularia regum Francorum 1–2. Hanover, 1883–1897.

Monumenta Germaniae Historica: Epistulae 4–6. Berlin, 1895–1925.

Monumenta Germaniae Historica: Poetae 1. Berlin, 1881.

Monumenta Germaniae Historica: Scriptores 3, 19. Hanover, 1839, 1866.

Monumenta Germaniae Historica: Scriptores rerum Merovingicarum 7. Edited by Bruno Krusch and Wilhelm Levison. Hanover, 1919–1920.

Morgan, David. *The Mongols.* Oxford, 1990.

Mühle, Eduard. *Die städtischen Handelszentren der nordwestlichen Rus: Anfänge und frühe Entwicklung altrussischer Städte (bis gegen Ende des 12. Jahrhunderts),* Quellen und Studien zur Geschichte des östlichen Europa 32. Stuttgart, 1991.

——. "Review of Srednevekovaia Ladoga." *Jahrbücher für Geschichte Osteuropas* 35 (1987): 585–590.

Müller-Wille, Michael. *Das wikingerzeitliche Gräberfeld von Thumby-Bienebek (Kr. Rendsburg-Eckernförde),* 1, Offa-Bücher 36. Neumünster, 1976.

Näsman, Ulf. "Sea Trade during the Scandinavian Iron Age: Its Character, Commodities and Routes." In *Aspects of Maritime Scandinavia AD 200–1200: Proceedings of the Nordic Seminar on Maritime Aspects of Archaeology, Roskilde, 13th-15th March, 1989,* edited by Ole Crumlin-Pedersen, 23–40. Roskilde, 1991.

Neff, Karl. *Die Gedichte des Paulus Diaconus: Kritische und erklärende Ausgabe*, Quellen und Untersuchungen zur lateinischen Philologie des Mittelalters 3:2. Munich, 1908.

Neill, Stephen. *A History of Christian Missions.* 2d ed., Pelican History of the Church. Harmondsworth, 1986.

Nelson, Janet. *The Annals of St-Bertin*, Ninth-Century Histories 1. Manchester, 1991.

———. "England and the Continent in the Ninth Century: II, The Vikings and Others." *Transactions of the Royal Historical Society, Fifth Series* 13 (2003): 1–28.

———. "The Frankish Empire." In *The Oxford Illustrated History of the Vikings*, edited by Peter Sawyer, 19–47. Oxford, 1997.

Niles, John D. "Beowulf's Great Hall." *History Today* 56 (2006): 40–46.

Niles, John D., Tom Christensen, and Marijane Osborn, eds. *Beowulf and Lejre*, Medieval and Renaissance Texts and Studies 323. Tempe, Ariz., 2007.

Nilsson, Bertil, ed. *Kristnandet i Sverige: Gamla källor och nya perspektiv*, Publikationer Projektet Sveriges kristnande 5. Uppsala, 1996.

———. *Missionstid och tidig medeltid*, Sveriges kyrkohistoria 1. Stockholm, 1998.

Noonan, Thomas S. "European Russia, c. 500–c.1050." In *The New Cambridge Medieval History*, vol. 3, *c. 900-c. 1024*, edited by Timothy Reuter, 487–513. Cambridge, 1999.

———. "The Impact of the Silver Crisis in Islam upon Novgorod's Trade with the Baltic." *Bericht der römisch-germanischen Kommission* 69 (1988): 411–447.

———. *The Islamic World, Russia and the Vikings, 750–900: The Numismatic Evidence.* Aldershot, U.K., 1998.

———. "The Vikings in the East: Coins and Commerce." In *Developments Around the Baltic and the North Sea in the Viking Age*, edited by Björn Ambrosiani and Helen Clarke, 215–236. Stockholm, 1994.

———. "Why the Vikings First Came to Russia." *Jahrbücher für Geschichte Osteuropas* 34 (1986): 321–348.

Nyberg, Tore. *Die Kirche in Skandinavien: Mitteleuropäischer und englischer Einfluss im 11. und 12. Jahrhundert: Anfänge der Domkapitel Børglum und Odense in Dänemark*, Beiträge zur Geschichte und Quellenkunde des Mittelalters 10. Sigmaringen, 1986.

Nylén, Erik. *Vikingaskepp mot Miklagård: Krampmacken i Österled.* Stockholm, 1987.

Nylén, Erik, and Jan Peder Lamm. *Bildstenar.* 3d ed. Stockholm, 2003.

O'Brien O'Keeffe, Katherine, ed. *MS C.* Vol. 5 of *The Anglo-Saxon Chronicle: A Collaborative Edition*, edited by David Dumville and Simon Keynes. Cambridge, 2000.

Ó Corráin, Donnchadh. "Ireland, Wales, Man, and the Hebrides." In *The Oxford Illustrated History of the Vikings*, edited by Peter Sawyer, 83–109. Oxford, 1997.

———. "The Vikings & Ireland." Corpus of Electronic Texts (CELT), [ca. 1991]. http://www.ucc.ie/celt/General%20Vikings%20in%20Ireland.pdf.

Oddr Snorrason. *The Saga of Olaf Tryggvason.* Translated by Theodore M. Andersson. Ithaca, N.Y., 2003.

Ólafur Halldórsson, ed. *Færeyinga saga: Ólafs saga Tryggvasonar eptir Odd munk Snorrason*, Íslenzk fornrit 25. Reykjavik, 2006.

Olsen, Magnus, and Aslak Liestøl. Norges innskrifter med de yngre runer. Norges indskrifter indtil reformationen, afd 2. Oslo, 1941–.

Olsen, Olaf. *Hørg, hov og kirke: Historiske og arkæologiske vikingetidsstudier.* Copenhagen, 1966.

Orrman, Eljas. "Church and Society." In *The Cambridge History of Scandinavia*, edited by Knut Helle, 421–462. Cambridge, 2003.

Osborn, Marijane. "Legends of Lejre, Home of Kings." In *Beowulf and Lejre*, edited by John D. Niles, Tom Christensen, and Marijane Osborn, 235–254. Tempe, Ariz., 2007.

Østergård, Else. "Textilfragmenterne fra Mammengraven." In *Mammen: Grav, kunst og samfund i vikingetid*, 123–138. Viborg, 1991.

Padberg, Lutz von. *Christianisierung im Mittelalter.* Stuttgart, 2006.

Page, R. I. *Chronicles of the Vikings: Records, Memorials, and Myths.* Toronto, 1995.

Palm, Rune. *Vikingarnas språk 750–1100.* Stockholm, 2004.

Peirce, Ian G. *Swords of the Viking Age.* Rochester, N.Y., 2002.

Perez de Urbel, Justo, and Atilano Gonzales Ruiz-Zorrilla, eds. *Historia Silense*, Consejo superior de investigaciones científicas, Escuela de estudios medievales: Textos 30. Madrid, 1959.

Perkow, Ursula. "Wasserweihe, Taufe und Patenschaft bei den Nordgermanen." PhD diss., Hamburg University, 1972.

Phelpstead, Carl, and Devra Levingson Kunin, trans. *A History of Norway, and the Passion and Miracles of Blessed Óláfr.* London, 2001.

Pirenne, Henri. *Medieval Cities: Their Origins and the Revival of Trade.* Translated by Frank D. Halsey. Princeton, N.J., 1925.

Poole, Russell. "Claiming Kin Skaldic Style." In *Verbal Encounters: Anglo-Saxon and Old Norse Studies for Roberta Frank*, edited by Russell Poole and Antonina Harbus, 269–285. Toronto, 2005.

———. "The 'Conversion Verses' of Hallfreðr vandræðaskáld." *Maal og minne* (2002): 15–37.

Price, Neil S. *The Viking Way: Religion and War in Late Iron Age Scandinavia.* Uppsala, 2002.

Pulsiano, Phillip, and Kirsten Wolf, eds. *Medieval Scandinavia: An Encyclopedia.* New York, 1993.

Radhe, Birgitta, ed. *Klenoder i Gotlands Fornsal*, Gotländskt arkiv 75. Visby, 2003.

Raffel, Burton. *Beowulf.* New York, 2008.

Ralph, Bo. "Gåtan som lösning—Ett bidrag till förståelsen av Rökstenens runinskrift." *Maal og minne* (2007): 133–157.

Raudvere, Catharina. "Popular Religion in the Viking Age." In *The Viking World*, edited by Stefan Brink, in collaboration with Neil Price, 235–243. London, 2008.

Rausing, Gad. "Barbarian Mercenaries or Roman citizens?" *Fornvännen* 82 (1987): 126–131.

Reallexikon der germanischen Altertumskunde. 2d ed. Berlin, 1967–2007.

Regesta pontificum Romanorum: Germania pontificia 6. Göttingen, 1981.

Regino of Prüm. *Reginonis abbatis Prumensis Chronicon cum continuatione Treverensi.* Edited by Fridericus Kurze, MGH SS rer. Germ. Hanover, 1890.

Reuter, Timothy. *The Annals of Fulda*, Ninth-Century Histories 2. Manchester, 1992.

———. "Plunder and Tribute in the Carolingian Empire." *Transactions of the Royal Historical Society* 35 (1985): 75–94.

Riché, Pierre. *The Carolingians: A Family Who Forged Europe.* Translated by Michael Idomir Allen, Middle Ages Series. Philadelphia, 1993.

Rimbert. *Vita Anskarii auctore Rimberto: Accedit Vita Rimberti.* Edited by G. Waitz, MGH SS rer. Germ. Hanover, 1884.

——. *Anskar, the Apostle of the North 801–865.* Translated by Charles H. Robinson, Lives of Early and Mediæval Missionaries. [London], 1921.

Roesdahl, Else. "Dendrochronology in Denmark, with a Note on the Beginning of the Viking Age." In *Developments around the Baltic and the North Sea in the Viking Age,* edited by Björn Ambrosiani and Helen Clarke. Stockholm, 1994.

——. *The Vikings.* 2d ed. London, 1998.

Rosenwein, Barbara H. *Reading the Middle Ages: Sources from Europe, Byzantium, and the Islamic World.* Peterborough, Ont., 2006.

Russell, James C. *The Germanization of Early Medieval Christianity: A Sociohistorical Approach to Religious Transformation.* New York, 1994.

"Samnordisk runtextdatabas." Uppsala University, 2009. http://www.nordiska.uu.se/forskn/samnord.htm.

Samson, Ross. "Fighting with Silver: Rethinking Trading, Raiding, and Hoarding." In *Social Approaches to Viking Studies,* edited by Ross Samson. Glasgow, 1991.

Sandwall, Ann, and Björn Ambrosiani. *Vendeltid,* Historia i fickformat. Stockholm, 1980.

Sanmark, Alexandra. *Power and Conversion: A Comparative Study of Christianization in Scandinavia,* Occasional Papers in Archaeology 34. Uppsala, 2004.

Sauer, Jonathan D. *Historical Geography of Crop Plants: A Select Roster.* Boca Raton, Fla., 1993.

Sawyer, Birgit. *The Viking-Age Rune-Stones: Custom and Commemoration in Early Medieval Scandinavia.* Oxford, 2000.

Sawyer, Birgit, and Peter Sawyer. "Scandinavia Enters Christian Europe." In *Cambridge History of Scandinavia,* edited by Knut Helle, 147–159. Cambridge, 2003.

Sawyer, Birgit, Peter Sawyer, and Ian Wood, eds. *The Christianization of Scandinavia: Report of a Symposium Held at Kungälv, Sweden 4–9 August 1985.* Alingsås, Sweden, 1987.

Sawyer, P. H. "Kings and Merchants." In *Early Medieval Kingship,* edited by P. H. Sawyer and I. N. Wood, 139–158. Leeds, 1977.

——. *Kings and Vikings: Scandinavia and Europe, A.D. 700–1100.* London, 1982.

Sawyer, Peter. *Da Danmark blev Danmark: fra ca. år 700 til ca. 1050.* Translated by Marie Hvidt. Vol. 3, *Gyldendal-Politikens Danmarkshistorie.* Copenhagen, 1988.

——, ed. *The Oxford Illustrated History of the Vikings.* Oxford, 1997.

——. "The Process of Scandinavian Christianization in the Tenth and Eleventh Centuries." In *The Christianization of Scandinavia: Report of a Symposium Held at Kungälv, Sweden 4–9 August 1985,* edited by Birgit Sawyer, Peter Sawyer, and Ian Wood, 68–87. Alingsås, Sweden, 1987.

Saxo Grammaticus. *Saxonis Gesta Danorum.* Edited by Jørgen Olrik and Hans Raeder. Copenhagen, 1931.

Schneider, Gerhard. *Erzbischof Fulco von Reims (883–900) und das Frankenreich,* Münchener Beiträge zur Mediävistik und Renaissance-Forschung 14. Munich, 1973.

Scholz, Bernhard W., and Barbara Rogers. *Carolingian Chronicles: Royal Frankish Annals and Nithard's Histories.* Ann Arbor, Mich., 1970.

Schön, Volkmar. *Die Mühlsteine von Haithabu und Schleswig: Ein Beitrag zur Entwicklungsgeschichte des mittelalterlichen Mühlenwesens in Nordwesteuropa*, Berichte über die Ausgrabungen in Haithabu 31. Neumünster, 1995.

Schücking, Levin L. "Wann entstand der Beowulf? Glossen, Zweifel, und Fragen." *Beiträge zur Geschichte der deutschen Sprache und Literatur* 42 (1917): 347–410.

Seaver, Kirsten A. *Maps, Myths, and Men: The Story of the Vinland Map.* Stanford, Calif., 2004.

Seegrün, Wolfgang. *Das Papsttum und Skandinavien bis zur Vollendung der nordischen Kirchenorganisation*, Quellen und Forschungen zur Geschichte Schleswig-Holsteins 51. Neumünster, 1967.

Sigurðsson, Jón Viðar. See Jón Viðar Sigurðsson.

Sjøvold, Thorleif. *Vikingeskipene i Oslo.* Oslo, 1985.

Skree, Dagfinn. "Missionary Activity in Early Medieval Norway: Strategy, Organization, and the Course of Events." *Scandinavian History Review* 23 (1998): 1–19.

Smedt, C., ed. "Translatio sancti Germani Parisiensis secundum primaevam narrationem." *Analecta Bollandiana* 2 (1883): 69–98.

Smyth, Alfred P. *Scandinavian Kings in the British Isles, 850–880*, Oxford Historical Monographs. Oxford, 1977.

——. *Scandinavian York and Dublin: The History and Archaeology of Two Related Viking Kingdoms.* Dublin, 1987.

Snorrason, Oddr. See Oddr Snorrason.

Snorri Sturluson. *Heimskringla.* Edited by Bjarni Aðalbjarnarson, Íslenzk fornrit, 26–28. Reykjavik, 1941.

——. *Heimskringla: History of the Kings of Norway.* Translated by Lee M. Hollander. Austin, Tex., 1964.

Söderberg, Sven, and Erik Brate. *Ölands runinskrifter*, Sveriges runinskrifter 1. Stockholm, 1900.

Solli, Brit. "Narratives of Encountering Religions: On the Christianization of the Norse around AD 900–1000." *Norwegian Archaeological Review* 29 (1996): 89–114.

Somerville, Angus A., and R. Andrew McDonald. *The Viking Age: A Reader.* Toronto, 2010.

Spurkland, Terje. *I begynnelsen var fuþark: Norske runer og runeinnskrifter*, LNUs skriftserie. Oslo, 2001.

Squatriti, Paolo. "Digging Ditches in Early Medieval Europe." *Past and Present* 176 (2002): 11–65.

Staecker, Jörn. "Jelling—Mythen und Realität." In *Der Ostseeraum und Kontinentaleuropa 1100–1600: Einflußnahme—Rezeption—Wandel*, 77–102. Schwerin, 2004.

Stefánsson, Jón. "The Vikings in Spain: From Arabic (Moorish) and Spanish Sources." *Saga-Book of the Viking Club* 6 (1908–1909): 31–46.

Steuer, Heiko. "Der Handel der Wikingerzeit zwischen Nord- und Westeuropa aufgrund archäologischer Zeugnisse." In *Der Handel der Karolinger- und Wikingerzeit: Bericht über die Kolloquien der Kommission für die Altertumskunde Mittel- und Nordeuropas in den Jahren 1980 bis 1983*, edited by Klaus Düwel, 113–197. Untersuchungen zu Handel und Verkehr der vor- und frühgeschichtlichen Zeit in Mittel- und Nordeuropa 4 = Abhandlungen der Akademie der Wissenschaften in Göttingen: Philologisch-historische Klasse, 3. Folge, 156. Göttingen, 1987.

———. "Eine dreieckige Bronzeschale aus Haithabu bei Schleswig." *Archäologisches Korrespondenzblatt* 3 (1975): 89–93.

Stjernquist, Berta. "Offerplatsen och samhällsstrukturen." In *Uppåkra: Centrum och sammanhang*, edited by Birgitta Hårdh, 3–28. Lund, 2001.

Storm, Gustav. *Monumenta historica Norvegiae: Latinske kildeskrifter til Norges historie i middelalderen*, Skrifter utg. for Kjeldeskriftfondet. Kristiania, 1880. Reprint, Oslo, 1973.

Ström, Jonas. "Världens största vikingatida silverskatt." Historiska museet, 2002. http://www.historiska.se/historia/manadensforemal/2002/mfjuni2002/.

Strömbäck, Dag. *The Conversion of Iceland: A Survey*. Translated by Peter G. Foote. [London], 1975.

Strömberg, Märta. *Untersuchungen zur jüngeren Eisenzeit in Schonen: Völkerwanderungszeit, Wikingerzeit*. Bonn, 1961.

Sturluson, Snorri. See Snorri Sturluson.

Sullivan, Richard E. *Christian Missionary Activity in the Early Middle Ages*, Variorum Reprints: Collected Studies Series 431. Aldershot, U.K., 1994.

Sundqvist, Olof. "Cult Leaders, Rulers and Religion." In *The Viking World*, edited by Stefan Brink, in collaboration with Neil Price, 223–226. London, 2008.

Sveinbjörn Egilsson, and Finnur Jónsson. *Lexicon poeticum antiquæ linguæ Septentrionalis: Ordbog over det norsk-islandske skjaldesprog*. 2d ed. Copenhagen, 1931.

Svenskt biografiskt lexikon 33. Stockholm, 2009.

Swanton, Michael, trans. *The Anglo-Saxon Chronicle*. London, 1996.

———. *Anglo-Saxon Prose*, Everyman's Library. London, 1993.

Talbot, Charles H. *The Anglo-Saxon Missionaries in Germany; being the Lives of SS. Willibrord, Boniface, Sturm, Leoba, and Lebuin, together with the Hodoeporicon of St. Willibald and a Selection from the Correspondence of St. Boniface*. New York, 1954.

Theliander, Claes. *Västergötlands kristnande: Religionsskifte och gravskickets förändring 700–1200*. New ed., GOTARC, series B: Gothenburg archaeological theses 41. Göteborg, 2005.

Theodoricus. *Historia de antiquitate regum Norwagiensium: An Account of the Ancient History of the Norwegian Kings*. Translated by David McDougall and Ian McDougall, Viking Society for Northern Research: Text series 11. London, 1998.

Thietmar of Merseburg. *Die Chronik des Bischofs Thietmar von Merseburg und ihre Korveier Überarbeitung*. Edited by Robert Holtzmann, MGH SS rer. Germ. NS 9. Berlin, 1935.

Todd, J. H. *War of the Gaedhil with the Gaill, or, The Invasions of Ireland by the Danes and Other Norsemen*, Rerum Britannicarum medii aevi scriptores 48. London, 1867.

Togan, Ahmed Zeki Velidi. *Ibn Fadlan's Reisebericht*, Islamic geography 168. Frankfurt am Main, 1994.

———. *Ibn Fadlan's Reisebericht*, Abhandlungen für die Kunde des Morgenlandes, 24.3. Leipzig, 1939.

Turville-Petre, Gabriel, and Christopher Tolkien, eds. *Hervarar saga ok Heiðreks*, Viking Society for Northern Research: Text series. London, 1976.

Udolph, Jürgen. "'Handel' und 'Verkehr' in slavischen Ortsnamen." In *Der Handel der Karolinger-und Wikingerzeit: Bericht über die Kolloquien der Kommission für die Altertumskunde Mittel- und Nordeuropas in den Jahren 1980 bis 1983*, edited by Klaus Düwel, 570–615. Untersuchungen zu Handel und Verkehr der vor- und frühgeschichtlichen Zeit in Mittel- und Nordeuropa 4 = Abhandlungen der Akademie der Wissenschaften in Göttingen: Philologisch-historische Klasse, 3. Folge, 156. Göttingen, 1987.

Van Houts, Elisabeth M. C. *The "Gesta Normannorum ducum" of William of Jumièges, Orderic Vitalis, and Robert of Torigni*, Oxford Medieval Texts. Oxford, 1992–1995.

Vésteinsson, Orri. *The Christianization of Iceland: Priests, Power, and Social Change, 1000–1300*. Oxford, 2000.

Vogel, Walther. *Die Normannen und das fränkische Reich bis zur Gründung der Normandie (799–911)*, Heidelberger Abhandlungen zur mittleren und neueren Geschichte 14. Heidelberg, 1906.

Wallace, Birgitta L. *Westward Vikings: The Saga of L'Anse aux Meadows*. St. John's, NF, 2006.

Wamers, Egon. "Kristne gjenstander i tidligvikingtidens Danmark." In *Kristendommen i Danmark før 1050*, edited by Niels Lund, 43–59. [Roskilde], 2004.

Wamers, Egon, and Michael Brandt. *Die Macht des Silbers: Karolingische Schätze im Norden*. Regensburg, 2005.

Warner, David. *Ottonian Germany: The Chronicon of Thietmar of Merseburg*, Manchester Medieval Sources Series. Manchester, 2001.

Weber, B. "Norwegian Reindeer Antler Export to Orkney: An Analysis of Combs from Pictish/Early Norse sites." *Universitetets Oldsaksamlings Årbok 1991–1992*, 1993, 197–205.

Webster, Leslie. "Archaeology and *Beowulf*." In *Beowulf: An Edition with Relevant Shorter Texts*, edited by Bruce Mitchell and Fred C. Robinson, 186–187. Oxford, 1998.

Webster, Leslie, and Michelle P. Brown. *The Transformation of the Roman World AD 400–900*. London, 1997.

Weibull, Lauritz. "Ansgarius." *Scandia* 14 (1942).

———. "Den skånska kyrkans älsta historia." In *Nordisk historia: Forskningar och undersökningar*, 2:1–130. Stockholm, 1948.

———. *Historisk-kritisk metod och nordisk medeltidsforskning*. Lund, 1913.

———. *Kritiska undersökningar i Nordens historia omkring år 1000*. Lund, 1911.

———. *Nordisk historia: Forskningar och undersökningar*. Lund, 1948.

———. "Skånes kyrka från älsta tid till Jacob Erlandsens död 1274." In *Lunds domkyrkas historia*, edited by Ernst Newman, 141–356. Stockholm, 1946.

———. "Upptäckten av den skandinaviska Norden." *Scandia* 7 (1934).

Welinder, Stig. *Sveriges historia 13000 f.Kr.–600 e.Kr.*, Norstedts Sveriges historia. Stockholm, 2009.

228   Bibliography

Wessén, Elias. *Runstenen vid Röks kyrka*, Kungl. Vitterhets-, historie-och antikvitet-sakademiens handlingar: Filologisk-filosofiska serien, 5. Stockholm, 1958.

Wessén, Elias, and Sven B. F. Jansson. *Upplands runinskrifter*. Vol. 3, Sveriges runinskrifter 8. Stockholm, 1949.

———. *Upplands runinskrifter*. Vol. 2, Sveriges runinskrifter 7. Stockholm, 1943.

Whaley, Diana. "The 'Conversion Verses' in Hallfreðar Saga: Authentic Voice of a Reluctant Christian?" In *Old Norse Myths, Literature and Society*, edited by Margaret Clunies Ross, 234–257. Odense, 2003.

———. *Heimskringla: An Introduction*, Viking Society for Northern Research: Text series 8. London, 1991.

———. *The Poetry of Arnórr Jarlaskáld: An Edition and Study*, Westfield Publications in Medieval Studies 8. Turnhout, 1998.

———. *Sagas of Warrior-Poets*, World of the Sagas. London, 2002.

Whitelock, Dorothy. *The Anglo-Saxon Chronicle: A Revised Translation*. New Brunswick, N.J., 1962.

———. *English Historical Documents*. Vol. 1, *c. 500–1042*. London, 1979.

Wickham, Chris. *Framing the Early Middle Ages: Europe and the Mediterranean, 400–800*. Oxford, 2005.

Widukind of Corvey. *Die Sachsengeschichte des Widukind von Corvey*, edited by Paul Hirsch and Hans-Eberhard Lohmann, MGH SS rer. Germ. Hanover, 1935.

Williams, Gareth. "Raiding and Warfare." In *The Viking World*, edited by Stefan Brink, in collaboration with Neil Price, 193–203. London, 2008.

Williams, Henrik. "Runjämtskan på Frösöstenen och Östmans bro." In *Jämtlands kristnande*. Uppsala, 1996.

———. "Vad säger runstenarna om Sveriges kristnande?" In *Kristnandet i Sverige: Gamla källor och nya perspektiv*, 45–83. Uppsala, 1996.

Wilson, David M. *Vikingatidens konst*. Translated by Henrika Ringbom, Signums svenska konsthistoria. Lund, 1995.

Winroth, Anders. "Christianity Comes to Denmark." In *Reading the Middle Ages*, by Barbara Rosenwein, 166–167. Peterborough, Ont., 2006.

Wood, Ian. "Christians and Pagans in Ninth-Century Scandinavia." In *The Christianization of Scandinavia: Report of a Symposium Held at Kungälv, Sweden 4–9 August 1985*, edited by Birgit Sawyer, Peter Sawyer, and Ian Wood, 36–67. Alingsås, Sweden, 1987.

———. *The Missionary Life: Saints and the Evangelisation of Europe, 400–1050*. Harlow, U.K., 2001.

Wormald, C. Patrick. "Viking Studies: Whence and Whither?" In *The Vikings*, edited by R. T. Farrell, 128–153. London, 1980.

Zettel, Horst. *Das Bild der Normannen und der Normanneneinfälle in westfränkischen, ostfränkischen und angelsächsischen Quellen des 8. bis 11. Jahrhunderts*. Munich, 1977.

Index